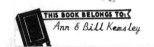

THE COMMUNIST PARTY

vs.

THE C.I.O.

THE
COMMUNIST PARTY

VS.

THE C.I.O.

A STUDY IN
POWER POLITICS

By MAX M. KAMPELMAN

FREDERICK A. PRAEGER
New York

PREFACE

The author of this book is a close friend and associate of mine. It is, therefore, a great personal pleasure for me to have an opportunity to write the preface to his work. More than personal considerations are involved, however, in these chapters for I feel strongly that Dr. Kampelman has made a valuable contribution to the understanding of one of our democracy's great modern problems, that of Communism within our society.

My first occasion to read an early draft of this study came in 1951 when I was Chairman of the Senate Subcommittee on Labor and Labor Management Relations. The author, who was serving as my legislative counsel, was kind enough to make his doctoral dissertation available to the Subcommittee which was investigating the problem of Communism in the labor movement. The background information which it provided was invaluable. Dr. Kampelman has since revised and added to his original work and the literature on the problem is enriched as a result of his consent, after a number of years of hesitation, to make the manuscript available for publication.

Dr. Kampelman brings a happy variety of talents and experiences to his task. An able attorney, he served for nearly seven years in a key legal and political advisory position in the United States Senate. A political scientist, he has taught problems of American democracy at the University of Minnesota, Bennington College and Howard University. His work over the years has brought him close to the trade union movement and has provided him with an insight vitally necessary for the proper fulfillment of his task. All these, added to his basic integrity, intelligence and dedication to a democratic way of life, demonstrate his qualifications beyond question.

The book covers a vital era in American history. Its main theme begins with the birth of the CIO in 1936; and it appropriately writes fini to its story twenty years later with the merger of the AFL and the CIO. The Communist infiltration of the CIO was a direct threat to the survival of all of our country's democratic institutions. The CIO victory over the Communist party was a significant victory for our nation. It was also a crucial defeat for the international Communist conspiracy.

This is the first time to my knowledge that this story has ever been told. It should be told and retold, for it is a story of American men and women, members and leaders of our trade unions, and their successful struggle against our totalitarian enemies. Every American should know this story and award it a place in the annals of our nation.

HUBERT H. HUMPHREY
U.S. Senator from Minnesota

FOREWORD

> We can (and must) begin to build Socialism, not with imaginary human material, not with human material invented by us, but with human material bequeathed to us by capitalism. . . . The art of politics (and the Communist's correct understanding of his tasks) lies in correctly gauging the conditions and the moment when the vanguard of the proletariat can successfully seize power. . . . (You) must imperatively work wherever the masses are to be found. You must be capable of every sacrifice, of overcoming the greatest obstacles in order to carry on agitation and propaganda systematically, perseveringly, persistently and patiently, precisely in those institutions, societies and associations—even the most reactionary—in which proletarian or semi-proletarian masses are to be found. . . . We must be able to withstand all this, to agree to any sacrifice, and even—if need be—to resort to all sorts of stratagems, artifices, illegal methods, to evasions and subterfuges, only so as to get into the trade unions, to remain in them, and to carry on Communist work within them at all costs.
>
> V. I. Lenin
> *"Left-Wing" Communism,*
> *An Infantile Disorder*

"Trade-unionism is the conservative movement of our time," is the theme of a recently published philosophical study of the labor movement.[1] "American labor is not 'working-class conscious.' It is not 'proletarian.' It does not believe in class war." So conclude the editors of *Fortune* in their analysis, *U.S.A.: The Permanent Revolution.*

A study of American labor history lends weight to these conclusions. The early American unions were impregnated with the middle-class aspiration for self-employment. From the beginning, the American labor movement had its spiritual and material roots in the existing order. Professor Selig Perlman observed this characteristic and related trade unionism to the "wide diffusion of private property" as moderating influences upon society. The gains of trade unionism to the worker are on a par with private property. This "property" is regarded as a protective dike between himself and a ruthless struggle for existence. The trade unionist too is a "protectionist." When he can count among his trade union gains decent wages and living conditions, reasonable job security, and perhaps even a partial voice in management, so that he can share the material fruits of capitalism, he becomes reluctant to destroy the existing economic and political system on the gamble of building up a better one in its place. Trade unionism, therefore, acts as society's policeman and watch-dog against revolutionary and catastrophic change.[2]

It would be an error, however, to rest with these analyses. Trade unions have on occasion produced politically militant leadership. There have likewise been constant efforts from within and without to radicalize American labor. These have helped shape both labor and society and cannot be ignored for a full understanding of labor's role in the American society.

This is the study of one—the most recent—attempt to change the character of American trade unions: The effort of the Communist party in the United States to control and direct unions of the Congress of Industrial Organizations. The effort was to control the unions in their *political* expression, not as instruments of collective bargaining.

The Marxist aim is to convert unions into political organizations so that they can be used as instruments for producing revolutionary change. This program is the outcome of the Marxist assumption that there is an inherent tendency in capitalist society for the position of the workers to deteriorate.

Trade unions, however were started earlier than, and have always existed independently of, the Marxist movement. They became strong and their leaders have often self-consciously resisted active Marxist domination. Early western European Marxists, recognizing the legitimate role of trade unions as organs of self-defense for the workers, reluctantly accepted the fact of trade union autonomy and independence. They were satisfied with a loose type of intellectual domination over the trade unions. This understanding was formalized at the Mannheim Congress of 1906.[6] Lenin dramatically altered this orientation and rejected the notion that there could be a parity between the trade unions and the revolutionary Marxist political party. This was interpreted in the United States as follows:[4]

> It goes without saying that it is in the trade unions that we in the United States must show our greatest activity. This must be done through organized and well disciplined fractions. Without any exceptions whatever all Communist fractions must work under the immediate leadership and control of the Party Committees...doing all possible to carry out the Party Policy in all organizations wherein they function. The party's instructions and decisions are obligatory in fraction work, and no member of the fraction, once a decision is made and a policy laid down, can in any way take a stand against such a decision or policy, no matter what his opinion may be regarding the correctness of the policy.

This approach guided the activity of the Communist Party in the American labor movement. That activity varied with the changing strategy of international communism, but the objective of communist domination remained constant. This was not too serious a threat to American democracy so long as the Communist party remained isolated and outside the mainstream of American politics. With the birth of the CIO, however, the Communist party made a serious and successful bid for entry into the fabric of the American labor movement for political purposes. In an address to the convention of the Young Communist League in 1937, William Z. Foster said:[5]

> It is not enough to support the CIO. . . .
> We must become leaders in these movements. We will then march forward with giant strides in the revolutionary movement that is growing like a snow ball in all parts of the United States.

It was this development which created a problem for the American labor movement and for our democratic society. It was one with which the unions had to deal themselves, for employers were not strategically placed to act and the government could only assist.

The formation of the CIO, and the split in the American labor movement that took place in 1936, was one of the most significant social, economic, and political events of American history.

Coming at a period when the New Deal was captivating the imagination of the American people, the CIO spirit and organizational activity seemed in harmony with the changes taking place all over America. An emphasis on solidarity replaced individualism. Sheer numbers rather than job scarcity constituted the weapon which the CIO had against the employer's armory of legal and economic resources. It was difficult to attempt to arrest thousands of working men and women for contempt of court if they ignored an injunction. Company guards hesitated before huge unorganized parades of pickets. The sitdown strike became a technique. It was first used on a large scale in the plants of the Goodyear Tire Company in November, 1935, and spread to the Bendix Corporation plant, General Motors, Chrysler, and to the hosiery plants in Reading, Pennsylvania. Organized industrially and coming from large plants, the new members of the labor movement developed a discipline of acting together in great bodies. They allowed themselves to be drawn into widespread sympathetic strikes. Their slogan became, "Organize the unorganized."

The spirit which animated the CIO in this period is characterized by a pledge which many of its new members took upon joining. It read as follows:[6]

> I do sincerely promise, of my own free will, to bear true allegiance to, and keep inviolate, the principles of the Committee for Industrial Organization; never to discriminate against a fellow worker on account of creed, color, or nationality; to defend freedom of thought, whether expressed by tongue or pen; to defend on all occasions and to the extent of my ability the members of our organization. . . .That I will not accept a brother's job who is idle for advancing the interests of the union or seeking better remuneration for his labor; and as only by standing together can workers improve their lot, I promise to cease work at any time I am called upon by the organization to do so. And I further promise to help and assist all brothers in adversity, and to have all eligible workers join the Union that we may all be able to enjoy the fruits of our labor; and that I will never knowingly wrong a brother or see him wronged, if I can prevent it.

The CIO spirit was also expressed in an old I.W.W. song which became the rallying anthem of the organization. It was sung to the tune of the "Battle Hymn of the Republic":

SOLIDARITY

When the Union's inspiration through the workers blood
                          shall run
There can be no power greater anywhere beneath the sun.
But what force on earth is weaker than the feeble strength
                          of one?
But the Union makes us strong.

It is we who plowed the prairies, built the cities where
                       they trade,
Dug the mines and built the workshops, endless miles of
                       railroads laid,
Now we stand outcast and starving 'mid the wonders we
                       have made,
But the Union makes us strong.

In our hands is placed a power greater than their hoarded
                          gold,
Greater than the might of armies magnified one thousand
                          fold;
We can bring to birth the new world from the ashes of
                       the old,
For the Union makes us strong.

Solidarity forever, solidarity forever,
Solidarity forever, for the Union makes us strong.

The growth of industrial unionism had inevitable repercussions along the political front. The CIO, composed largely of unskilled workers, could not depend solely on the benefits it could derive from direct collective bargaining The collective principle of industrial organization lent itself quite easily to political action. John L. Lewis expressed this well when he said:[7]

Time was, before the depression, when the representative labor leader would have said: 'Guarantee labor the right to organize and we shall do the rest.' Now he knows that modern mass-production industry—not only natural resources industries but manufacturing and mechanical industries as well—are uncoordinated, uncorrelated and overcapacitated. With the guarantee of 'the right to organize' such industries may be unionized, but, on the other hand, better living standards, shorter working hours and improved employment conditions for their members cannot be hoped for unless legislative or other provision be made for economic planning and for price, production and profit controls. Because of these fundamental conditions, it is obvious to industrial workers that the labor movement must organize and exert itself not only in the economic field but also in the political arena.

In the very first days of the CIO, therefore, Labor's Nonpartisan League was formed. John L. Lewis was elected chairman of the League's executive board and Sidney Hillman was made treasurer. During the 1936 Presidential campaign, the League spent, through all of its affiliated organizations, many hundreds of thousands of dollars to elect Franklin Roosevelt and a number of Congressmen who were considered friendly to labor. John L. Lewis stated the objective of labor's political activity in his closing speech before the 1937 CIO convention as follows:[8]

We are not only fighting for the economic emancipation of the millions of Americans who work for a living, but we are fighting also for their political emancipation, for the right to live in communities free from corporation's domination to a point that limits and circumscribes their political rights and political actions.

The league believed that the primary cause of organized labor's early failures to establish a unified and effective political movement was the absence of any widespead working-class psychology in America. The CIO, therefore, from the outset fostered the idea of class solidarity:[9]

Industrial unionism develops a new conception of our class duty. . . . In craft unions, steam-fitters talk as steam-fitters, plumbers as plumbers, and so on down the line in all the trades. But in industrial unions, workers talk and act in relation to their class identity, irrespective of trades. In industrial unionism we do not develop craft trade, religions, political, or race ideas. We develop class solidarity.

This was a climate in which the Communists thought they could thrive.

[1] Frank Tannenbaum, *A Philosophy of Labor* (Knopf: New York, 1951).
[2] Selig Perlman, *A History of Trade Unionism in the United States* (MacMillan: New York, 1937) pp. 302, 303.
[3] Philip Taft, "Attempts to 'Radicalize' the Labor Movement," *Industrial and Labor Relations Review,* July, 1948, pp. 580-583.
[4] M. Jenkins, *The Communist Nucleus* (Workers' Library Publishers: New York, 1928) pp. 55, 56.
[5] *The New York Times,* May 4, 1937.
[6] Edward Levinson, *Labor on the March* (Harper: New York, 1938) p. 299.
[7] John L. Lewis, "What Labor is Thinking," *The Public Opinion Quarterly* Vol. 1, no. 4., October, 1937, pp. 27, 28.
[8] Lois MacDonald, *Labor Problems and the American Scene* (Harper: New York, 1938) p. 470.
[9] CIO, *Union News Service* (mimeographed) June 15, 1936.

TABLE OF CONTENTS

PART I
Chapter 1-4

THE COMMUNISTS PENETRATE

THE C.I.O.

1 | THE C.I.O. AND THE COMMUNIST PARTY

> To carry on a war for the overthrow of the international bourgeoise, a war which is a hundred times more difficult, prolonged and complicated than the most stubborn of ordinary wars between states, and to refuse beforehand to maneuver, to utilize the conflict of interests (even though temporary) among one's enemies, to refuse to temporize and compromise with possible (even though transient, unstable, vacillating and conditional) allies—is not this ridiculous in the extreme? Is it not as though, in the difficult ascent of an unexplored and hitherto inaccessible mountain, we were to renounce beforehand the idea that at times we might have to go in zigzags, sometimes retracing our steps, sometimes abandoning the course once selected and trying various others? . . .
>
> V. I. Lenin

The American labor movement has had the experience of being irresponsibly labeled as "Red" or "dangerous" ever since the first group of Philadelphia shoemakers organized themselves into a union in 1787. While the AFL in recent years had managed to achieve a reputation for respectability in the eyes of even a reader of *The Wall Street Journal,* the CIO is still equated with militant radicalism. By recklessly yelling "Communist" at signs of militant labor activity, anti-union employers and their editorial echoes nearly succeeded in distorting the use of the term in the eyes of both liberal and fair-minded conservatives.

The organized labor movement is probably the largest and most active non-governmental economic or political body in the American society. It has become an integral part of the delicate mechanism of modern life. Primarily dedicated to improving the working conditions and raising the living standards of its members,

3

the labor movement with its economic program permeates all aspects of American life. Its influence, political, social and economic, reaches far beyond its 15 million members and their families.

The power relationships within the organized labor movement, therefore, are, in a real sense, directly of interest to the American people. This is particularly the case insofar as those power relationships involve the influence of the Communist party on the labor movement.

With European experience vividly in mind, it is unnecessary for us to elaborate the assertion that what Communists do in the trade unions of any country vitally affects the welfare and security of that country's entire citizenry and not merely its organized labor movement.

The traditional area of concentration for Communist trade union activity has been the fields of transportation, shipping, fuel, metal trades, and other industries vital to a nation's economy. We shall see that this was the pattern in the United States, as it has been in Europe. In France, for example, Communist unions in those industrial areas dominated the General Confederation of Labor, and through that control played a large role in French politics.[1] This role is damaging to the national interests of any society, since the primary loyalty of a Communist is to the Soviet Union. For example, the Communists took to resistance in France during World War II, not when their own country was attacked, but only after Russia was invaded.[2]

The study of this problem, therefore, is one which merits serious attention. This is so, in spite of the fact that the Communists have never been a significant numerical factor in American life or within the unions. The largest number of members which the Communist party has had in recent years is probably 70,000. Assuming that of this number one-half belong to unions—and that would probably be an exaggeration—they would have had a maximum numerical strength of .0024 of the 15 million labor union members. Yet at the height of this power drive within the CIO, they dominated 12 to 15 of the 40 international CIO unions.[3]

The technique of this Communist domination is not easy to describe. Yet basic to the domination is the application of the Bolshevik principles of minority control.

The basic unit of Communist organization is the same whether in Berlin, Belgrade or Brooklyn.[4] It is the "cell," consisting of from three to ten card-holding members of the Communist Party who know each other well and work closely together. If the assigned project is to penetrate and control a union by "boring from within," either an existing cell will be assigned the task, or the few Communist members already in the union will form a new cell. The cells meet for advice with Party officials, called "functionaries," who are organizationally experienced and expert. The emphasis within a cell is on the need for following a "line" and acting as a rigidly disciplined group. Family and all other personal considerations must be subordinated to cell responsibility and Party loyalty.

The cell will frequently broaden to include "fellow-travelers" and "sympathizers," but as a hard core, it never surrenders its identity and never genuinely merges with the larger "leftist caucus."

The next larger unit above the cell in the Party organization is a "section." A number of sections constitute a state organization. Above the state organization will frequently be a regional or district organization, depending upon geographic and population factors. Each unit chooses one or more representatives to send to the next higher group. A meeting of the full membership of any level above the cell is called a "Party plenum."

Communist strength in any community or organization is based upon five basic types of individuals:

(a) The Party member, who actually holds a membership card and is a cell member, openly or in secret.
(b) The fellow-traveler, who is not a member of the Communist party but who is prepared to follow every policy of the Communist party.
(c) The sympathizer, who is either emotionally influenced by the Soviet Union or is essentially in agreement with its general objectives, even while he may disagree with one or more of the Communist party policies.
(d) The opportunist, who believes that Communists can be effectively used for the achivement of his own ends but who, himself, remains completely unaffected by them.
(e) The liberal, and sometimes the "civil-libertarian" conservative,

who has fundamental disagreements with the Communist party but who is willing to associate politically with Communists in attaining some of the immediate demands urged by the Communists which they share.

In a power struggle for control of a trade union or "program organization," a basic pattern is usually followed by the Communist Party. It begins with a conscious drive toward colonization. Party members are urged to enter the industry and either help organize or join the union. Where there is a trade union in existence and its leaders are friendly, Party members are generally assured of good jobs unless the needs of the moment call for their placement elsewhere. Where there is a friendly trade union administration, therefore, the effect is to give the Party control over the jobs of large numbers of workers, thus incidentally not only strengthening control over the trade union but also assuring contributions to Party funds and causes. Where colonization must take place without the knowledge of the trade union leaders or where there is no trade union, the Communists, acting as a disciplined core, move at first on the basis of personal contacts and direct individual solicitation alone. Not until the group can give the impression of having some members does it begin to act formally by issuing leaflets and otherwise making appeals for support—with its Communist identity, however, carefully concealed.

Once within a trade union or other kind of organization, the Communist group usually has some advantage over most other members. Most union members, for example, are indifferent to union business other than that directly related to wages and working conditions. The Communists, on the other hand, function as a disciplined body, constantly exhorted to attend to every duty, and usually assured of funds for expenses. They operate through caucuses, deception, and prearranged decisions. They are well organized in advance and arrive at meetings with their policies and strategies thoroughly mapped out. They are frequently helped by "a leading comrade" who specializes in the problems of their union or industry and who directs strategy. They caucus during recess and all other available hours to decide on tactics and to be assigned their roles in debates. Disciplined and organized as a solid phalanx, they join freely in argument and parliamentary maneuver for which they are well trained. They are good at fighting delaying actions and often succeed in wearing out the opposition. When they are not able to out-maneuver their opponents, they are likely to prolong union meetings until many members, exhausted and sleepy, leave for home. As they do, the Communist tide rises. Communists arrive early and stay late. The later the hour of the vote, the greater the likelihood of the Communist Party bloc prevailing. With few exceptions a cardinal principle of Communist policy is to deny charges of Communist identity or influence. In this technique they have often been aided by non-Communist liberals within and without the labor movement who have been the objects of reckless "smear" campaigns by irresponsible opponents of the labor movement or of liberalism. Thus for many years anyone charging a Communist trade union officer with being a Communist was likely to be accused of red-baiting and denounced as a reactionary. A careful and objective study of this problem is, therefore, difficult to achieve. But the CIO did have a serious Communist problem. No careful investigation of the CIO can fail to give it the prominent attention which the facts warrant.

World War I strengthened the conservative leadership of the American labor movement. Critical groups, such as the IWW, the Socialist Labor Party, and the Socialist Party found their remnants clipped of strength in the AFL and often broken of heart—partly, of course, because of wartime prosecutions by the government.

On this scene the American Communist movement was born within the ranks of the Socialist Party. Influenced by Leninism and the success of the Bolshevik revolution of 1917 in Russia, a small dedicated band of militant radicals attempted to gain control of the Socialist Party and begin preparing the country for revolution. The deep inconsistencies between democratic socialism as expressed by the gradualist Socialist Party majority, and Leninist elitism, was early apparent, and the Communists were expelled. In September 1919 the Communist Party of America came into being. Its trade union policy was one of opposition to the American Federation of Labor and sympathy with the Industrial Workers of the World.

A policy of "revolutionary unionism" espousing the overthrow of capitalism was enunciated. Unions were looked upon as "schools of communism." At ordinary strikes leaflets urging the worker to overthrow the goverment and establish Soviets were distributed. The revolution, however, did not come as quickly as expected and different tactics had to be used. With a more moderate appeal, unions established and run by Communists gained some following, particularly among foreign born workers in the needle trades, food, and metals and among laborers, thus illustrating what was called "dual unionism."

This line was followed until May, 1920 when Lenin, for reasons that had nothing to do with America, published his pamphlet, *Left Wing Communism: An Infantile Disorder*, in which he urged Communists to go into existing unions and criticized the German Communists for not doing so. Benjamin Gitlow, writing of this period, said: "The publication of Lenin's pamphlet turned the trade union policy of our Party upside down."[5] It was clear that the activity of the Communists in the trade unions was to be major. Gitlow, at the time an important functionary of the movement, described it as follows:[6]

> The Bolsheviks from the time of Lenin to the present have never given up hope of capturing the trade union movement of the United States. Our Party received more assistance, more advice, more decisions on the trade union question than on almost any other question. Lenin was particularly anxious to win over the American trade unions. It was Lenin who conceived the idea that it would be possible for the Communists in the United States, by hiding their identity, to form an opposition bloc in the trade unions, which would enable them to dislodge the reactionary forces in control of the American Federation of Labor.

In December, 1921, the Workers Party was formed at a New York convention, and the Communists emerged from underground. Four years had passed since the October Revolution and there was no indication that the mass of American workers would accept Communist leadership. Led by William Z. Foster, a prominent labor organizer in steel and meatpacking, the Communists began a policy of penetrating the AFL. Foster had been a Socialist and a

member of the syndicalist IWW. He had a reputation as a successful
labor organizer, having led the great Steel Strike of 1919. The
Communists dropped the policy of overtly promoting revolution and
adopted the strategy of obtaining a place for themselves in ordinary
trade union activity. In 1922 they formed the Trade Union Educational League (TUEL), intended as a rallying center for all progressive groups and individuals within the trade union movement.

The head of the TUEL was William Z. Foster and the managing
editor of its first publication, *The Labor Herald,* was Earl Browder.
It called itself "a left progressive bloc of all revolutionary and
progressive elements in the trade union." It hoped to act as a
revolutionary wing of the AFL and remain within it. This strategy
was difficult to maintain. The Communist (Third) International
had again proclaimed the Lenin thesis of "permanent revolution"
and the impossibility of establishing lasting socialism in one country
within a capitalist world.[7] The League and its leaders were
from the outset obliged to subordinate trade union policies to
political objectives. The Workers Party became increasingly aggres-
ive as a left wing opposition; it began to attempt to gain control of
unions through active participation in union elections; it nominated
its own opposition candidates. This lost the Party the support of
non-Communist progressives, and left the TUEL and its leader,
Foster, in 1923 exposed as Communist and nothing more.[8] This, in
turn, led to a great many expulsions from the AFL on the ground
of dual unionism.

The TUEL now spearheaded an attack upon the AFL. The
League's program called for a reorganization of the labor movement
through a program of amalgamation, under which craft unions
were to be merged into industrial groupings.[9] AFL reaction to the
new policy was immediate. Drastic punitive measures against TUEL
adherents were undertaken. Many unions insisted on loyalty
pledges.[10] TUEL members were removed from union offices and
others were expelled.

To meet these attacks, Foster advised his followers to sign
membership pledges against the TUEL so as to avoid expulsion.
The Communists remained a conspiratorial minority group, a policy
of "boring from within" began.[11] This program lasted until 1928,

when the Communists appeared with another dual labor organization, the Trade Union Unity League,[12] designed to follow a more independent policy.

The TUUL began what came to be known as the "Third Period" of the Communist Party. It lasted until 1935. It was a "revolutionary period," characterized in the U.S. by a few spectacular TUUL-led strikes, but otherwise it made a scant impression upon the labor scene. In following this pattern, the American Communist movement was in harmony with Communist practice all over the world. Social Democrats were called "social fascists," and new "red" trade unions were formed to compete with existing organizations.[13] Among the new unions so formed were the National Miners Union, the Building Trades Industrial League, the National Textile Workers Union, and the Needle Trades Workers Industrial Union.[14]

With the rise of the Nazis in Germany and the growing realization that the Hitler regime was not an interregnum before the Communist revolution but rather a real threat to the Soviet Union as well as to a free Europe, the line began to waver. The period between 1933-1935, therefore, was a transitional one toward the creation of a "United Front."

In March, 1933, for example, the Executive Committee of the Communist (Third) International addressed a Manifesto to all labor organizations and Social-Democratic parties asking them to unite. On March 30, the Communist Party in the U.S. followed suit and addressed a call for united action to the AFL Executive Council, to the National Executive Committee of the Socialist Party, and to other labor organizations. Some joint activity with the Socialist Party began in late 1934 with the Joint Committee to Aid the Herndon Defense.[15] Full acceptance and support of liberal capitalism as expressed by the New Deal, however, was slower to come and in fact didn't come until 1935 and the Laval-Stalin Pact in May of that year.[16] In the meantime, villification of the New Deal and the AFL continued.

In 1934, the New Deal was still a "fascist conspiracy" against the workers and for war. Sidney Hillman, to become during World War II an apparent hero of the Communists, was now repeatedy called an "NRA strikebreaker."[17] One of the Communist front labor publications, for example, wrote of the NRA in that year:[18]

> The NRA has fixed wages at the low crisis levels, turned the 'right of collective bargaining' into a federal legalization of the open shop, and bulwarked company unions. The countrywide and regional boards of conciliation are taking away the right of the workers to strike and organize into their own unions; together with the leaders of the American Federation of Labor the NRA has become a national strike-breaking agency supplemented by an intensified use of legal and extra-legal terror. The 'New Deal' is placing the whole burden of the crisis upon the shoulders of the workers, having launched a new attack upon them with the object of preventing general resistance to the capitalist program. It is a program of fascization and the most intense preparations for imperialist war.

A resolution passed by the 8th Convention of the Communist Party of the USA in April, 1934 declared:[19]

> The workers are rapidly learning the lessons of the strike-breaking role of the NRA and the betrayals of the AF of L leadership. The NRA, which promised without struggle better wages, shorter hours, and the right to organize, is more and more being exposed as the instrument of the capitalists for the greater, more intensive exploitation and oppression of labor. . . .

> The goverment is attempting to bolster up the NRA in which large sections of the workers have already lost confidence, with new demagogy embodied in the Wagner Bill which, in the name of outlawing company unions, in reality is legislation aiming to fasten compulsory arbitration upon the workers, giving a monopoly to the AF of L bureaucrats where the employers can no longer keep the workers in check through the company unions.

This was a far cry from statements in the same publication two years later in favor of "progressive New Dealers" and the plea to "help re-elect President Roosevelt because of his support of collective bargaining, wages and hours, relief, social security, and other measures vital to labor."[20]

The change in the international scene, which now dictated closer cooperation with "reformist "elements, led to the dissolution of the TUUL on March 16, 1935.[21] Once again the Communists resorted to "boring from within"[22]

The most dramatic evidence of the change was provided at the Seventh World Congress of the Communist International in August, 1935, in Moscow by Georgi Dimitrov, general secretary and "hero of the Reichstag fire trial," who defined "the immediate and central task of the international proletarian movement: the establishment of unity of action amongst all sections of the working class in the struggle against fascism."[23]

Anticipating this declaration of a policy which had been developing for two years, the central Committee of the American Communist Party in January, 1935 declared itself against dual unionism.[24] The futility of "building an Independent Federation of Labor" was admitted by the 1935 "plenum" of the Central Committee. The April, 1934 Convention of the Party had resolved:[25]

> ... The whole Party must be mobilized for work in the AF of L, and a decisive turn towards winning the millions of workers organized in the AF of L unions and the Railroad Brotherhoods and isolating the bureaucrats. ...

> Every Communist to carry on bolshevik work must establish and maintain contact with the non-Party workers. The Eighth Congress obliges every eligible Party member to become organized in a trade union and imposes upon the C.C. (Central Committee) the task of checking up on the fulfillment of this decision within three months.

Now in January, 1935 the Party Central Committee demanded concentrated work by its members in the AFL "... in view of the changing conditions of trade union work." Communists within independent unions were urged to "carry out... tactics of struggle for trade union unity and affiliation to the American Federation of Labor." The Communist press was also ordered to change its tone with regard to the AFL.[26]

Earl Browder, who had seen in the New Deal "the clearest example of the tendencies toward fascism" and who had said that Roosevelt's labor policies were the "American brother to Mussolini's Corporate state with state-controlled labor unions closely tied up and under the direction of the employers,"[27] now led his party members into the American Labor Party in New York and der support of FDR. He also began talking about Jefferson, J. and Lincoln; and "fellow travelers" were freely recruited, at ting the significance of the term. They marched into a growing ber of "front" organizations, including the Scottsboro Defense Committee, the National Negro Congress, the American Student Union, the Workers Alliance of America, and the American League against War and Fascism. It was Communists following this "line" who moved on the C.I.O. *en masse.*

[1] See A. Rossi, *A Communist Party in Action,* translated and edited with an introduction by Dr. Willmoor A. Kendall (Yale University Press: New Haven, 1949) Chapters XII and XXXII.

[2] David Dubinsky, "A Warning Against Communists in Unions." *The New York Time Magazine,* May 11, 1947, p. 64.

[3] *Ibid.*

[4] See Rossi, *op. cit.;* and James O'Neal and G. A. Werner, *American Communism* (E. P. Dutton & Co.: New York, 1947).

[5] Benjamin Gitlow, *I Confess* (E. P. Dutton: New York, 1939) p. 170.

[6] *Ibid.,* p. 391

[7] See *The Communist International:* Documents 1919-1922, Jane Degras, Ed. (London 1956).

[8] J. B. S. Hardman, *American Labor Dynamics* (New York, 1928).

[9] Philip Taft, *Economics and Problems of Labor,* (Harrisburg, 1942), p. 488.

[10] "Drive Against Left Wing In Trade Unions," *Daily Worker,* December 5, 1925.

[11] Meanwhile the Workers' Party changed its name in 1925 to The Workers' (Communist) Party, and in 1929 to The Communist Party of the U.S.A.

[12] Taft, *op. cit.,* p. 489.

[13] Frederick J. Lang, *Maritime* (New York, 1943).

[14] Benjamin Stolberg, *The Story of The CIO* (Viking: New York, 1938) p. 145.

[15] Labor Research Associates, *Labor Fact Book* (New York) Vol. 2, 1934, p. 147.

[16] Lang, *op. cit.*

[17] E.g., *Daily Worker,* February 5, 1934.

[18] Labor Research Associates, *op. cit.,* Vol. 2, p. 70.

[19] Communist Party of the U.S.A., *The Way Out,* 1934, pp. 48, 49, 62.

[20] Labor Research Associates, *op. cit.,* Vol. 4, 1938 pp. 22, 23.

[21] Stolberg, *op. cit.,* p. 146.

[22] Taft, *op. cit.,* p. 489.

[23] Labor Research Associates, *op. cit.,* Vol. 3, 1936, p. 147.

[24] Harry A. Millis and Royal E. Montgomery, *Organized Labor,* (McGraw Hill: New York, 1945) p. 230.

[25] *The Way Out, op. cit.* pp. 48, 49.

[26] Stolberg, *op. cit.,* p. 146.

[27] Dubinsky, *op. cit.,* p. 62.

2

THE C.I.O. MEETS
THE COMMUNIST PARTY:
1937-1940

The Communist Party directed all of its attention early in the new "United Front" period to the AFL. This drive continued even while and after the CIO was breaking away from the AFL and becoming independent. In spite of the fact that the CIO's program for industrial unionism agreed with the traditional Communist trade union policy, for almost two years the Communists ignored, chided, and opposed the efforts of the young CIO. Unity within the AFL had been the declared slogan of the CP Convention and its Central Committee in 1935 and unity within the AFL it would be, said the Communist trade union leaders, regardless of the CIO. This lasted until May, 1937, by which time the CIO had also become attractive bait.[1]

When the CIO started to move forward in 1936 and 1937, it found thousands of workers anxious to join its ranks. Even though it had originally intended to concentrate on the steel industry, the CIO found itself active on a dozen different fronts at once. The dramatic and spontaneous sit-down strike of December, 1936—February, 1937 in the automobile industry, for example, dumped a problem in the laps of the CIO leaders which they had not anticipated. Even today, those students, teachers, and lawyers, who had unexpectedly found themselves enlisted as union organizers, fondly recollect the storms of feverish union activity which characterized that period. Men and women assigned to help organize steel companies or hosiery mills found themselves with groups of waiters or laundry workers on their hands, organized, on strike, and asking for support and CIO charters. One man, now a well-known novelist but then an unemployed part-time student and volunteer organizer of textile workers, has nostalgically told this story: "I remember getting to our one-room office in Chicago at 8:00 one morning and receiving a feverish telephone call from a waiter at one of the fancier of Chicago's hotels downtown: 'Come quick, the chambermaids are on strike. They want to join the CIO.' I rushed down to do what I could—and the chambermaids became members of the textile union." In such an atmosphere, beset on all sides at once, short of trained manpower, this new union movement, lacking a staff, and without political direction, was ready to utilize the services of speakers, writers, and executives wherever it could find them.[2]

At first, young Socialists, eager to join the class struggle, welcomed an opportunity to express their idealism in action and jumped into the fray. By 1937, they were followed by the Communists, who stopped concentrating on the AFL and turned attention to the still virgin, young, active, and developing CIO.

The signal for the shift was given by William Z. Foster.[3]

". . . CIO's significance far outruns the question of the organization of the unorganized, fundamental though this may be. It is a movement which has potentiality of profoundly altering the whole structure, leadership, policies, and social outlook of the trade union movement. . . . It carries within it the possibility of a great advance of Labor on every front—ideologically, industrially, politically—during the oncoming period. It can serve as the means to unite all the present scattered struggles of the workers, farmers, middle class, Negroes, youth, etc., into one mighty progressive mass movement; into a great American People's Front against fascism and war. But it remains to be seen if its leaders, who are only now beginning to break with their past of many years' long ultra-conservatism, will display the understanding and initiative to realize the objectives that history opens up before the CIO.

John L. Lewis, faced with the problems of leading a movement whose rapid growth he had not anticipated, at first acted like a stupified father of quintuplets, but he quickly assumed the airs of a proud parent. Confident of his own power and destiny, he accepted the proffered aid of the Stalinists. They were experienced with organization and fully trained for their tasks, more so than the young Socialists, who had been earlier accepted by the CIO because of their sponsorship by the International Ladies' Garment Workers Union. The Stalinists knew how to make speeches, write reports, run mimeograph machines, prepare leaflets, set up a picket line, hold the chair in turbulent meetings, and manipulate parliamentary procedure.[4]

Chanting "CIO" like three notes in a new litany, the Communists found a home in 1937. And even though they were frequently to emphasize collective security rather than collective bargaining, John L. Lewis, parading Henry of Navarre's proverb, "In a battle I make arrows from any wood," asserted: "I'll work with anyone who'll work with me."[5]

It took a great deal of stretching and pulling and convenient forgetting to fit John L. Lewis and the Communists into an alliance. From the beginning, Lewis had been considered an enemy by the Stalinists. In 1927, William Z. Foster had showered abuse on Lewis in the pages of his book, *Misleaders of Labor*.[6] In *Toward a Soviet America*, Foster wrote in 1932:[7] "In the AFL the process of fascization is far advanced. In fact, the top leadership of this organization—the Greens, Wolls, Lewises, etc.—are already practically open Fascists. They have become the chief strike-breaking agency of the employers." On his side, Lewis during these years waged ruthless warfare against the Communist-inspired National Miners Union.

But in 1937, the *New Masses* was saying, "In a series of remarkable speeches . . . he (Lewis) demonstrated that the leadership of the progressive trade union movement was his by right of ability and program." In September, 1938, following an address by Lewis at a Mexico City Congress Against War and Fascism, Earl Browder exclaimed: "Lewis emerged with this speech not merely as the greatest American trade union leader, not only as one of the most potent representatives of American democracy, but as a leader of world democracy."[8] No matter how you viewed him, however, Lewis remained Lewis.

With Lewis willing to accept them, it was not too difficult for the Communists to become an integral part of the CIO organization, particularly since most of them disguised themselves as liberals or as American radicals in the democratic tradition. The Communist party itself, as we have seen, encouraged disguise in the interests of building a "democratic front." And even though the Party proclaimed its allegiance to "the Communist International" and to "the establishment of Socialism according to the scientific principles enunciated by the greatest teachers of mankind, Marx, Engels, Lenin and Stalin," its open appeal was increasingly an American one designed to be in harmony with the interests and locale of American workers. At its 10th national convention in New York City, May 26-31, 1938, the Communist party called for the "unity of all trade unions into a single, united, powerful American labor movement," and declared itself in its constitution to be a:[9]

> working class political party carrying forth today the traditions of Jefferson, Paine, Jackson, and Lincoln, and of the Declaration of Independence; it upholds the achievements of democracy, the rights of 'life, liberty, and the pursuit of happiness' and defends the United States Constitution against its reactionary enemies who would destroy democracy and all popular liberties; it is devoted to defense of the immediate interests of workers, farmers, and all toilers against capitalist exploitation, and to preparation of the working class for its historic mission to unite and lead the American people to extend these democratic principles to their necessary and logical conclusions.

A few voices protested the growing influence of the Communists in the CIO. As early as December, 1937, Professor John Dewey, a devoted friend of the organized labor movement, wrote:

> It is common knowledge that the CIO in its eagerness for rapid growth at the beginning accepted many members and even used organizers who belonged to one or another of these Communist factions . . . The danger lies in the fact that the tactics employed by these Communist groups have invaded the forces of labor and are attempting to divide it.[10]

But such warnings were disregarded, frequently with anger and impatience.

Even as alert an historian, student, and participant in the labor movement as Edward Levinson, allowed his CIO partisanship to interfere with his objective observation of the facts when he said in 1938:[11]

'Communist influence in the CIO' is a figment of imagination. Lewis' opposition to Communism is well known. The large CIO unions—miners, steel workers, rubber and needle trade workers —have no trace of Communist influence in their ranks. In the auto union, the Communists are an active faction, but their party is so opportunistic and self-effacing, politically, that the final stage of the internal conflict of 1937 found it wooing the good will of the conservative Frankensteen. In a few unions where Communists held positions of influence they were checkmated by memberships which are by no stretch of the imagination Communist . . . American Communism, in or out of the labor movement, is most frequently a red herring used by political or economic demagogues . . . As a major aspect of American political or labor life, it does not exist.

Yet at the time John Dewey was expressing his fears, and Edward Levinson his hopes, Communists were already acting as a caucus within the CIO and had begun doing so in 1937. Michael Quill, head of the Transport Workers Union and a member of the Communist caucus during this time, later reported that a Communist Party representative always met with that CIO caucus and was "assigned to dish out the instructions." He said:

> I don't recollect Atlantic City very well in 1937, but I do know, Harry (Bridges), in 1938 in Pittsburgh you and I met with Roy Hudson and a dozen others. Roy Hudson was a Party functionary at the time. He was assigned to the Pittsburgh one. . . . At the Detroit Convention (1941) the man that was there was Ebert. He is now (1950) in the Polish government. He was the Party functionary at that time.[12]

Quill testified that from 1937 "the left-wing bloc was and is controlled by the Communist Party of the United States. . . . They got their instructions and have voted down the line almost 100 percent every time they got their instructions." This control even extended to the assignment of speaking roles in debate at the CIO conventions.[13]

By 1938, Communists had obtained positions of trust, responsibility, and authority giving them complete or partial control in at least 40 percent of the CIO unions,[14] including the United Automobile Workers; the Transport Workers; the American Communication

Association; the Newspaper Guild; the United Electrical Workers; the Federation of Architects, Engineers, and Technicians; the State, County, and Municipal Workers, the National Maritime Union; the Office and Professional Workers, the Woodworkers of America; and the Cannery, Agricultural, Packing, and Allied workers.

Just as significant, Communist influence extended itself to Lewis' own kitchen cabinet. Lee Pressman, CIO general counsel, and Len DeCaux, editor of the *CIO News*, were quite influential with Lewis[15] and became prominently identified with the pro-Communist faction in the CIO. Pressman, in fact, who from the first CIO convention in 1938 was secretary of the important resolutions committee, became known as "one of the key Communists in the labor movement of this country," and "a member of the Communist party since the early days of the New Deal when he was a member of a Washington, D.C. unit of the party while employed with the federal government."[16] Pressman and De Caux, in addition to exerting personal influence over policy within their jurisdiction, were also able to "place" people elsewhere in the CIO structure and with many of the internationals. Through Pressman, for example, even so anti-Communist a union as Sidney Hillman's Amalgamated Clothing Workers, engaged as their general counsel John Abt, "a member of the Communist Party of long standing. Mr. Abt's wife and sister are also Communists, each of whom holds an important spot in the Communist movement."[17]

When the Communists began turning their eyes toward the CIO in 1937 they were, as remarked earlier, in their "united front" period which stemmed from the growing Nazi threat to the Soviet Union. Thus at its 10th Convention in 1938, the Communist Party called for "concerted action with France, Great Britain, the Soviet Union, and the other democratic peoples and governments of the world, in order to halt and isolate the fascist war-makers, to assist their victims, and to guarantee world peace," and on the domestic scene set the task of building a "democratic front" so as to defeat "the forces of reaction, fascism, and war." To accomplish the latter, they called for the building of an "independent political organization of the workers, and the uniting with them(of) the farmers and middle classes, as the means to preserve the unity of the majority which moved against monopoly capital and reaction in the 1936 elections, and the strengthening of that majority—in order to guarantee at all costs the defeat of the reactionary forces."[18] (It is interesting to contrast the Communist characterization here of the 1936 Roosevelt victory as that of "the majority . . . against monopoly capital" with its earlier characterization of the New Deal as "the American brother to Mussolini's corporate state."[19] With the Nazi-Soviet pact in August, 1939, however, and the change in the Soviet Union's international policy, the alliance with the New Deal was again shattered, Earl Browder in a Madison Square Garden speech exclaiming: "The Rooseveltism of the New Deal has capitulated to reactionaries.")[20]

The effect of this new international "line" on many sections of the CIO was soon apparent. Just prior to the invasion of Poland in September, 1939, the National Maritime union resolved in convention:[21]

> WHEREAS: Our Democracy demands the support of all democracies in the fight against fascist aggression;
>
> RESOLVED: that we urge upon our Congress the introduction and passage of legislation that will distinguish the aggressor from its victims and will provide for the complete stoppage of all trade relations with such aggressors.

In February, 1941, the *Pilot*, official publication of the National Maritime Union reported:[22] "On behalf of the NMU and the Greater New York Industrial Union Council, Joe Curran told the Senate Foreign Relations Committee that American labor was opposed to the Lend-Lease bill because it was Fascist and would help drive us into war."

And an NMU Statement of Policy issued in June, 1941, a few days after the Nazi invasion of the Soviet stated:[23]

> We recognize the present struggle of Great Britain and the Soviet Union against the forces of Fascism to be sincere and requiring the full support of liberty-loving people throughout the world.

These rapid changes in policy placed an added strain on the relationship between the Communist and non-Communist forces within the CIO. In a measure, even though each position of the line attracted sympathizers and allies who agreed with the particular policy of the Communist group at the particular time, the constant changes tended to label Communist those who swerved with the Communists at every turn of the road, and also tended to remove doubts as to the primary loyalty of the Communist group to the USSR.

However in 1939, the foreign policy of the Communist Party seemed in harmony with the general "isolationist" position which permeated America and the labor movement as well.[24] Opposition to war, therefore, and opposition to steps leading to war, was an easy cause to sell. Sharp differences between Communists and anti-Communists thus did not express themselves through foreign policy debates. Nevertheless, the Communists within the CIO took no chances and thoroughly prepared themselves to be effective at the 1939 CIO convention.

M. Hedley Stone, treasurer of the NMU, attended the Communist caucus meetings held during the convention. Following his split with the Communists in 1946, he told the National CIO that the caucus meetings had taken place at the Whitcomb Hotel, San Francisco, and that one of the chief agreements entered into "was to press for the isolationist program, not to get involved in a war...." When asked:"Do you recall who the Party representatives were at that particular meeting,?" he answered: "Schneiderman was there, and besides that there was the group that is well known in the CIO, Flaxer, Selly, Gold, Potash, Merrill."[25] Stone later added the name of Quill, head of the Transport Workers Union, as one of those present.[26]

The tension within the CIO was intensified when the Communists, in their eagerness to conform to the Nazi-Soviet pact pattern, undertook an intensive villification of Roosevelt, who was fashioning American foreign policy in an anti-Nazi-direction. As late as March 22, 1941, for example, only three months before the Hitler attack against the Soviet Union, Vito Marcantonio was telling an "anti-war rally" in Madison Square Park in New York that the four horsemen of the Apocalypse threatening the world were "Hitler, Churchill, Roosevelt, and Mussolini."[27] All during this period, the Communists were chanting this doggerel:

Oh Franklin Roose-e-velt
Told the people how he felt
We damn near believed what he said.
He said 'I hate war,
And so does Elinor,
But we won't be safe till everybody's dead.'

CIO leaders who supported the Roosevelt foreign policy were
taken severely to task. The Communist Party Campaign Book for
the 1940 election singled out Sidney Hillman, later constantly
praised, as the symbol of what was to be opposed. The "Hillman
wing" was charged with "subordinating the labor movement to
Wall Street's war program." A United Press dispatch from Moscow[28]
quoted a similar charge in the Communist International magazine:

> The American bourgeoise is using Hillman in a vicious campaign
> against the working class. . . . Hillman knows how to act to deal
> the workers vicious blows. He is an enemy of the working class,
> an enemy of the Communist party and a ferocious enemy of the
> Soviet Union.

Hillman retaliated by urging a resolution at the 1940 Atlantic City
CIO convention prohibiting Communists, Nazis, and Fascists from
holding union office. Defending the resolution, he said that
Communists[29] "cannot participate in the democratic process" and
give their "loyalty. . . . to an organization outside of this organization. . . . These people are a menace to the labor movement. . . .
I say that the oldest organization has incorporated it into their
constitution and I say that what is good enough for the United Mine
Workers is good enough for the CIO. . . ."[30]

At the same time John L. Lewis was pursuing a personal
vendetta with Roosevelt based upon other motives. The coalition
between Lewis and the Communists, therefore, became stronger.
The latter, seeing an opportunity to gain further influence within
the CIO through the forceful personality and prestige of the CIO
president, used flattery and even went through what many have
considered to be contortions in order to "butter" Lewis' ego. When
Lewis, for example, decided in the presidential election of 1940 to
support Willkie, rather than Roosevelt, the Communist line within

the CIO was to encourage and support Lewis. On the night of Lewis' famous radio broadcast, therefore, congratulatory telegrams poured in from the CIO Communist supporters. Harry Bridges, ILWU head, attributed to Lewis the "courage of a lion." Arthur Osman, who headed a pro-Communist faction within the Retail, Wholesale, Department Store Union, wired: "your radio speech of last night was a masterful indictment of the Roosevelt administration. We fully agree with your denunciation of its war-mongering and its abandonment of the New Deal program.... Those who have heard the words of Roosevelt and who have studied the public addresses of the President, from his Chicago 'quarantine' speech to his Charlottesville 'stab in the back' address, will understand his true objective. It is war."[31]

The Lewis pro-Willkie radio speech was a significant landmark in CIO history. He had publicly announced that he would leave his post as CIO president if his choice of Willkie was rejected by his followers at the polls. Willkie lost the election. The Communists, however, at the 1940 CIO convention, following Roosevelt's decisive victory, would have none of it and attempted to rally the convention in support of a "draft Lewis" move. Hoping to keep Lewis and their influence they began "Lewis is our leader" chants to develop a steamroller. One year later, following Russia's entry into the war, Lewis was to become "reactionary" and an "appeaser," but at the 1940 convention, Lewis was the champion of the Communists.[32]

It was too late, however. The anti-Communist revolt was developing and even though Lewis himself was still all-powerful and not to be attacked, the anti-Communists in the CIO were ready for a change in policy and a change in leadership. At the 1940 convention the issues and personalities, however, were still far from clear to large segments of the leadership and membership. The CIO, fully conscious of the need for internal unity if it was to maintain itself in the constant industrial warfare in which it was engaged, made strong efforts to avoid the impending internal strife.

[1] Stolberg, *op. cit.*, p. 146; Millis and Montgomery, *op. cit.*, p. 239.
[2] Taft, *op. cit.*, p. 489.
[3] William Z. Foster, *From Bryan to Stalin* (New York, 1937) p. 336.
[4] Herbert Harris, *Labor's Civil War* (New York, 1940) pp. 129-133.

[5] Heywood Broun, "Shoot The Works." *The New Republic,* Vol. 93, January 12, 1938, p. 280.

[6] William Z. Foster, *Misleaders of Labor* (TUEL: 1927) pp. 132-137.

[7] William Z. Foster, *Toward Soviet America* (Coward-McCann: New York, 1932) pp. 177-185.

[8] James A. Wechsler, *Labor Baron* (Morrow: New York, 1944) p. 124.

[9] Labor Research Associates, *op. cit.,* Vol. 4, 1938, pp. 37-39.

[10] Broun, *op. cit.* p. 280.

[11] Edward Levinson, *Labor On The March* (New York, 1938) p. 282.

[12] Congress of Industrial Organizations, *Hearings Before The Committee to Investigate Charges Against The International Longshoremen and Warehousemen's Union* (transcript), May 17, 18, 19, 1950, Washington, D.C., pp. 168, 169.

[13] *Ibid.* pp. 158-160, 166, 167.

[14] Harris, *op. cit.,* p. 135.

[15] *Ibid.*

[16] Nelson Frank *New York World Telegram,* August 25, 1947. These allegations were corroborated on August 27, 1950 in a statement issued by Mr. Pressman which appeared in *The New York Times,* August 28, 1950.

[17] Nelson Frank, *New York World Telegram,* August 25, 1947.

[18] Labor Research Associates, *op. cit.,* Vol. 4, 1938, p. 38, 39.

[19] *Supra,* p. 63.

[20] Dubinsky, *op. cit.,* p. 62.

[21] Lang, *op. cit.,* p. 137.

[22] *The Pilot,* February 14, 1941, p. 1.

[23] Lang, *op. cit.,* p. 140.

[24] See Langer and Gleason, *The Challenge to Isolation,* 1937-1940 (New York, 1952).

[25] Schneiderman was a representative of the Communist party; Flaxer was the head of the State, County and Municipal Workers; Selly was head of the American Communications Association; Gold and Potash were heads of the Fur Workers; while Merrill was head of the United Office and Professional Workers of America.

[26] C.I.O., *Hearings to Investigate ILWU,* pp. 395, 396.

[27] Aaron Levenstein, *Labor Today and Tomorrow* (Knopf: New York, 1945; p. 167.

[28] *The New York Herald Tribune,* March 19, 1941.

[29] Congress of Industrial Organizations, *Daily Proceedings of the Third Constitutional Convention* (Atlantic City, New Jersey, November 18-22, 1940) p. 30.

[30] This refers to a provision of the United Mine Workers of America's constitution prohibiting Communists from holding union office.

[31] Levenstein, *op. cit.,* p. 166. On Wilkie, see *Wilkie,* by Joseph Barnes (New York, 1952)

[32] Taft, *op. cit.,* p. 481.

3 | THE C.I.O.
THE COMMUNISTS
AND WORLD WAR II

Philip Murray, successor to Lewis as CIO president, was a trusted lieutenant and loyal friend of Lewis, and did not feel that differences with Lewis over the Roosevelt candidacy in 1940 was sufficient cause for breaking off friendship and association. He made every effort to maintain good relations with his predecessor. Lee Pressman, who had served as CIO general counsel and had become an integral part of the CIO "brain structure," was kept in office by Murray, who needed his experience, as was Len DeCaux, the editor. Murray's assumption of office, therefore, meant no change at all in the power relationships within the CIO. Quite confident of themselves, their strength and their influence, the Communists continued to pursue their political objectives within the CIO and did not allow the succession of Murray to the presidency to interfere with their plans.

To carry out their "isolationist" political objectives during the period from the Nazi-Soviet Pact in 1939 until the invasion of Russia in June, 1941, Communist-led trade unions began a series of strikes designed to hamper and embarrass America's defense efforts.

One of the earliest and most famous took place in November, 1940, at Vultee Aircraft, a plant of 4000 workers at Downey, California. Active in that strike was Wyndham Mortimer, called "a man who has played a large role as a Stalinist agent in American labor for many years."[1] Mortimer, then an international representative of the UAW, was placed in charge of West Coast aircraft organizing in 1938.[2] The original dispute between the company and the union was over wages and that was speedily settled. Mortimer, however, broke off negotiations over grievance procedure and a no-strike clause. A 12-day strike ensued[3] which was finally settled after pressure by the War and Justice Departments, and a hurried flight by UAW President R. J. Thomas to California, on substantially the same basis offered earlier by the company.[4] U.S. Attorney General Robert H. Jackson charged Communist inspiration of the strike.[5]

The same Wyndham Mortimer was also prominent in a second West Coast aircraft dispute on June 6, 1941, when 12,000 workers went out at North American Aircraft.[6] To end this strike it was necessary for Richard Frankensteen, head of the UAW Aircraft division, to fly to California and remove Mortimer from office. Frankensteen labeled the strike Communist-inspired: ". . . infamous agitation, the vicious maneuverings of the Communist Party is apparent."[7]

A strike of 12,000 International Woodworkers Association members in logging camps and sawmills in the Puget Sound area broke out on May 9, 1941. This strike illustrated very clearly the split within the CIO during this period. The National Defense Mediation Board, of which Philip Murray was a member, attempted to settle the dispute. O. M. Orton, head of the union, walked out of the hearing, calling the Board an "all-out labor-busting and strike-breaking device." Murray immediately excoriated him publicly.[8]

Probably the most serious Communist-inspired defence strike was the 76-day affair at Allis-Chalmers in Milwaukee, February to April, 1941. It was sponsored by Local 248 of the UAW, headed by Harold Christoffel, who later went to jail in connection with the case and his testimony with regard to it. The strike began after eight months of wrangling during which there were 17 work stoppages called.[9] No issue of wages, hours, or conditions was at stake.

Christoffel had for a number of years been associated with Communist leaders. Testimony of a former Communist party member alleged that Christoffel had discussed with the Wisconsin organizer of the Communist party the strategic value of organizing Allis-Chalmers, a vital navy defense plant, as a way of furthering the anti-war activities of the Communist party.[10] After investigating this strike, the House of Representatives Committee on Labor and Education in 1947 officially labeled it Communist inspired:[11]

At the direction of the Communist Party and for the purpose of carrying out its program, Harry Christoffel called a seventy-six-day strike at the Allis-Chalmers plant. In doing this he used over 2,000 fraudulent ballots and betrayed his country, his employer and his fellow workers.

In operating within the Milwaukee CIO, incidentally, Christoffel was operating as part of a heavily concentrated apparatus which kept pace with Communist policy from the very beginning. In October, 1937, for example, it sent a delegation to the Communist inspired American League Against War and Fascism; in December, 1938, it was represented in the Communist Congress for Peace and Democracy; in 1939 it harmonized with the Communist isolationist line by joining the Committee to Defend America by Keeping Out of War; and it continued those policies throughout that period including the passage of a resolution on January 8, 1941, opposing lend-lease. When Russia was invaded in 1941 the Milwaukee CIO joined the Communist party furor in behalf of the war. As an interesting sidelight demonstrating its loyalty, the Milwaukee CIO, on March 17, 1943, adopted a resolution expressing "the resentment of Milwaukee production workers over Admiral Standley's cheap and unworthy criticism of the Soviet Union" when the Admiral suggested that Russia had not given the U.S. proper credit for the lend-lease material it was getting.[12]

ALL OUT FOR WAR

The invasion of Russia by the Nazis produced an immediate upheaval in Communist policy and had the same immediate repercussions within the Communist caucus in the CIO. In a sense this change of policy served to postpone further conflict within the CIO. In the main, the non-Communists within the CIO accepted the leadership of Roosevelt in his "defense" program so that in the period between the Russian invasion and Pearl Harbor the difference between the groups was over the rate at which America would enter the war rather than over the more fundamental question of "isolation" versus "intervention." The pro-Communists, therefore, now found themselves in the position of urging America rapidly to enter a conflict which they had once opposed as "imperialist." Furthermore, once Pearl Harbor brought the United States into the war, the pro-Communists were again in the lead, urging the opening of a "second front" to relieve the Russian front.

In New York, for example, the American Labor Party, official representative of the CIO, took an active role in arousing public support for a "second front."[13]

> The New York County Committee of the American Labor Party yesterday announced the first of a series of meetings at which the crucial need for the invasion of Europe will be brought to the people of every Assembly District. The slogan of the meetings will be 'Invade Europe Now.'

The United Electrical Workers Union at its 1942 Annual Convention adopted the following resolution after turning down a vigorous opposing speech by James B. Carey, Secretary-Treasurer of the National CIO and the UE's former president.[14]

> RESOLVED: That we condemn vigorously and without compromise the pro-Nazi appeasers, fifth columnists, enemy agents, and those who speak for them wittingly or unwittingly, delaying the opening of the western front by spreading rumors against the power of the armed forces of the United Nations to which this union is contributing so much in material, labor, and fighting men, and be it finally
>
> RESOLVED: That we, together with the overwhelming majority of the American people are ready to shoulder the responsibilities of putting this basic military strategy into action now; and that we, representing 435,000 war production workers who have already produced tremendous quantities of arms, pledge ourselves to give everything we can in fighting men, in production, in money and in patriotism to keep the Second Front open, so that our country and our allies may achieve a military defeat of the Fascist Axis.

Examination of the issues of conscription and selective service will briefly illustrate some of the difficulties which the new "patriotic" policy of the Communist created within the CIO. Prior to Pearl Harbor, the official CIO position was opposition to peacetime conscription. This stemmed from a widespread "liberal" reluctance to advance the power of government over the individual, associated with a pacifist orientation in the CIO "intellectual" ranks.[15] This policy, of course, met with the approval of the pro-Communist faction as well. Joseph Curran, head of the National Maritime Union, for example, testified in 1940 that the Burke-Wadsworth Conscription bill was a "step toward fascism" and "in fact very little removed from downright slavery."[16] These views were endorsed by Lewis Merrill, head of the United Office and Professional Workers of America. Arthur Osman, head of the pro-Communist Local 65 in New York of the URWDSE, attacked conscription in September, 1940 as[17]

a death sentence on the trade union and all democratic institutions. A conscription bill is being shamelessly rushed through Congress in utter disregard for the wishes of the people. Thus in one fell swoop democracy is to be completely destroyed. Our freedom, dead as a door nail, is to be 'preserved' in the intoxicating alcohol of war hysteria.

Following the change in Communist foreign policy, however, not only did the Communists embrace conscription, they also enthusiastically endorsed the principle of permanent selective service. This new enthusiasm proved embarrassing to the National CIO because it also meant that a number of the CIO unions were actively in favor of the labor conscription program and the National Service Act recommended by Roosevelt in January, 1944 and again in the President's message to the Congress in January, 1945. The National CIO, which strongly opposed these recommendations, found it necessary to rebuke sharply those pro-Communist unions which did not follow its lead.[18] But legislative representatives from pro-Communist unions continued their attempts to persuade Congressmen to support labor conscription in spite of the National CIO position.[19] This frequently produced confusion in the minds of Congressmen and resulted in a great deal of friction in the National CIO office.[20]

One of the first activities of the pro-Communist unions following America's entry into the war, in addition to agitating for a "second front" was to call for the release of their leader, Earl Browder, from jail, where he was serving a term for a crime involving his unlawful use of a passport. Meetings were held all over the country urging that his services were needed for the common cause in the war against Hitlerism. A Citizens Committee to Free Earl Browder was formed, which was later cited as a Communist organization by Attorney General Francis Biddle.[21] Endorsing the National Free Browder Congress arranged for March 28–29, 1942, New York City CIO Industrial Union Council secretary-treasurer, Saul Mills, said:[22]

> You cannot divorce the Browder case from the political party which he heads. There is no question that Browder and those who are associated with him are a part of the united fighting front of freedom-loving peoples against the Axis. . . . The National Free Browder Congress should be fully supported . . .

The hidden assumption of this "Free Earl Browder" movement, of course, was that his conviction in January, 1940, was "political" arising out of differences over the war question. The President, probably not as a result of these pressures, in May, 1942 commuted Browder's four year sentence, which had begun in March, 1941. Immediately, the pro-Communist leaders in the CIO acclaimed the act, thereby again openly associating themselves with the Communist leader. Saul Mills immediately wired Mr. Roosevelt:[23]

> The commutation of the sentence of Mr. Earl Browder is welcome and cheering news for every trade unionist who has been looking to your leadership for the attainment of the greatest degree of national unity behind the war effort for the defeat of Hitlerism and Japanese militarism.

A similar telegram was sent by Joseph P. Selly, president of the American Communications Association. Arthur Osman, who but a year and a half back in a telegram to Lewis indicted Roosevelt for "war mongering"[24] this time used Western Union to congratulate the President: "You have struck a powerful blow for national unity against the defeatist fifth column in our country."[25]

Not all of the war period was one of harmonious cooperation, however. Some CIO leaders were convinced that even though the exigencies of war might call for international unity on the war front, democratic principles and democratic trade unionism were incompatible with the totalitarian nature of the Soviet Union and its fumbling but eager satellite in the United States, The Communist party. One of these leaders was C.I.O. Secretary-Treasurer James Carey, who had been ousted as UE president after he supported Roosevelt in 1940 and thus broke with his mentor, John L. Lewis. Carey featured in a significant conflict with Communists at this time. Victor Alter and Henryk Ehrlich, internationally known socialist leaders in Poland, were arrested in 1939 by the invading Soviet armies on the charge that they had collaborated with fascists. These charges were considered absurd by democratic leaders in the United States because the men were leaders of anti-Nazi opinion in Poland. After first being condemned to death and then having the sentence reduced to ten years at forced labor, they were suddenly released after a general agreement with Poland calling for amnesty of Polish prisoners. Just as suddenly, however, in 1941, they mysteriously disappeared. Inquiries brought only the information that they had been arrested again. Early in 1942, the Russian NKVD ominously declared that the two men were Soviet citizens.[26]

In February, 1943, Molotov ordered Ambassador Litvinov to inform William Green, president of the AFL, that Alter and Ehrlich had been rearrested after manifesting hostility to the Soviet regime by making "appeals to the Soviet troops to stop bloodshed and immediately to conclude peace with Germany." He said they had been sentenced to death and concluded,"Their sentence has been carried out in regard to both of them." Later, it was learned that they had been killed as early as December, 1941, soon after their arrest, so that they were dead even during the time the Soviet was apparently considering protests against their death.[27]

In the course of these developments, liberals and labor leaders all over the world intervened. In the United States distinguished persons, led by Albert Einstein and Eleanor Roosevelt, protested to the Russian government.[28] In New York, a mass protest rally was organized to express America's indignation; after the announcement of the deaths, a memorial meeting was arranged. Mayor La Guardia, William Green, Senator Mead, and other distinguished leaders lent their names as sponsors and were asked to speak. James Carey accepted an invitation and spoke for the CIO.

The Greater New York Council, through Joseph Curran, its head and Saul Mills, its secretary-treasurer, issued a statement declaring the Alter-Ehrlich meeting motivated "only by a deliberate effort of disruption" against the war effort. They said:[29]

> While called ostensibly as a memorial meeting, there is no ques-
> tion of the underlying motive being to create dissension among
> the United Nations and to involve American labor in a con-
> troversy which detracts from its contributions to the war effort.

The New York City CIO Council later, by a vote of 200-2 outvoted an attempt made by Jack Altman, representing the Retail Union, to support the Alter-Ehrlich memorial. At the Council Meeting, Max Perlow, manager of the Furniture Workers Union, Local 76B, compared the Alter-Ehrlich protests to the "hysteria" following the 1937 Moscow trials. "This is part of an organized campaign to smear our Soviet ally and disrupt United Nations unity," he echoed.[30]

A controversy on this issue also took place within the American Newspaper Guild. The strong New York Guild chapter accused Carey and those who associated with him in the Alter-Ehrlich protests of destroying UN unity. They were then chastised by the International American Newspaper Guild which itself protested the Russian action as a "cruel and unnecessary execution." In fact, the official newspaper, the *Guild Reporter*, carried a cartoon in which a man, labeled "OGPU", is holding a smoking revolver with which he has just murdered Alter and Ehrlich. He is looking in a mirror and his reflection is labeled "Communist Party of America."[31]

The war period, therefore, although it was in the main one of growing "unity" on the surface, did little more than postpone the power struggle within the CIO. A brief examination of an incident within the United Retail, Wholesale and Department Store Employees Union, will illuminate this matter further. The president of the Union, from the very beginning, was Samuel Wolchok, a retail salesman from the Bronx, New York, who presided over a strife-torn union. Wolchok had a reputation as a militant anti-Communist. Within his organization, however, there was a very strong Communist minority, principally centered in New York under the leadership of Arthur Osman, head of Local 65, the Warehousmen's local of the union. Local 65, frequently characterized as "one of the most completely Communist-controlled trade unions in the entire United States."[32] was also one of the most militant.[33] In the "isolationist" period, for example, it swung completely from a collective security position to support of the "Yanks are not Coming Committee" in New York. Carrying out these principles, Osman, himself, ran for public office in New York as a "peace candidate" on the ALP ticket and his union recruited members of the Communist sponsored "Round-the-Clock Peace Vigil" White House picketing demonstration.[34]

This background is particularly relevant because Local 65 and the pro-Communist element in the RWDSEU, with equal fervor, following the Nazi invasion of Russia, plunged into total support of the war and a "no-strike" pledge by labor to aid the war effort.[35] When Samuel Wolchok, head of the parent international union, called a strike in 1944 against Montgomery-Ward, he was accused by Osman of "in effect helping Sewell Avery's treasonable activities."[36] This, in spite of the fact that the strike was called only after that firm had persistently refused to abide by an order of the National War Labor Board. A banner headline in *The Union Voice,* organ of Local 65, announced the strike in these terms, "Wolchok opens War on No-Strike Pledge."[37]

Harry Bridges, many of whose warehousemen worked for Montgomery-Ward, refused to join Wolchok in the strike. Those employed in St. Paul worked on orders transferred from the struck plants of the Montgomery-Ward chain. In spite of repeated requests to cooperate and not act as a strike-breaker, he ordered his members not to strike and wrote a letter to President Roosevelt on December 22, 1944, repeating the no-strike pledge.[38]

In Michigan, the Wayne County Council, controlled by the pro-Communists, adopted a resolution as follows:[39]

We urge the Montgomery Ward workers not to be further incited by Avery into repudiating labor's voluntary no-strike pledge.

By coincidence, a resolution on the subject adopted by the Greater New York Industrial Union Council, contained the same wording with the exception that the word "further" was omitted—thus demonstrating the origin of the resolution![40]

The Communist-led group in the Chicago CIO Industrial Union Council condemned the secretary of the Council, Michael Mann, leader of the anti-Communist group, on the charge that he "was more concerned with expressions of support for the Montgomery-Ward workers than with the (reaffirmation) and defense of the no-strike pledge."[41] It became necessary for John Brophy, representing the National CIO headquarters, to investigate the Chicago affair. He concluded that:

> the Council and its Secretary were not only within their rights in declaring their support for the Montgomery-Ward employees, but might well have been regarded as remiss in their duty to organized labor had they failed to take a strong stand on that issue.

During this period, a working alliance was developed by Sidney Hillman between his traditionally anti-Communist Amalgamated Clothing Workers and the pro-Communist faction. Hillman, to whom Roosevelt gave much of the responsibility for supervising America's wartime manpower needs, took his task seriously. The winning of the war was the paramount objective. Unity was the means of attaining that objective, and he made up his mind to foster unity. Hillman sided with the pro-Communists in the American Labor Party and thus caused the irrevocable and noisy breach which led to the creation of the Liberal Party. In New York, too, the Amalgamated locals affiliated themselves, after many years of disagreement, with the actively pro-Communist Industrial Union Council.[42] Hillman did all this even though the Communists had, in earlier years, attacked him as "the real fifth column in labor's ranks. . . . The employer's representative in the C.I.O."[43]

The New York Industrial Union Council was probably one of the most brazen of the pro-Communist CIO groups and undoubtedly proved to be a source of great embarrassment to Hillman and to the other leaders of the Amalgamated. In 1943, it officially endorsed the Communist party leaders and candidates, Benjamin J. Davis and Peter V. Cacchione, for the New York City Council.[44] The official endorsement letter to Davis, signed by Joseph Curran as president and Saul Mills[45] as secretary-treasurer, read:[46]

You received the unanimous endorsement of the Council delegates because of your uncompromising support of the win-the-war program of President Franklin D. Roosevelt and your fight for the rights of the Negro people.

Again in 1945, after the Amalgamated Clothing Workers were a part of the Industrial Union Council, Davis was once more endorsed as a "symbol of the unity between the Negro people and people of all races."[47]

THE WAR ENDS

All ties of "unity" within the C.I.O. strained and eventually broke as the war came to an end and tension developed between the United States and the Soviet Union. Signs of the split on foreign policy first appeared in late 1945 with regard to the China question. The New York CIO Council, always a willing sounding board for the Communist program, sent a telegram to President Truman describing "the presence of American troops in China and the use of U.S. lend-lease arms and equipment by Kuomintang troops to fight other Chinese troops as constituting armed intervention in the internal affairs of one of our allies."[48] Washington Congressman Hugh DeLacy introduced a resolution of similar intent in the House of Representatives and a drive was begun in support of it within many of the CIO unions and councils. The matter came to the attention of the national CIO office when R. A. Hayes, President of the Omaha-Council Bluffs City Industrial Union Council, wrote the national office for guidance. On December 18, after a number of high level conferences, Nathan Cowan, CIO legislative director, replied as follows:

The National CIO has taken no action regarding the Foreign Policy of the United States Government in the affairs of the Chinese Government thus far. It is a well known fact, however, that the Government of the United States continues to recognize the National Government of China as the legitimate Government of China and as the central instrument for achieving Chinese unity; therefore, the CIO Legislative Committee, in a meeting held last week, voted unanimously to take no action on the resolution . . .

The New York CIO Council began to protest more actively against American foreign policy in 1946. When Winston Churchill visited New York in March, 1946, the *Daily Worker* carried the following story:[49]

> The City CIO will throw a mass picket line against the Waldorf-Astoria banquet the city is tendering Winston Churchill at 6 p.m. today in protest against his call for a U.S.-British military alliance against the Soviet Union.

The story also quoted the CIO as characterizing Churchill as the "greatest danger to world peace and security."

The end of the war and the Communist shift in foreign policy gave the anti-Communists in the CIO the cue actively to organize for the internal struggle. In New York, a CIO Committee for Democratic Trade Unionism was formed by 34 trade union leaders representing the UAW, segments of the United Retail, Wholesale, Shipbuilders, the Plaything and Novelty Workers, the Textile Workers Union, the Oil Workers, and the Utility Workers.[50] Stimulus for the organization came from the fact that the Communists were acting to oppose the election in New York of Senator James M. Mead for Governor and of former Governor Herbert H. Lehman for Senator.[51] Alleging that the Communist purpose was to "serve the ends of a foreign nation and its idealogy," these C.I.O. leaders also criticized the use of strikes or picketing "for the purpose of fostering the interests and policies of any political party or foreign power."

One of the leaders of the CIO Committee for Democratic Trade Unionism was Jack Altman, director of department store organization, who was also in the midst of a struggle against Local 65 and the Communist elements within his own international union. In an article in his union's newspaper,[52] he explained his anti-Communist activity as follows:

> I believe that Communism is in conflict with the democratic philosophy and the interests of the working people of this country. It must be fought wherever it is put forward with a positive democratic program.

The intensified anti-Communist activity within the New York CIO was matched in other areas and within the national CIO as well.

One of the nation's leading business and management journals, the *Chicago Journal of Commerce*, commented about this time on the Communist problem within the CIO. The article realistically reported:[53]

> Speaking moderately there is at least a hundred times as much vigorous and intelligent opposition to the Communist Fifth Column in organized labor as there is in business. For it is in organized labor that men and women learn who the Fifth Columnists are, how they maneuver, and how they must be fought . . .
>
> The Communists in the CIO are not strong enough to have their own way regularly, but, by their threats, and their totalitarian contempt for conscience, they are often as effective, as if they controlled 51 per cent of the membership. They command a veto power over almost any action, and Philip Murray submits to it . . .

Philip Murray's role was a strange and a difficult one. A devout Catholic and an unequivocal anti-Communist, he nevertheless had as his chief objective, the avoidance of a split within the CIO. At this time, the pro-Communists within the CIO controlled international unions with a membership of about a million, or about 15 per cent of the CIO's total.[54] Murray feared that a split within the CIO would significantly weaken the organization, encourage AFL raiding, and lead toward eventual destruction. Murray, who continued to feel the need to prove himself in the eyes of history, certainly had not inherited Lewis' mantle to preside over the liquidation of the CIO! Therefore, he continued to resist the anti-Communist pressure within the CIO and also continued Pressman and DeCaux as lieutenants. For this he was critized; many of the more rabid and impatient anti-Communists called him the Neville Chamberlain of American labor.[55] Murray's supporters urged patience.

A reporter for the *Chicago Journal of Commerce*, placing the CIO problem within the milieu of 1946 America, urged a proper perspective:[56]

> Certainly it is very naughty of Mr. Murray to appease the Communists, but when one considers those California business leaders who anxiously opposed the deportation of Harry Bridges, and that New York shipping magnate who was honorary chairman of the huge banquet in honor of Communist Ferdinand Smith

of the National Maritime Union one is led to suspect that Mr. Murray's naughtiness has its counterparts in other places than the labor movement.

Prior to the 1946 convention of the National CIO there was a great deal of feverish activity on both sides and much confusion as to what the future held in store. Speaking before the convention of his United Steel Workers, in May, Murray virtually ignored the importance of the Communist issue and so disappointed many of the anti-Communists. He took note of the problem only by saying the CIO would not tolerate "outsiders" and listed them "whether they be Communists, Socialists or any other group to infiltrate, dictate, or meddle."[57] Murray's speech, which at least indicated that he was aware of the sharp controversy within his organization, was criticized as indicating a lack of comprehension of the basic essentials which made the Communists a threat to the American labor movement. By associating Socialists "or any other group" with Communists, he alienated a number of the anti-Communists leaders who felt a kinship with the socialist tradition albeit not with the Socialist Party, and who felt that the basic issue was a belief in democracy.

The Communists, on the other hand, seemed relieved by the speech. Ben Gold, the head of the CIO International Fur and Leather Workers, claimed the speech barred anti-Communist witch hunts in the CIO.[58] He said Murray had "smashed the hope of those who sought to divide, weaken and undermine unions by eliminating Communists and progressives and other honest union members from office and from the unions themselves."[59] Speaking before the Fur Workers Union convention which was meeting at this time, Lee Pressman, CIO general counsel, praised the union as "one of the organizations that has lived up to the principles of the statement of policy expressed by Murray."[60] in spite of the fact that Gold and Potash, the union's leaders, were avowed members of the Communist party. This was accompanied by a *Daily Worker* story praising Murray's speech for reaffirming the right of any CIO member to "harbor such views as he chooses."[61]

The drive to rid the CIO of Communists continued, however. James B. Carey, secretary-treasurer of the CIO, was, as we have seen, particularly active in the campaign. His efforts were effective because he was frequently presumed to speak for Mr. Murray as well as for himself, and it was known he certainly would not speak *contrary* to Murray's wishes. In the war of nerves, therefore, Carey's speeches assumed significance. Communists in the CIO, remembering Mr. Murray's speech which they had praised in May, read Mr. Carey's speech before the 12th Annual Convention of the Industrial Union of Marine and Shipbuilding Workers, on September 24, 1946, and wondered indeed whether Mr. Murray loved them in September as he had in May. Carey said:[62]

> There are in this country a number of forces actuated by differing motives. For example, the American Communist Party has appointed itself advance agent for a certain formula for world government and establishment of a certain type of economy. It is vastly different from the American type of economy which the CIO favors. Events during the last several months certainly have made it clear to all members of your union that the Communist Party does not favor the economy favored by your international officers and the programs adopted at your last convention. The fight against the policies of your international union, which are traditional CIO policies, has not been limited to healthy, open discussion and democratic procedures on the floors of your local union. The war against you has been waged in accordance with outside political views, and while those political views openly belittle American constitutional processes, your opponents have not hesitated to invoke the aid of American courts which they hate and despise. Underlining the whole procedure is their basic desire to operate your international union solely as a political club in the interest of the foreign policies of Soviet Russia. If we are critical of American foreign policy, as well we can be, there are certainly other alternatives available than adoption of the foreign policy of some other government. As I see this problem our task is to do our utmost to correct our foreign policy, not discard it. That is our American way of doing things . . .

There was a great deal of confusion, however, when Murray, a few days later, addressing the UE convention, went out of his way to place on record his praises for that union's leadership. He was "proud" and "pleased" and "deeply appreciative" of "the splendid support" which "your organization and its officers" gave "for all national policies."[63]

This was followed by a Murray speech the following month in Chicago before a conference of progressives (not to be confused with the Progressive Party formed later on, although some delegates were to be associated with both). In this speech, Murray made clear the place of the Communist within his own United Steel Workers:[64]

> We've got no more use for any damn Communist coming over here meddling in our affairs than you would welcome our meddling in your affairs. And so far as I am concerned, the same thing goes for any damn Communist meddling in the affairs of the independent Progressive movement in America. We want only to be left alone to work out our affairs without any intrusions from outside.

1946, therefore, was a year of sparring, waiting, and much grumbling on the part of the CIO factions—with Murray attempting to maintain internal strength and unity.

One of the most serious political consequences of the internal split and of the Communist strength within the CIO appeared in Wisconsin, where the Communists had a pocket of power in the Milwaukee and Wisconsin Industrial Union Councils.

Wisconsin's U.S. Senator Robert M. LaFollette, Jr., one of the nation's outstanding liberals, was also a strong critic of the Soviet Union. In 1946, he faced a primary battle within the Republican Party for renomination, against Joseph McCarthy, representative of the Old Guard Republicans in the state. LaFollette, who had always run as a Progressive with the support of organized labor, had decided earlier that his Progressive Party had outlived its usefulness and that his political future called for him to join and liberalize the Republican Party. He looked for support in the primary and election from organized labor, whose friend he had always been.

But the Milwaukee CIO began to spread the word around that LaFollette was anti-labor. Charges appeared in the Milwaukee newspapers, attributed to a CIO union official, that LaFollette had favored attempts to weaken the bill calling for a 65¢ an hour minimum wage. The Communists in the CIO were intent on defeating LaFollette regardless of the political alternative available.

In an attempt to thwart these plans, the National CIO, which championed the Wisconsin senator, sent its representative to Milwaukee and made public an official letter of support. Over the signature of Nathan Cowan, legislative director for the CIO, the letter branded the rumor "completely in error" and characterized the attitude of the local CIO officials as "in no way. . .(representing) the feelings of President Philip Murray or of the national CIO."[65]

> The record is clear that in the course of debate and voting on the 65¢ Minimum Wage Bill you consistently took a place among those waging the fight for a decent bill free from crippling amendments.

It noted that Senator LaFollette, on two occasions, had voted for defeat of labor-opposed ammendments.[66]

> Your vote on all these issues was fully in consonance with the position of the CIO and other labor and liberal organizations supporting the 65¢ Minimum Wage Bill and in line with your own good record on legislation affecting labor's rights, civil liberties, and the social welfare of the people. Equally untrue is the statement attributed to the CIO union official that you failed to support previous legislative activity in behalf of a Fair Employment Practices Commission, as is also the charge that 'on the one hand he (Senator LaFollette) sold out the Negro people and on the other hand he voted against labor.'
>
> Please rest assured that the CIO is highly appreciative of your votes in behalf of recent legislation favored by this organization.

LaFollette's defeat in the Wisconsin Republican primary intensified the hostilities within the CIO and helped sharpen the issues as the CIO entered its 1946 convention in November.

---

1 Benjamin Stolberg, "Inside Labor," *The American Mercury,* Vol. 53, August, 1941, p. 177.
2 Testimony before the House of Representatives Special Committee on Un-American Activities alleged that Wyndham Mortimer had been a member of the Communist Party, under the alias of Baker, since 1933. Joseph Zack, former member of the Communist Party Central Committee, testified he had approved Mortimer's application. Earl Browder, to a direct question as to Mortimer's membership, said: "I am not sure. He is a very close friend, at least. . . ." Mortimer's early UAW activities from 1936 identified him with the Communist caucus; these activities brought con-

stant praise and recognition from the *Daily Worker* (January 21, 1937; August 20, 1937; August 1, 1940; December 1, 1940; January 3, 1941). See House Report No. 1311, *Investigation of Un-American Propaganda in the United States,* 1944, 78th Congress, Second Session, on H. Res. 282.

[3] The *Daily Worker,* December 1, 1940, greeted the Vultee strikers as "heroes."

[4] Stolberg, "Inside Labor," *op. cit.*

[5] Jack Barbash, *Labor Unions in Action* (Harpers: New York: 1948) p. 214.

[6] Associated with Mortimer in the UAW on the West Coast was Lew H. Michener, West Coast Director, who was likewise actively associated with Communists, and accused by many of being a Communist Party member. Another member of this West Coast team was Philip M. (Slim) Connelly, secretary and president of the Los Angeles American Newspaper Guild, secretary of the Los Angeles CIO Industrial Union Council, and president of the California State Industrial Union Council. He was reported to have participated in the aircraft strike decisions. The Special House Committee on Un-American Activities has listed a number of his pro-Communist affiliations and activities. See House Report 1311, 78th Congress, 2nd Session, *op. cit.,* pp. 131, 98, 99.

[7] Stolberg, "Inside Labor," *op. cit.,* p. 180.

[8] *Ibid.,* p. 179.

[9] *Ibid.* p. 178.

[10] Donald A. Schwartz, *The 1941 Strike at Allis Chalmers* (an unpublished thesis for an M.A. degree, University of Wisconsin: Madison, 1943).

[11] *The New York Times,* June 1, 1947, p. 1.

[12] *The Milwaukee Journal,* February 22, 1948, Standley's remarks of course occasioned an international episode and led to his recall in appeasement of the U.S.S.R. Yet his remarks were essentially correct.

[13] *Daily Worker,* April 11, 1942.

[14] United Electrical, Radio, and Machine Workers of America, *Proceedings of the Eighth Constitutional Convention* (Cleveland, Ohio, September 7-11 1942) pp. 120, 121, 127.

[15] Kermit Eby, CIO Director of Education and Research during this period, was an ordained Brethren minister. The Brethren is one of the historic pacifist denominations.

[16] *Daily Worker,* July 27, 1940.

[17] *The Retail, Wholesale and Department Store Employee,* January 1, 1945.

[18] Alfred Braunthal, "American Labor in Politics," *Social Research,* Vol. 12, No. 1, February 1945, p. 11.

[19] William J. Smith, *Spotlight on Labor Unions* (New York, 1946) p. 79.

[20] The background for this analysis comes from an interview in July, 1947 with Mr. Nathan Cowan, national legislative director of the CIO.

[21] *Congressional Record,* September 24, 1942, p. 7687.

[22] *Daily Worker,* March 9, 1942, p. 3.

[23] *Daily Worker,* May 19, 1942.

[24] *Supra* p. 81.

[25] *Daily Worker,* May 19, 1942.

[26] Julien Steinberg, *Verdict of Three Decades* (Duell, Sloan and Pearce: New York, 1950) pp. 424, 425.

[27] *Ibid.,* p. 425.

[28] Jerzy Gliksman, *Tell The West* (Gresham Press: New York, 1948) p. 358.

[29] *Daily Worker,* March 31, 1943.

[30] *Daily Worker,* April 3, 1943.

[31] *New York World Telegram,* April 28, 1943.

[32] In addition to Osman, the union had the following pro-Communist leaders: Kenneth Sherbell, vice-president, who in 1942 supported Israel Amter for Governor of New York on the Communist ticket; David Livingstone, organization director, listed by the Yearbook of the Young Communist League as an active leader who became New York State Chairman of the Communist-front American Youth for Democracy; Irving Baldinger, editor, who joined 27 other officers and staff of the union in sending greetings to the *Daily Worker* on its 20th anniversary in 1944; Jack Paley, secretary-treasurer, a member of the Communist May Day Committee in 1946; Mollie Genser, director of the hardware division and an avowed member of the Communist Party.

[33] For much of this material I am indebted to Frederick Woltman and Nelson Frank, staff writers of the *New York World Telegram,* who made their files available for my examination.

[34] Levenstein, *op. cit.,* p. 165.

[35] In 1942 and 1943, negotiations took place, under the auspices of the Communist Party, between Harry Bridges and Arthur Osman for Local 65 to withdraw from the RWDSE and affiliate with the International Longshoremen's and Warehousemen's Union. Local 65 was in per capita dues arrears to the International. This would have brought Bridges to the East Coast and created a strong Communist front. See CIO, *Hearings to Investigate ILWU, op. cit.,* pp. 597, 598.

[36] *Retail, Wholesale and Department Store Employee,* January 1, 1945.

[37] Levenstein, *op. cit.,* p. 167.

[38] *Ibid.,* p. 161; and *PM,* December 22, 1944.

[39] Levenstein, *op. cit.,* p. 165.

[40] *Ibid.*

[41] Barbash, *op. cit.,* p. 214.

[42] *Daily Worker,* March 15, 1945.

[43] Levenstein, *op. cit.,* p. 165. A rather unsatisfactory biography of Hillman is *Sidney Hillman* by Matthew Josephson (New York, 1952).

[44] *Daily Worker,* October 9, 1943.

[45] Mills, a member of the American Newspaper Guild, had a long record of pro-Communist activities. See House Report 1311, 78th Congress, 2nd Session, *op. cit.,* pp. 132, 133.

[46] *Daily Worker,* October 14, 1943.

[47] *Daily Worker,* July 21, 1945.

[48] *Daily Worker,* November 10, 1945.

[49] *Daily Worker,* March 15, 1946. This was after Churchill's speech at Fulton, Mo.

[50] Press release, October 3, 1946.

[51] The Political Action Committee Director for the New York CIO at this time was Daniel Allen, recently elected. In sworn testimony before the New York State Department of Labor, reported in the *New York World Telegram,* a municipal home relief employee and ex-Communist, Affie Hammond, testified on August 8, 1941 that Allen had been a leader of the Communist party faction within the CIO State, County and Municipal

Workers Union while acting as secretary-treasurer. There was evidence that Allen was active in the American Peace Mobilization before the war and had declared the war to be "a war for market-grabbing which is Fascist and anti-labor and anti-people on both sides." Allen had also, prior to becoming CIO-PAC Director in New York, taught at the School for Democracy, a Communist training school, and had been a member of the Citizens Committee to Free Earl Browder, and of the Morris U. Schappes Defense Committee. On April 25, 1946, prior to the 1946 elections, and the formation of the CIO Committee for Democratic Trade Unionism, Allen was quoted in the *Daily Worker* in favor of a resolution introduced at the April convention of the United Federal Workers Union accusing Great Britain and the United States of "imperialist ambitions," praising Russia, and demanding the immediate withdrawal of British and American troops from China, France, Greece, the Philippines, Indonesia, Belgium and Iceland.

[52] *The Retail, Wholesale and Department Store Employee*, November, 1946.

[53] Andrew Avery, "The Communist Fifth Column," *Chicago Journal of Commerce*, June 25, 1946 pp. 1, 7.

[54] It is again necessary to warn that this number bears no relationship to the number of Communists within the CIO. The Communists, by acting as an effective disciplined minority, exercised a power acutely disproportionate to their numbers.

[55] Avery, *op. cit.*

[56] *Ibid.*

[57] *The New Leader*, May 18, 1946.

[58] *Daily Worker*, May 16, 1946.

[59] *The New York Times*, May 21, 1946.

[60] *Ibid.*

[61] *Daily Worker*, May 17, 1946.

[62] James B. Carey, "Address at Twelfth Annual Convention of the Industrial Union of Marine and Shipbuilding Workers of America," (mimeographed) September 24, 1946.

[63] *Sunday Worker*, September 29, 1946.

[64] *The New York Times*, November 17, 1946.

[65] CIO, Press Release, April 10, 1946.

[66] LaFollette's defeat in the Republican Primary cannot be attributed solely to the action of the Communists in the Wisconsin CIO. A number of the AFL leaders were also quite critical of LaFollette, primarily because he concerned himself rather exclusively with national affairs and seldom took the time to "mend his fences" at home. Some of the craft leaders had also developed a close relationship with the Old Guard state Republican machine. In addition to these factors, LaFollette's decision to abandon the Progressive Party and join the Republicans met with the disapproval of many Progressives, particularly the younger people who felt the action was irresponsible and selfish. A number wanted the Progressive party to continue, while others felt closer to the Democratic party nationally and wanted to help build a liberal Democratic party in their state.

4 | A CRITICAL
CONVENTION: 1946

The 1946 CIO Convention found the generals ready but the battle-lines and armies ill-formed. The Communists had control of international unions representing about 15 percent of the total CIO membership but they could not be certain of the loyalty of the members in case of a split. They were, in the main, able to control the policies of the union, but only because they were a disciplined minority rather than because they represented the views of the membership.

The lineup appeared to be as follows:[1]

IN THE COMMUNIST CAMP:

American Communications Association
Food, Tobacco, Agricultural & Allied Workers
International Longshoremen's & Warehousemen's Union
Inland Boatmen's Union of the Pacific
International Union of Fisherman and Allied Workers
International Union of Fur and Leather Workers
International Union of Mine, Mill and Smelter Workers
National Marine Cooks and Stewards Association
National Maritime Union
Transport Workers Union
United Electrical, Radio, and Machine Workers
United Farm Equipment and Metal Workers
United Furniture Workers
United Office and Professional Workers (which had just absorbed the Federation of Architects, Engineers, Chemists, and Technicians)

United Public Workers (formed by a recent merger of United Federal Workers and the CIO State, County and Municipal Workers)

United Shoe Workers

UNCERTAIN AND SHIFTING:

Amalgamated Clothing Workers

United Gas, Coke and Chemical Workers

United Packinghouse Workers

International Woodworkers of America (formerly Communist-controlled; anti-Communists coming into power)

National Marine Engineers' Beneficial Association

Optical and Instrument Workers Organizing Committee

Retail, Wholesale and Department Store Union

United Automobile Workers

United Stone and Allied Products Workers

Barbers and Beauty Culturists

Oil Workers International Union (President O. A. Knight anti-Communist, but some other leaders are not)

ANTI-COMMUNIST AND LEANING AGAINST COMMUNISTS:

Federation of Glass, Ceramic and Silica-Sand Workers

Industrial Union of Marine and Shipbuilding Workers

United Paperworkers of America

United Steel Workers of America

United Rubber, Cork, Linoleum and Plastic Workers

International Union of Playthings, Jewelry, and Novelty Workers

American Newspaper Guild (but New York and Los Angeles chapters controlled by Communist Party)

Textile Workers Union

United Transport Service Employees

United Railroad Workers of America

Utility Workers Union (recently granted CIO charter. Its new constitution contained one of the most drastic bans against Communists ever adopted by a labor union, specifically excluding Communists and providing for their expulsion from membership. Article II, Sec. 5, reads "Any member accepting

membership in the Communist, Fascist, or Nazi party shall
be expelled from the Utility Worker's Union of America
and is permanently barred from holding office... and no
member of the Communist, Fascist, or Nazi party shall be
permitted to have membership in our union unless they withdraw from the Communist, Fascist, or Nazi party and forfeit
their membership therein.")

On the eve of the Atlantic City convention, the CIO Executive
Board met and there faced a Phillip Murray, somewhat hurt at the
criticism levelled against him and the CIO, determined to do something to defend himself against that criticism and yet anxious to
preserve organic unity by not going too far too fast. He demanded
a resolution which he was determined to have unanimously accepted
by the Executive Board and then by the convention.

To draft the resolution, he appointed a committee of six, evenly
divided among the two factions. On the committee were Benjamin
Gold, president of the Fur and Leather Workers, an acknowledged
Communist; Abram Flaxer, president of the United Public Workers,
pro-Communist;[2] and Michael Quill, head of the Transport Workers.
The right wing representatives were Walter P. Reuther, president
of the United Automobile Workers, he had just defeated R. J.
Thomas for the office and was considered one of the most fervent of
the anti-Communists; Emil Rieve, president of the Textile Workers,
and from the first a steady and dependable ally of the anti-Communists; and Milton Murray, president of the American Newspaper
Guild.

Phillip Murray joined the committee, which was in session most
of the week end, and helped to direct it to a unanimous decision.
The resolution was, in the main, similar to Murray's May speech—a
non-controversial reaffirmation of democratic faith followed by a
final paragraph which would make some of the Communists swallow
a little hard when accepting it. The last paragraph seemed incidental
and associated the "efforts of the Communist Party" with "other
political parties and their adherents" who would "intervene in the
affairs of the CIO," although this time the Socialists were not
specifically mentioned.[3]

The following day, on November 18, immediately after the

President's Report and as the first item of business, Murray asked that the convention rules be suspended so that he could present the "special statement of policy" adopted by the Executive Board. It is important to quote from the *Proceedings* of the convention at this point for Mr. Murray's presentation:[4]

> It might be opportune at this moment for the presiding officer to give to the delegates the benefit of such information as he may have in his possession regarding the need for the introduction of this resolution today.
>
> For some weeks prior to the convening of this convention, and particularly in the course of the past few days, the news organs of the nation, in so far as their columns are concerned, were literally deluged with a great amount of material concerning the position the CIO convention might take with regard to an extremely important issue, that issue being one with which the delegates are fully conversant.
>
> It deals primarily with the allegations contained in the newsprints and disseminated throughout the land that this organization of yours and mine, this great big mighty trade union movement, was Communistically dominated.
>
> I have consistently, in the course of my incumbency as President of your Union, taken occasion to deny such charges, contending that these statements were not true. However, the propaganda disseminated throughout the nation, particularly in the newspapers, created in certain sections of our country a kind of hysteria over the subject, and in the course of the last Congressional election many aspirants for public office, taking advantage of these misrepresentations, denounced and slandered this movement of ours to win votes at the polls.
>
> As I have stated before, I have taken occasion repeatedly to assert that this Union, the Congress of Industrial Organizations, was not and must never be Communistically controlled or inspired. However, that statement again was one of fact (sic), an incontrovertible fact.
>
> Hence, due to these wild and wholly irrational statements I thought it proper in the course of this convention to have the matter brought to the attention of the CIO Executive Board. Last Friday, without consulting anyone, any officer of this organization or any member of this Union, I assumed the personal responsibility for directing the attention of the Executive Board to this all-important matter ...
>
> It should not be misconstrued to be a repressive measure, calculated to do certain things of a repressive nature, but it does

provide definitely certain charts and certain courses, that when this subject matter is disposed of, should be and in fact must be adhered to within the councils of the National CIO and all of its affiliates . . .

In presenting the Resolution to the convention, Murray did not ask for discussion. He hoped the delegates would respond with a "rising vote of thanks" to the Executive Board. He said this would "obviate the necessity of needless debate . . . because that has already been taken care of" by the Executive Board. He made it clear in his comments that he was associating himself with the vigorous anti-Communists in the CIO when he said, "This organization is not and must not be Communist-controlled and inspired." But he then paid his respects to the moderates and attempted to attract the support of the pro-Communists for the resolution when he also said that the statement is "designed to chart a course for the overall conduct of our International unions. . . . It should not be misconstrued to be a repressive measure. . . . As the President of this organization . . . I am definitely opposed to any form of repression in this movement of ours."

The minutes of the convention read, however:[5]

PRESIDENT MURRAY: Those favoring the motion will rise to their feet.

The delegates will all be seated.

Those opposed to the motion will rise to their feet.

There are two delegates who have arisen to their feet and voted against the motion. It seems, therefore, that the resolution recommended by the Executive Board to this convention has been adopted by a 'faint' majority.

(Later, just before adjournment, President Murray announced that the two delegates who had voted against the adoption of the statement of policy had appeared on the platform and indicated their desire to withdraw their opposition, and that the statement had therefore been adopted by unanimous vote of the convention.)

Observers at the convention who saw the incident have reported that the two temporary dissenters were Joseph Stack and Howard McKenzie, vice-presidents of the NMU. A number of others did not rise from their chairs to accept the resolution, but neither did they dissent. As soon as the two dissenters made their presence known, Joseph Selly, head of the American Communications Association, "immediately went into earnest conversation with Mr. Stack."[6] It was clear that the Communists had no desire to irritate or further alienate Mr. Murray. A few moments later, the dissenters reversed their position, making the vote unanimous.

It was also clear that the Communists, as always, were operating as a caucus. The exact nature of the caucus was confidentially revealed some time later by Michael Quill of the Transport Workers Union, who participated in it. He said that the caucus met daily with John Williamson, labor secretary of the Communist Party, who had a hotel room in Atlantic City; ". . . it was called of the leaders of all the left wing unions," he explained. "Whether they were members of the Communist Party or not I don't know. But they got their instructions at these meetings from John Williamson, the Secretary of the Communist Party."[7]

There was one other indication of disunity which brought the convention close to an open break. The convention was scheduled to elect nine vice-presidents, one of whom was to be newly-elected President Walter Reuther of the UAW. R.J. Thomas, who had been supported by the pro-Communists within that union was, therefore, to be relieved of his vice-presidential post. The CIO "right wing" was also planning to make one other change in the officer's slate by fighting against the re-election of Reid Robinson, head of the Mine, Mill, and Smelter Workers, to a CIO vice-presidency. Their opposition was ostensibly based on Mr. Robinson's acceptance of a $5,000 loan from an employer, but no less important was their desire to displace a pro-Communist. They were hopeful of replacing Robinson with O. A. Knight, "right-wing" head of the Oil Workers Union. Murray was likewise determined to have Robinson withdraw and so notified the left-wing. When the pro-Communists balked, however, and threatened a fight, Murray, after a series of discussions agreed upon a plan with the left-wing, whereby Robinson would be replaced by R. J. Thomas, in spite of the fact that he was defeated for office within his own international union and it would mean two CIO vice-presidents from the UAW. The left-wing, in turn, agreed not to run a candidate against Carey, secretary-treasurer.

When this agreement reached the ears of the right-wing leaders, there was consternation. They regarded it as a virtual cancellation of Mr. Reuther's vote on the executive board and considered making an issue of it, which would have shattered the veneer of harmony which Murray was struggling to preserve. Within a few minutes after Murray's speech accepting re-election, the difficulty began.[8]

Murray, in his acceptance speech, had pointedly said:[9]

> Let no one create conflict within this movement. It has a God-given task to perform for the men, the women, and the children of America. So, carry forward, my friends; demonstrate, as you have demonstrated in the course of this convention, that spirit of accord, that spirit of unity so essential to the well-being of the people whom you are privileged to represent.

This speech was met with vigorous applause. The convention immediately proceeded to the election of vice-presidents.

Nominations proceeded smoothly until David J. McDonald, secretary-treasurer of the Steel Workers, nominated R. J. Thomas for the ninth spot to replace Robinson. (The other eight were Reuther; L. S. Buckmaster, of the Rubber Workers; Joseph Curran of the National Maritime Union; Albert J. Fitzgerald of the Electrical Workers; John Green, of the Shipbuilding Workers; Allen S. Haywood of the Steel Workers; Emil Rieve of the Textile Workers; and Frank Rosenblum of the Amalgamated Clothing Workers.) This itself was unusual in that Thomas was the only candidate not nominated by a member of his own union. Murray's strategy in designating one of his own associates to make the nomination was clearly to make it a personal issue.

Following Thomas' nomination, T. M. McCormick, of the Oil Workers International Union, stood up and in the longest nomination speech placed Knight's name before the convention. The situation became tense in the convention hall, according to Joseph A. Loftus, who attended the convention as the *New York Times* correspondent.[10] The parliamentary procedure usually followed was to elect the nine vice-presidents en bloc—but now there were ten candidates. Quickly, Knight, who had been put on the spot by Murray's personal intervention in the election, took the rostrum and withdrew, saying he "did not want to delay the convention by a roll-call."[11] On this, George Baldanzi, vice-president of the Textile Workers Union, and bitter foe of the Communists, stepped to the microphone. Speaking moderately, he said:[12]

> I have no desire nor wish to inject any controversial questions in this convention that has gone along so harmoniously for the past week, but I do want to state for the record, without necessarily discussing personalities, that we of the Textile Workers Union of America have always been very proud to belong to the CIO. We still are, and we will, I assure you, support the policies of this Union and its officers in every respect. But one of the things that has contributed to the greatness of CIO has been that feeling, that concept which has given representation to all the Unions, large or small, within the confines of this organization; and we of the Textile Workers Union of America wish to state for the record that we think it is not proper departure when we begin to elect more than one Vice President from any one International Union.
>
> I have the greatest admiration for Brother Reuther and for Brother Thomas, but I don't believe that that organization is entitled to two Vice Presidents in the National CIO, and I want that merely, as I say, as our point of view, and I don't want it to be misunderstood, but we do feel quite strongly about it, and I wanted the opportunity in this democratic assembly of stating my point of view.

There was substantial applause, according to Mr. Loftus, whereupon Murray, also speaking softly, said:[13]

> I might say for the information of the convention there is nothing before the convention now but the regular election of these candidates. It is needless to indulge in the luxury of filling up the record with our personal convictions about these matters. The Chair is compelled to rule under the circumstances that the delegates take their chairs and we proceed with the regular election.

Ross Blood, of the Shipbuilding Workers, now approached the microphone to support Baldanzi. He was greeted with shouts of "You tell him, Ross," but retreated when Murray warned the delegates, "Don't get noisy." Baldanzi later told reporters his chief purpose had been to "make a record." Loftus, continuing his report, wrote:

The right wing was furious about the entire performance. Except for Mr. Baldanzi's remarks, they contained themselves on the convention floor only out of loyalty to Mr. Murray and deference to his wish for avoidance of open hostilities. For like reasons did the left refrain from nominating an opponent to Mr. Carey for secretary-treasurer. When Mr. Carey was elected there was a rising ovation, but delegates from his own union, the Electrical Workers, remained in their seats.

Another indication of the tight rope walked by the CIO at the 1946 convention can be seen from the following report by Mr. Loftus dealing with the foreign policy resolution adopted by the convention and written by the resolution committee, chaired by anti-Communist Van Bittner but under the secretaryship of Lee Pressman.[14]

A foreign policy resolution submitted to the Congress of Industrial Organizations convention today with the approval of the resolutions committee called for an end to the stockpiling of atomic bombs and for progressive universal disarmament.

Some evidence of Communist inspiration in the document evoked mutterings of dissatisfaction. Nevertheless the statement met some of the demands of the Right Wing, too, and it was so carefully worded in other respects that opposition on the convention floor . . . was not expected to be serious.

The only criticism of the resolution came from Jack Altman, representing the RWDSU, who was also chairman of the New York Committee of Thirty-Four to Fight Communism. He did not oppose the resolution, however, choosing rather to demur in part. He particularly questioned the CIO policy calling for an end to bomb stockpiling. He said:[15]

. . . the United States made the greatest gesture that any nation made in the history of the world. We feel this weapon is so dangerous to mankind we are willing to have control of this weapon shared by mankind through the United Nations. There is one condition. We say there must be a system of control and inspection. The only sound position our Government can take is to yield its own sovereignty and for others to do the same.

Van A. Bittner, chairman of the resolutions committee, replied that a 28 man resolutions committee approved the resolution. "This resolution, from end to end, backs up every action of the United States of America." On adoption, there was a scattering of 'no' votes heard in the auditorium, but it was difficult to ascertain the sources.

Interestingly enough, this resolution—though defended by Van Bittner—was used by the Communists the following year at the New York State CIO convention, when Mr. Altman was again one of the leaders against the powerful Communist wing. The "right-wing," for the first time organized and on the road to solidification, supported a foreign policy resolution at the 1947 Saratoga Springs Convention which endorsed the Marshall Plan, called for the abolition of the veto power, and condemned all forms of totalitarianism. Their program went on to accuse the USSR of utilizing its veto power "to reinforce its reactionary nationalistic position in the United Nations." To meet this attack, the pro-Communists pointed to the 1946 CIO Atlantic City resolution calling on the U.S. to stop the stockpiling of atom bombs, urging the renewal of Big Three unity, and calling for the severing of diplomatic relations with Spain.[16] They, therefore, criticized the right-wing program as being opposed to CIO policy.

The 1947 New York convention did not settle the right-wing, left-wing dispute in that state. A compromise was reached condemning the "excessive use of the veto power" and urging that vetoes be subject to a three-quarter over-riding vote by the General Assembly. With regard to the controversial Marshall Plan, the adopted resolution went on to say: "there is an overwhelming and immediate need for American help to the war-torn countries of Europe, Asia, and Africa. We must extend that help in the fullest measure that our resources allow and we must act without delay."[17]

The 1946 National CIO Convention would have been quite a disappointment to the anti-Communists had it not been accompanied by other indications that the CIO would put a halt to Communist activity and carry out its stated intent. The most important of these was the adoption of an amendment to the CIO Rules for Industrial Union Councils, which was, incidentally, also unanimously adopted by the CIO Executive Board. Industrial Union Councils, within the CIO, are organizations of various CIO locals in the same area, usually a state or large city, which join together

to sponsor legislation and other forms of mutual aid[18] and obtain a
CIO charter for that purpose.[19]

Since this form of union activity is, in the main, secondary to the
bread and butter activity of running the day-to-day work of a local
union, a great many local unions merely went through the form
of belonging to an industrial union council without putting too much
time into the activity. This made many councils easily subject to
manipulation by Communists. Hence, an unusually large number of
the councils were under Communist domination and, as we have
seen, associated the name of the CIO with a great many pro-
Communist resolutions and activities.

Taking one geographical area, for example, the Central West,
we find the Communists in control of the following city industrial
union councils: Detroit, Des Moines, Omaha, Milwaukee, St. Louis,
Minneapolis and St. Paul. Chicago, Cincinnati, Columbus, and
Kansas City (Mo.) were in the non-Communist camp. Taking states
in the Central West, the line up was Indiana, Wisconsin, Missouri,
Iowa-Nebraska, Minnesota, and North Dakota in the pro-Communist Camp; and in the non-Communist column were Ohio, Michigan, and Kansas.[20]

It was, therefore, quite significant to have the CIO Executive
Board on November 15, 1946, adopt an amendment to Rule #81[21]
which read as follows:

> Local and state industrial union councils shall confine their activ-
> ities and statements to issues of *local or state* concern and to
> matters of general policy that have been passed upon by the
> national CIO. Councils shall take no action *or* issue statements in
> conflict with CIO policy. They shall send no delegates *or* make
> any contribution to *national* organizations not recognized by the
> CIO. In case of doubt as to CIO policy or recognition, and on
> problems of procedure and structure, councils shall consult with
> and be guided by advice of the national office of the CIO. Noth-
> ing in this paragraph shall prevent any council from making
> recommendations on any subject at any time to the national CIO
> through CIO channels.
>
> The national office of the CIO shall have the power to
> assign *duly accredited* CIO Representatives to work closely with
> local, state and industrial union councils for the purpose of having
> such councils comport themselves to the requirements of the pol-
> icies herein provided.

In his Report to the convention, Philip Murray specifically chastised
a number of the Industrial Union Councils. He said:[22]

> Public statements by local Councils on developments in distant
> foreign lands, in relation to which the CIO has not taken a
> position, are too often based on faulty information, sometimes
> conflict with policy formulation which is the responsibility of
> designated agencies of the national CIO, and should not be in-
> dulged in by Industrial Union Councils. The proper procedure is
> for Councils to make their views known in appropriate statements
> or communications to the Director of Councils for transmission
> to the executive officers and the appropriate CIO agencies deal-
> ing with these questions. Due consideration can then be given to
> such recommendations by the national organization.

To the press, Murray explained that "some laxity in operation in
these councils" has occurred, and that "oftentimes strangers have
gotten into their midst and offered destructive propaganda" in the
form of statements "not as trade union issues or not in conformity
with national CIO policy."[23]

It is interesting to note that the *Daily Worker*, in reporting the
new Rules Change, limited its explanation to the fact that it was
necessary because of interference by "strangers."[24] John Brophy,
director of Industrial Union Councils for the national CIO office,
however, was quite specific as to the meaning of the amendment.
Soon after the end of the convention, he sent a letter to all of the
industrial union councils ordering them forthwith to drop all association with and activity for the National Negro Congress, an
organization which had been listed in 1943 by Attorney-General
Biddle as "sponsored and supported by the Communist Party."[25]
The National Negro Congress had been organized in 1935 and had
attracted a great many Negro and labor leaders. By 1940, however,
its pro-Communist character was clear, leading to the resignation of
a great many of its members and leaders, including A. Philip
Randolph, international president of the Brotherhood of Sleeping
Car Porters, who issued a statement alleging that the organization
was "deliberately packed with Communists and CIO members
who were either Communists or sympathizers with the Communists."

There was no doubt but that the CIO had supported the NNC

actively. In fact, the very year of Randolph's resignation, John L. Lewis spoke at their 1940 convention expressing CIO support for their activities. Nevertheless, as the opposition to the Communists within the CIO developed, so did support for the NNC disappear. By the May, 1946 convention, only pro-Communists in the CIO like Donald Henderson, president of the Food, Tobacco, and Agricultural Workers, remained active sponsors. In that context, therefore, Brophy's letter to the industrial union councils was quite significant. In his letter, Brophy said: "You will please note that the national office of the CIO has never indorsed the National Negro Congress and that our councils should not engage in membership solicitation, fund raising, or other activities in support of this organization." He went on to say, "The organization with which we work very closely and successfully is the National Association for the Advancement of Colored People, on whose Executive Board is President Philip Murray."

In summarizing the effect of the 1946 CIO convention, both factions felt that the decisions made there were inconclusive. The *Daily Worker* greeted the convention decisions with a whistle-in-the-dark editorial called "A Rebuff to Reaction."[26] The editorial reflected the public position of the Communists at the time, which was one of strengthening Murray's attitude of caution and siding with him in his determination to maintain unity. The editorial said: "Fully aware of the real goal behind the red-baiting diversions, the Communists and Left forces had no hesitation whatsoever in refusing to make themselves a party to any kind of internal struggle which would lead the convention away from the real tasks at this crucial moment." It evaluated the convention action as follows: "The intrigues and hopes of reaction with regard to splitting the CIO have been again frustrated."

The *New York Times* correspondent concluded in his summary;[27] "few believe it (the issue of communism in the CIO) was finally resolved." He said:

Communists and their associates, whatever their strength or weakness, are still there. No material change was made in the personnel in key positions. Resentments seemed to run even deeper as the convention closed. . . . What the right wing undertook in the CIO convention this week was to curb the Communist base of operation. They succeeded to some extent, but it is too early for an accurate assessment ... the convention revised the preamble of their consitution. The new language, in part, is: 'We oppose all those who would use power to exploit the people in the interest of alien loyalties.' The right yielded, however, to President Murray's strongly expressed wish for outward harmony. The price of their refusal to yield might have been Mr. Murray's refusal to accept the presidency again. They did not want to risk the consequences at this time.

In one sense, there was little more that the anti-Communists could have expected. It was true that there were no barriers to the removal of Lee Pressman, Len DeCaux,[28] and the other pro-Communists staff members other than Murray's reluctance to do so. But there were constitutional and power limitations to doing much more.

Furthermore, the anti-Communists had reason to feel assured that Murray was moving closer to their side. But he was most anxious to keep the fight from the floor and from the public view and many CIO leaders agreed with his objectives in this respect. Most important, the anti-Communists felt that, imperfect as the CIO convention resolution on Communism was, it did, for a time, condemn Communist interference. They could now meet taunts of "red-baiter,"usually leveled against them, by quoting CIO policy.

The convention showed the main left-wing strength to be in the United Electrical Workers, the third largest CIO union in numerical strength, followed by the Mine, Mill and Smelter Workers, the National Maritime Union, Longshoremen, Fur Workers, and Public Workers. Left-wing strength in the CIO came to between 92-100 out of 305 delegates to the convention.[29] The strength of the right-wing was centered largely in the Steel Workers, the Automobile Workers, Textile Workers, Shipbuilding Workers, Rubber Workers, and Retail and Wholesale Clerks. The right-wing strength in the CIO was greater than its proportion of convention delegates would indicate. Most of the Communist-controlled unions were small and the convention rules gave a larger proportionate delegate strength to them. For instance, memberships up to 5,000 were allowed two delegates; but with a 100,000 membership, the allotment was only eight, with an additional delegate for each 50,000 members.

Effectively controlling Communism would have meant inter-ference with the internal operations of the left-wing international unions or their expulsion and the resultant weakening of the whole movement. Intervention on a large scale was constitutionally impossible. The CIO recalling its own expulsion from the AFL, originally created for itself an organization with decidedly limited powers in the national headquarters. It was the international unions which controlled the CIO and not vice-versa. Murray apparently began to develop the strategy of depending upon a growing anti-Communism within the rank and file of the CIO international unions, which would intensify resistance to Communist leadership, and perhaps persuade some of the fellow travelers and innocents that they were on the wrong side.

The New York Times, commenting on this, wrote an interesting editorial on November 23 in which it characterized the resolution on communism as one which "swept the issue of Communist in-filtration under the bed." The editorial said:

> In recent months rank and file revolts have been breaking out against this party-line leadership. It is hard to get rid of, from the bottom, because the Communists are good organizers and tireless union workers. It is hard to eliminate from the top because of fears that the national organization may be disrupted. Never-theless, the movement appears to be growing and is bound to affect the future course of the CIO. In Atlantic City the matter was merely side-stepped.

1 Avery, *op. cit.*, and "Communist Power in U. S. Industry," *Chicago Journal of Commerce*, January 13-31, 1947.
2 The CIO's State, County and Municipal Workers Union had combined with the CIO United Federal Workers earlier in the year to form the United Public Workers. Flaxer had been head of the SCMWU and "Repeatedly identified as a member of the Communist Party" without ever denying it (*The Columbus Citizen* November 29, 1946.) He had been a member of the National Council of the American Peace Mobilization during the Soviet-Nazi Pact. Following the invasion of Russia, he is quoted as saying: "I am for all aid to the Soviet Union. The Soviet Union has a really democratic form of government and any aid to the Soviet Union would really be aid against Fascism." At the first convention of the UPW in April, 1946, the union adopted a resolution asking President Truman to "halt the present policy of attempting to isolate the Soviet Union in the UN and world affairs." They called for the withdrawal of US troops from China, the Philippines, France, Greece, India, Indonesia, Belgium and Iceland. They rejected a suggestion that the Soviet withdraw

its troops from Eastern Europe. (*Daily Worker*, April 25, 1946; Avery, "Communist Power in U. S. Industry", *op. cit.*)

[3] *The New York Times*, November 18, 1946.

[4] CIO, *Daily Proceedings of the Eighth Constitutional Convention* (Atlantic City, New Jersey, November 18-22, 1946) pp. 111-113.

[5] *Ibid.*, p. 114.

[6] *The New York Times*, November 19, 1946.

[7] CIO, *Hearings To Investigate ILWU*, *op. cit.*, p. 86.

[8] *The New York Times*, November 23, 1946.

[9] CIO Eighth Constitutional Convention, *op. cit.*, p. 317.

[10] *The New York Times*, November 23, 1946.

[11] CIO Eighth Constitutional Convention, *op. cit.*, p. 320.

[12] *Ibid.*

[13] *Ibid.*, p. 321.

[14] *The New York Times*, November 20, 1946.

[15] *The New York Times*, November 23, 1946.

[16] *The New York Times*, September 3, 1947.

[17] *The New York Times*, September 6, 1947.

[18] Barbash *op. cit.*, p. 29.

[19] At the time of the 1946 convention there were 231 state, city, and county industrial union councils engaging in political action, legislation, public relations, labor and public education, community services, housing, health, race relations, economic and social planning, as well as assistance in organizing and collective bargaining. See "Report of President Murray" in CIO Eighth Constitutional Convention, *op. cit.*, p. 58.

[20] Avery, "Communist Power in U. S. Industry" *op. cit.*

[21] CIO "Letter from CIO National Office to All Industrial Unions and Organizing Committees, State and Local Industrial Union Councils, CIO Regional Directors, and Local Industrial Unions," (mimeographed) November 26, 1946.

[22] CIO Eighth Constitutional Convention, *op. cit.*, p. 59.

[23] *The New York Times*, November 16, 1946.

[24] *Daily Worker*, November 16, 1946.

[25] *New York World Telegram*, December 6, 1946. In October, 1947, Max Yergan, president of the National Negro Congress "Quietly left" with the explanation that "the Communists sought to sabotage decisions of the Board." *Current Biography*, September, 1948, pp. 57-59.

[26] *Daily Worker*, November 20, 1946.

[27] *The New York Times*, November 24, 1946.

[28] There continued to be a very strong feeling on the part of many of the anti-Communist leaders that the *CIO NEWS* was a mouthpiece of the left wing. A number of the delegates at the convention seemed particularly incensed at what they considered to be one example of Mr. DeCaux's personal pro-Communist editorializing. There was a cartoon in the issue of April 22, 1946 with a caricature of Hoover standing over an emaciated family of starving people and captioned: "So They Send Us A Man Who Believes In Depressions." This cartoon found its way into the *Daily Worker* of May 13, 1946.

[29] *The New York Times*, November 24, 1946.

PART II

Chapter 5-11

INTRA-UNION STRUGGLES
OVER COMMUNISM

5 | THE COMMUNISTS FACE OPPOSITION

Whether so planned by Murray or not—probably because it was inevitable from the nature of the developing international crisis and the increased activity of the right-wing—anti-Communist activity within the international unions and within the industrial union councils now began in earnest.

The 8th convention of the Massachusetts CIO, meeting immediately after the Atlantic City national CIO convention, passed a constitutional amendment barring Communists from holding state office within the organization.[1]

At about the same time, the New Jersey CIO State Industrial Union Council passed a resolution which went beyond the national resolution. It declared that "communism is alien to the philosophy and desires of the American people." Furthermore, even though it felt obliged to recognize the strength of the UE within the state by electing actively pro-Communist James McLeish, president of the Union's District 4, as a 3rd vice-president of the state CIO, the New Jersey Council went on to express "resentment of the Communist Party and its adherents and their efforts to interfere in the affairs of the CIO."[2]

In Cleveland a breach within the industrial union council there, made it necessary for the national CIO to place a temporary administrator in charge of the affairs of the council.

In the elections which took place in Milwaukee on December 4, 1946, the anti-Communists took control by winning every office. A few days later the victory was duplicated on the state level as the pro-Communists were defeated in the Wisconsin State Industrial Union Council.[3]

63

The battles in Chicago and in the Illinois State Council were quite prolonged. Somewhat at stake, in addition to the obvious power relationships, was the future of the *Chicago Star,* Communist launched weekly. There was reason to believe that a Communist victory in the city and state would have raised a sufficient sum in the unions to convert the weekly into a daily, which would have been of immense value to the Communists in the mid-west.[4] The president of the Chicago Industrial Union Council had been Herbert Marsh of the United Packinghouse Workers of America, a former district organizer for the Young Communist League. He had been a member of the Citizens Committee to Free Earl Browder and a contributor to the *Daily Worker.*[5] However, the anti-Communists, led by Michael Mann, Chicago secretary, had been able to win in 1945.

On the state level, much of the pro-Communist leadership was coming from Robert C. Travis, vice-president of the Illinois CIO Council, a man with a long pedigree of Communist activity.[6] However, in 1947 the powerful and numerous Steelworkers, with a green light from Philip Murray, actively joined the anti-Communists in the state and helped their forces capture all the official positions and all but one of the executive board seats. On taking office as president, Steelworker Joseph Germano declared:[7]

> If you don't believe in the objectives of the CIO, then you have no business here. I don't like Communism and I'm going to do everything in my power to prevent any small organized minority from taking over a union or taking over our country . . .

The national CIO office also went forward with its determination to place under closer control the activities of its local and state industrial union councils. Early in January, 1947, taking advantage of the new rules governing the councils, and following up on its instructions regarding the National Negro Congress, it prohibited all industrial union councils from making gifts or sending delegates to organizations other than those on a selected list of thirty-six organizations[8] "recognized by the CIO." This was clearly and unmistakably interpreted as an anti-Communist move even though the councils were told that "the fact that an organization is not listed does not reflect on the merits of the organization or its work in any way." The list, described as tentative and subject to revision, but also as "binding on all councils," was based on recommendations of various CIO departments and committees. Council officers were instructed to refrain from allowing their names to be listed on boards of directors or sponsoring committees of national organizations not listed.

The instructions made clear that solicitation of membership in unlisted organizations was also prohibited. Organizations operating in more than one state, or related primarily to national or international affairs, and their state or local affiliates, were to be regarded as organizations which must be approved by the national CIO before councils or council members could contribute or send delegates.

There were other rumblings. Desperate minorities within two of the leading pro-Communist unions were fighting the top leadership and making appreciable headway in the Mine, Mill and Smelter Workers Union particularly. We have already taken note of the fact that Reid Robinson's leadership was repudiated at the national level when the CIO refused to re-elect him a national vice-president. The reason alleged was his reported $5,000 "loan" from an employer, but it was also understood that his irresponsibility, frequent intoxication, and unexplained absences, made it particularly difficult, even within his own union, for the pro-Communists to defend him. The revolt therefore grew, but it was unorganized, unharnessed, and thus weak. A number of local unions, particularly in the Connecticut Valley, seceded from the parent organization and remained either independent or asked to join an anti-Communist CIO international, such as the United Steel Workers. Others remained within the international to fight for control, but since the secession by similarly minded locals lessened their number, they remained weak. We shall later examine in greater detail the internal difficulties of this union.

The powerful electrical and radio workers union also showed growing internal dissent, as we shall later report in more detail. James B. Carey, national secretary-treasurer of the CIO, but deposed as head of the UE in 1941 when he began actively to oppose Communist control, continued his anti-Communist activities. He used a 1946 convention resolution to rally increased opposition to the union leadership. A number of the locals joined his activities and ousted many of their officers deemed to be followers of secretary Julius Emspak and director of organization James J. Matles. In the main, however, the UE officers maintained organizational control in the large plants of General Electric, Westinghouse, and other concerns, and thus kept comfortable control over the national organization. Nevertheless, they were somewhat concerned and at a meeting of the CIO vice-presidents early in 1947, James Fitzgerald, UE president, brought charges against Carey for giving aid and comfort to the revolting minorities in the local unions. Mr. Carey, however, stood on his "civil rights" and Mr. Murray, who was present, significantly did not interfere.[9]

Labor commentators and experts also looked for and found other signs of changes within the national CIO. Louis Stark, veteran labor expert for *The New York Times,* saw significance in the fact that at a press conference following a CIO officers' meeting in February, 1947, Walter Reuther sat at Mr. Murray's right.[10] Personal relations in the CIO were very important, and there had been rumors that Reuther's impetuousness and flair for newspaper headlines did not sit well with Mr. Murray. Nevertheless, this gesture by Murray was interpreted as support for Reuther, who had just defeated Murray's friend, R. J. Thomas, for the UAW presidency, and who sat alone with his strong anti-Communist views on a board of four top officials in the UAW.

Another "straw in the wind" was the composition of a five-man committee appointed by Murray in early 1947 to discuss mutual problems and possible merger with the AFL. None of the five could be called "Communist" and Murray chose to replace Emspak, who had been a CIO representative on earlier similar boards, with Fitzgerald, who was not considered a Communist though he owed his election to the presidency to them.[11]

There was also no escaping Murray's intention, when early in 1947, he demoted the CIO West Coast Longshoremen's president, Harry Bridges, from the position of California director of the CIO. Murray did this by splitting the state into two principalities and awarding the southern half to a loyal Murray follower.

The precipitating factor leading to Murray's decision was Bridges' unwillingness to share in a CIO agreement to end inter-union jurisdictional fighting, but there was no question this was the culmination of a number of irritations arising from Bridges' political views.

THE FARM EQUIPMENT WORKERS UNION

One of the most serious jurisdictional disputes within the CIO— and the specific controversy which led Philip Murray to propose a plan for settling these disputes—involved the CIO Farm Equipment Workers and the UAW. We have already seen that the UAW was well on its way, under Reuther's leadership, to an anti-Communist orientation. The FE, on the other hand, was completely within the Communist orbit.[12] Since both unions covered much the same jurisdiction in the light of the UAW's entrance into the machine field, frequent and serious conflict developed.[13]

In 1945, the matter came before the Jurisdictional Committee of the CIO, which, after full hearings, recommended the immediate amalgamation of both unions as the solution of the problem. The recommendation was accepted by the CIO Executive Board and vice-president Allan Haywood, Director of Organization, was designated to assist the parties in working out the details. He failed when the FE Executive Board rejected the CIO Executive Board motion. A membership referendum, "Do you desire to maintain your union and reject affiliation with the UAW?," supported the officers.[14]

In 1947, a merger agreement was entered into by representatives of both organizations, subject to a referendum vote of the UAW locals and the approval of the FE locals. Walter Reuther, UAW president, had no hand in the making of the agreement and interpreted it as a Communist plan to add the FE membership strength to the next UAW convention, ally it to the Addes-Thomas faction, and upset the delicate balance by which Reuther maintained the presidency but remained in a minority on the union's executive board. He, therefore, opposed the plan as giving the FE too much independence within the UAW in violation of the UAW's constitution and the principles of industrial unionism. The membership sided with Reuther and rejected the proposal. Reuther later offered the FE a merger proposal with terms similar to those on which the Aluminum Workers of America had joined the United Steelworkers, but the FE never responded.

The president of the FE was Grant Oakes, who was considered to be a figurehead. His allegiances, however, were clear. His record showed him to be president of the Communist party's Peoples Publishing Association in Chicago, a director of the Party's Abraham Lincoln School, member of the national council of the American Peace Mobilization during the days of the Stalin-Hitler Pact, a sponsor of the Citizens Committee to Free Earl Browder, and a member of the Defense Committee for Morris U. Schappes, a Communist convicted of perjury, and a former member of the College of the City of New York College faculty.

The principal Communist leader in the FE was, however, Joseph Ruic, who was known within the union as Joseph R. Weber, and elsewhere under the aliases of Hudson, Judson, Ross and Ray. He was born in Yugoslavia and brought to the U. S. as a child, although he resisted deportation from the U. S. for a number of years by claiming American birth. After joining the Communist party, he was sent to Moscow for training. In 1937 he was assigned by the Communist party to organize the farm equipment industry.[15]

There seemed little question but that the UAW-FE controversy was thoroughly tangled with the Communist issue. This explains why Harry Bridges refused to go along with any agreement which would have subordinated the weaker and smaller FE to the UAW. Further evidence of Communist interest in this issue was the use of the FE as a pawn in UAW politics. The Communist hand in the struggle was also shown in the attitude of Robert C. Travis, vice-president of the Illinois CIO Council. He, too, had a record of pro-Communist activity as a director of the Abraham Lincoln School, a writer for the *Chicago Star*, a sponsor of the American Peace Mobilization, and a participant in the move to free Earl Browder. Travis had started as a UAW member, being a key figure in the 1937 Flint auto strike. He was now again a member of Local 543 of the UAW in Illinois, significantly called the "little Kremlin." In the intervening period, he had shifted to the FE where, during the Hitler-Stalin Pact period, he became leader of the important 1941 strikes at International Harvester. When the UAW in 1945, after he was again a UAW member and officer, tried to organize the McCormick Works, Travis openly campaigned for the FE and against his own union.

Further evidence of FE Communist domination was later revealed by a former Communist party member and ex-CIO Mine, Mill and Smelter Union official, Kenneth Eckert, who told the national CIO officers at a private hearing that the basic decision as to whether the FE officers were to sign the Taft-Hartley anti-Communist affidavit was made by the Communist party leaders.[16] The FE, like many other of the smaller unions, found that it was in an impossible position under the law in competing with other unions for membership unless its officers signed the affidavit. Since the UAW officers had signed, that union could be represented on the ballots in NLRB elections to determine union representation. So long as the FE did not sign, it could not be listed on the ballot and thus many elections would be lost by default.[17]

Eckert told of a meeting in New York in early 1948 at which he was present along with William Z. Foster, the Communist party national chairman, Eugene Dennis, national secretary, John Williamson, organizational secretary of the Party, and representatives from a number of the Communist-led unions such as the UE, Fur Workers, FE, and the Mine, Mill. The meeting was called to discuss strategy with regard to the Taft-Hartley anti-Communist affidavits. Williamson opened the meeting by saying he was tired of the increasing number of left-wing trade union leaders who were clamoring for the right to sign the affidavits in order to protect their unions. The Communist leaders had agreed earlier to allow the FE leaders to sign after they had discussed it with Gil Green, Communist party secretary in Chicago, but now the Party doubted the wisdom of extending the privilege to others. Foster expressed the same doubts when he spoke. The discussion that followed then led Dennis to say that it was even a mistake for the FE to sign.

The UE representatives, Matles and Emspak, and Ben Gold

of the Fur Workers[18] concurred in the feeling that none of the unions, including the FE, should sign the affidavits. The FE representative present tried to resist the tide by explaining that it was now too late for the union to reverse itself since a special Executive Board meeting had made the recommendation, following the clearance, and they had already called a special convention to approve the step. His only support, however, seemed to come from the Furniture Workers representative. The result was that when the special convention convened, it reiterated the previous decision not to sign the non-Communist affidavits.[19]

The UAW-FE jurisdictional problem within the CIO continued, with its persistent Communist overtones. Following the failure of the two unions to come to an agreement, the CIO Jurisdictional Committee in July, 1948, submitted a further report to the CIO Executive Committee pointing out in part that nothing had been done to enforce its 1945-1946 decisions. On November 27, 1948, the CIO Executive Board, meeting in Portland, Oregon, adopted a resolution directing the United Farm Equipment and Metal Workers of America "to take immediate steps to affiliate with the United Automobile, Aircraft, and Agricultural Implement Workers of America, CIO, on a basis which is organizationally sound, consistent with the structure of industrial unionism and in keeping with the provisions of the UAW-CIO, which guarantees membership rights and representation in accordance with democratic trade union principles." The CIO then appointed a committee consisting of Emil Rieve, chairman, Jacob Potofsky, and Joseph Curran to facilitate the amalgamation, investigate and report back to the executive board.

The following week, the executive board of the FE met in Chicago, and on December 3 and 4, adopted a policy statement which was made public declaring the actions of the CIO Executive Board to be arbitrary, dictatorial, and conspiratorially designed to dissolve the FE in disregard of its membership's welfare and contractual security. It stated the decision would require the FE "membership to pay the price of their contracts, their wages, their working conditions, and their union to satisfy the power-hungry, selfish purposes of UAW officials." The FE leadership then embarked on a campaign of criticism against the CIO for it decision.

In addition to press statements, resolutions passed by locals, and stories in its publication, *FE News,* the union distributed an eight-page pamphlet entitled *FE Rank and File Replies to Murray and Reuther.*

When the Rieve-Potofsky-Curran CIO committee met in Chicago on January 7, 1949, representatives of the UAW and FE were present. Grant Oakes, FE president, read a prepared statement which he released to the press, and then led the FE representatives from the committee meeting, The statement declared that the committee "carries absolutely no status with our organization" and characterized the executive board decisions as a "Pearl Harbor ultimatum to disband," "unprincipled," "union-wrecking vendettas," designed to "by-pass the desires, the objectives, and the well being of our membership."[20]

Meanwhile, tensions developed between the UAW and the FE, particularly at International Harvester, where both unions had members. On February 10, for example, a clash between members of both unions broke out near the Moline, Illinois plant, causing injury to more than a score of people.[21] As a result of these developments, the Rieve-Potofsky-Curran Committee, on April 4, 1949, again reviewed the facts, recommended amalgamation to the CIO Executive Board, and expressed its support of the UAW position. It severely criticized the FE leadership for "distorting and misrepresenting" the facts "maliciously," comparing that attitude with the UAW which "was at all times wholly cooperative and ready and willing to attempt to work out a satisfactory settlement of its differences with the FE." The Committee took note of the sporadic violence, with its "uncomplimentary" publicity which would do damage to both organizations involved and to the CIO as a whole, and would also retard the organizational work and weaken the union.

In support of its renewed recommendation of amalgamation, the Committee quoted from the "excellent statement" contained in the preamble to the 1947 written merger proposal, which the FE leadership had accepted in agreement with the Addes-Thomas group in the UAW. The statement referred to the inevitable "conflict" and "difficulties" which arise when the "two sister unions, both affiliated with the same parent body" seek "to organize and to service workers in the same industry, and frequently in the same plants in the industry." Such a condition, the preamble continued, "results in the duplication of organizational effort and entails expenditures of considerable magnitude which might otherwise be made in the direct interest of the workers involved." This, in turn, means "a lessening of the strength of the workers in the industry in their dealings with their employers."

In 1947 the FE leaders saw unity as a way of bringing increased "strength . . . to the advancement of the interests of the workers in the industry . . . higher wages, better working conditions and more efficient service for the workers in the plants." The "combined strength of the two unions" would also facilitate "organizing the unorganized workers in the industry."

Finally, the CIO Committee concluded that since the jurisdictional dispute "led to rivalry, conflict, and waste, thereby impairing the welfare of the workers," the close relationship between the automobile and farm implement industries made it economically desirable for the workers in both industries to belong to one union. The largest number of farm implement workers belonged to the UAW which was patterned and "well-equipped" in "experience, militancy, democratic structure and numerical and financial strength" to serve the workers involved. The decisions of 1945 and 1948 should be reaffirmed. They recommended, therefore, that the UAW should be given exclusive jurisdiction in the field, and further, that "the CIO Executive Board censure the officers and Executive Board members of the FE for their contumacious and unprincipled conduct and stubborn refusal to attempt to work out a solution of a situation which causes substantial injury to the workers they represent."

The CIO Executive Board accepted its Committee's recommendations on May 18, 1949 and recommended to the convention "that the charter of the Farm Implement and Metal Workers Union be revoked." The convention accepted its Executive Board's recommendation, expelled the FE, and urged the FE membership to join the UAW.[22]

Meanwhile, just prior to the CIO convention which expelled it, the FE had merged with the UE, which was also expelled by the CIO at the same convention.

THE UNITED AUTOMOBILE WORKERS UNION

The Farm Equipment Workers union was only one pawn in the politics of the UAW. We have seen that Walter Reuther was elected to the UAW presidency in 1946, but that he remained alone in his views among the four top union officers. The other three, R. J. Thomas, the defeated president, now vice-president, Richard Leonard, vice-president, and George Addes, secretary-treasurer, formed an anti-Reuther coalition.

The Stalinists, from the very beginning of the union's formation, had wanted to control its policies. They set about wooing Homer Martin, preacher and the UAW's first head. They promised to "build him up" into a figure second in presitige and prominence only to John L. Lewis, if he would follow their advice and leadership. During the negotiations the Communist party press hailed Martin as a "vigorous," "able," "crisp-spoken," and "militant" labor leader.[23]

The negotiations broke down when Martin refused to make the deal and particularly rebelled at the Communist demand that they name the central office staff for the union. He, therefore, set about with good intentions "but meager mental and political equipment" to eliminate their influence from the union. He failed dismally. The Communists fomented nearly 160 "wild-cat" strikes, and painted him as an irresponsible weakling. They broke up union meetings and created so much discord that the union lost more than a third of its original strength. It was only through the repeated efforts of Phillip Murray and Sidney Hillman, skilled labor diplomats, that some order was restored.[24] Martin left the union a tired and disillusioned man. Today he is in labor relations work for a private company.

By this time, the anti-Martin faction within the UAW included more than the Communists. Walter Reuther joined with George Addes in a "united front" against Martin. Both men, however, were strong and ambitious and very soon headed opposite camps, neither powerful enough to control the policies of the union alone. With this delicate power relationship, both groups accepted R. J. Thomas as president. Thomas played the balance of power game so well that without a following of his own, he managed to neutralize the opposing Reuther and Addes forces and hold the presidency for eight years. Toward the end of that time, however, he set out to be a general in his own right and in his "search for troops," he "accepted mercenaries of doubtful loyalty."[25]

Writing of this development, the *Wage Earner,* a reliable Detroit labor paper published by the Association of Catholic Trade Unionists said:

> Communists and Communist followers began to appear in key staff positions. The UAW's educational department became in-filtrated. Soon Thomas himself began to talk the language of the Party line. The same man who, four years ago, angrily rejected Communist support at the Buffalo convention, now declared he couldn't help it if the Commies like him.
>
> Strange things began to happen. Thomas caused a furor in a Senate Committee by an unexpected personal attack upon Senator Vandenberg.
>
> Other auto union leaders charged that this statement was written by a pro-Communist on the UAW staff and that the motive was to discredit Vandenberg's position on the United Nations Organization. It is doubtful if Thomas had any chance to analyze the statement before he made it.
>
> Thus gradually, R. J. Thomas was knitted into the so-called 'left-wing' of which Addes had been the leader.

Addes was the real leader of the anti-Reuther UAW bloc. As secretary-treasurer of the UAW from the early days, he was thought to be the most popular of the UAW officials—he was certainly, in view of his position, the most powerful. He and Reuther had maintained a balance of power by not running against each other for union office and by both supporting Thomas, but it was Addes who was best able to enlist Thomas' support. Addes was not a Communist, but the Communists in the UAW threw in their lot with him in a joint effort to defeat Reuther and he seemed so perfectly willing to associate with them in this effort that he became identified with them. The FBI, in fact, in a memorandum dated May 7, 1942, branded him a subversive.[26] He became a sponsor of the National Council for American-Soviet Friendship[27] and also sponsored the Communist front Michigan Civil Rights Federation in September, 1943. On April 29, 1945, his name was listed on page three of the *Daily Worker* as one of those sending anniversary greetings to that publication.

Richard Leonard, the third member of the anti-Reuther triumvirate, had been for many years associated with the Reuther anti-

Communist faction. His own leadership talents, however, and ambitions, led to a personal disagreement between the two and he broke with the Reuther group to run for vice-president. After his election, he sided with Addes.

The period following the 1946 UAW elections, therefore, was one of internal political sparring. Reuther, as president, did not control the executive board. He was thus in the extremely difficult position of acting as president of a union, the control of whose governing body was in an anti-Reuther coalition.

The three top officers prepared to defeat Reuther at the next union convention. They saw in the FE jurisdictional conflict a way to carry out their plans. They proposed with the aid of the Communists within the UAW and the FE, to merge the two organizations by having FE join the UAW in a semi-independent status. This would have solved the jurisdictional problem, preserved the FE leadership and autonomy, and yet added a sufficient number of anti-Reuther votes in the next UAW convention to defeat him and his group. Reuther countered with the allegation that the plan was a fraud, politically motivated, and designed to saddle the UAW membership with FE debts without proportionate benefit. He travelled to UAW local meetings around the country, speaking in opposition to the proposal and for a plan of complete merger only. A membership referendum on the subject sided with Reuther.

One interesting by-play of this intra-UAW struggle in 1946-1947 was the battle of words that took place. The Addes-Leonard-Thomas faction controlled the union's monthly newspaper and kept firing propaganda broadsides. Just prior to the 1947 convention, they issued a special edition of the *United Automobile Worker,* "Report on the State of Your Union," in which they took out after Reuther. In dealing with Reuther's charge of Communism, they said:

> Probably one of the most effective exposes of the red-baiting technique we have ever seen was made not long ago by a man known to all of us. He said:
>
> 'Many years ago in this country, when the bosses wanted to keep the workers from forming a strong union, they started scares of various kinds.
>
> 'One scare the bosses raised was the Catholics against Protestants.

'Another scare they used very successfully was the American-born against the foreign-born.

'Then they placed one foreign-born group against another, like the Poles against the Germans, and so on.

'All that is played out now. It has been worked too often.

'So now the bosses are trying a new stunt.

'They are raising a new scare: the red scare.

'They pay stools to go whispering around that so-and-so—usually a militant union leader—is a red. They think that will turn other workers against him.

'What the bosses really mean, however, is not that a leader is red. They mean they don't like him because he is a loyal, dependable union man, a fighter who helps his union brothers and sisters and is not afraid of the boss.

'So let's all be careful that we don't play the bosses' game by falling for their red scare. Let's stand by our union and our fellow unionists. No union man worthy of the name will play the bosses' game. Some may do so through ignorance. But those who peddle the red scare and know what they are doing are dangerous enemies of the union.'

The author of the above quotation was Walter Reuther himself. This was the militant Reuther of 1937, who then answered his own red-baiting charges of today.

We endorse his sentiments then and commend them to all trade unionists now, including Reuther.

Reuther's FE referendum victory had so strengthened his hand that at the 1947 convention of the UAW he was not only overwhelmingly re-elected himself, but was able to bring with him into office his own slate of top union officials and thus gain control of the executive board. To this day, Reuther has maintained and strengthened his control over the union, and with only a few local exceptions.[28] the Communist influence in the UAW has disappeared.

THE NATIONAL MARITIME UNION

One of the most significant developments which took place within the CIO at this time was a growing split within the National Maritime Union, leading to an open break between Joseph Curran and the Communist party. Curran's political metamorphosis, which culminated in 1947, was one of the most challenging and fortuitous developments for the anti-Communists within the CIO.

Students of labor and participants in the labor movement had always identified Curran with the Communist party. In 1938, soon after the NMU was organized, Curran had led the attack against an anti-Communist faction in the union headed by Jerome King. The King faction had won a majority of the union officers in 1938, but was inexperienced and indecisive. After King was elected secretary in 1939, Curran brought charges against him, alleging, among other things, disruption and AFL sympathies. As a result, King was expelled.[29]

Curran had also been head of the New York City Industrial Union Council during the period when that group slavishly adhered to the Communist position.

There was certainly no doubt that the NMU from its very beginning had pursued the Communist party line and had been under Communist influence. At the July, 1945, Fifth National Convention of the NMU, for example, a resolution was adopted on "red-baiting", identifying it as "Hitler's secret weapon," and as a "menace to democracy," which was aimed "primarily to split the unity of any progressive group." The resolution went on to say that anti-Communist activity was "aimed at smashing American-Soviet unity, discouraging democratic development in liberated Europe, and weakening world cooperation. . . . It is clearly bent on breaking the morale of our armed forces, and our determination to exterminate Fascism."[30]

During that year too the NMU continued to use its union organization for pro-Communist political demonstrations.[31] On December 3, the NMU stopped work on all ships for 24 hours unless those ships carried American troops home or engaged in legitimate relief activities.[32] One of the strike's purposes, according to Curran, was to popularize union demands to the Maritime Commission for a "certified list of troop carriers and relief ships," on the basis of which the maritime unions would set up manpower priorities in the ports.[33]

By July, 1947, Curran was publicly announcing: "I have been convinced for a long time that the Communist Party as it is today is a menace to the labor movement and particularly our union."[34]

The break came in 1946.

It is, of course, difficult to know whether Curran ever was

actually a card-holding member of the Communist party. It now seems as if he was not, in spite of the fact that he was emotionally and intellectually tied to them. Nevertheless, he apparently insisted on maintaining a position of personal independence from Party control.

Support for this conclusion appears in a statement by M. Hedley Stone, NMU treasurer, who was, at one time, a member of the party. He tells of a meeting in 1942 or 1943 at the home of Saul Mills, secretary-treasurer of the New York City Industrial Union Council. It was a Communist meeting to discuss ways and means of strengthening Bridges on the East coast by having Arthur Osman's Local 65 affiliate with the Longshoremen. Stone was assigned to bring Curran to the Sunday meeting. He describes the process he followed in this manner:[35]

> ... I went out and bought tickets for a ball game, and I called Joe earlier in the morning and told Joe I had tickets for the ball game that afternoon, but I had to run an errand in Brooklyn, and if we could make it early enough we would have time, and Joe came down, picked me up and drove me to Saul Mills' house. And Santos (Secretary of the CIO Transport Workers Union) was the Party leader of the group, and we had started to talk on the affiliation or merger already going then when Santos cracked open by saying the fraction decided, and when Joe Curran heard the fraction decided he said, 'Come on, let's go; I didn't come to any fraction meeting.' And that broke that up.

Stone, when asked specifically whether Curran had been a member of the Communist party said: "No. The only time Curran was brought to a meeting by me would be when I was asked specifically to bring him to a certain place, and I believed everybody at that meeting was told and briefed how to behave themselves at the time and what subject to raise."[36]

Stone himself, during his tenure as treasurer of the National Maritime Union, was an active Communist party member. He had joined the party about 1935 and continued his membership for about ten years. Some insight into the tight hold which the Communist party had on its union membership and the techniques by which it maintained control over unions within its orbit can be seen from an additional statement by Stone:[37]

I attended conventions of the Communist Party, which were closed, whenever it didn't interfere with my work in the union to such a degree as it would hinder the union. I attended plenary sessions which were usually called semi-annually, sometimes a little sooner. They weren't on scheduled dates, but most of the time these plenary sessions were sort of staged to coincide with our semi-annual Council meetings and conventions of our own union, and at various times during the ten years I would receive calls from the 9th floor that a meeting is being called at noon or 2:00 o'clock at a certain place, and to be there. I would attend whenever I was available.

When asked to identify the "9th floor," he answered: "The 9th floor was the executive offices or the router's office, and the secretary and president. The person in charge of the trade union work was located in the Communist Building on 13th Street in New York City." The Party, therefore, had a direct pipeline from its own office to the NMU headquarters.

The break between Curran and the Communists began as an NMU versus ILWU affair, but soon became an internal NMU controversy. It was precipitated by the formation of the Committee for Maritime Unity.

In 1945, Curran agreed to a proposal by Bridges to form within the CIO a seven-union Committee for Maritime Unity, to act as a "united-front" of off-shore and dockside seamen's unions all of which were under Communist domination. Bridges and Curran became co-chairmen.

Within a short time, Curran began to show signs of restiveness about Bridges' role within the organization. He began to mistrust Bridges and to look upon the CMU as an effort by Bridges to establish himself in the East coast maritime industry.

The most serious disagreement arose when Bridges proposed a general strike in the industry in 1946. The collapse of the wartime unity between the United States and the Soviet Union led the Communists into a period of labor militancy; Bridges adopted the slogan "Strike time is here." Curran was not anxious for a strike and felt he could come to a settlement with the industry, but Bridges persuaded the other members of the CMU that a general strike in the industry was necessary and desirable. M. Hedley Stone, in explaining the CMU decision, said: "... the Party had a line that whatever we do we try to have some kind of waterfront stoppage."[38]

Bridges also saw in a general strike a chance to increase his influence on the East coast—which was exactly what Curran feared. In reporting to his union membership during the summer of 1946, Curran made his fears known. While declaring his 100 percent support for the CMU, he insisted he would see to it that it became "a great unifying body providing strength for all unions and not a body for somebody to build castles on or take over any union."[39]

Once the strike started, the national CIO office, with Phillip Murray taking a personal hand, attempted to bring about a settlement quickly. Curran was likewise anxious to end the stoppage. Stone later claimed that the strike was prolonged because of Communist politics. He said that on September 17th, the operators were prepared to settle at terms satisfactory to the NMU, but that the CMU prevented a settlement, thus losing "millions of dollars" for the union membership.[40]

The strikes were, of course, finally settled, but not without serving to help separate Curran from the Communists. The Communist party was quite disturbed at this rift. In an attempt to come to an understanding, Bridges, in the fall of 1946, decided to confer with the NMU leaders. Again Stone's description of the event is our only available source:[41]

> I got a call from Harry on the West Coast to my office where he said he was coming East and he would like to talk with me and with Joe. I told him at the time that Joe was in the Dakotas, he was on his vacation, but I would be there; and he came in and we closeted ourselves in my room in our New York headquarters building for quite a number of hours, and the subject of the conversation was my relationship with the Party. And at that time they had a new section organizer by the name of Christianson, and they had shuffled over, the Browder line had gone out, and a new secretariat of three had taken over the proposition, and Harry said, 'We can't work this way.' He was primarily interested in getting things straightened out with Curran also, and he asked me to get hold of Curran in Dakota and make an appointment for him out there, that he would go out there and meet him, or Joe could meet him in Chicago, and he would go to the Party and see these things were straightened out.... I got Joe to come in to see Harry in Chicago, I believe it was ...

The attempted agreement failed and instead of reconciliation, added bitterness developed. In December, 1946, Curran resigned as co-chairman of th CMU, declaring:[42]

> Four craft unions, located 3,000 miles away, together with a fifth union, a shore-side organization, have been dictating all policies of CMU and have made our great industrial union virtually a stooge for their shot-gun 'unity'.

Curran also referred to the fact that the NMU was the chief financial supporter of the Committee, having contributed $30,000 out of a $43,000 total. "Under the set-up, the NMU treasury can be drained by CMU while our Union, which carries the main financial burden, does not have a decisive voice on how our money should be spent...."

The CMU dissolved in 1947.[43]

The Party was prepared for the possibility of a break with Curran. In fact, one of the things Stone had complained to Bridges about in their conversation was the villification beginning within Communist ranks against him and Curran. Stone had surrounded this complaint with charges that the Party itself had now deteriorated, perhaps stemming from the change in top leadership and the ousting of Browder. Bridges had promised to bring Stone's complaints to the party's attention.[44]

> Harry left me with the understanding he was to go to the party. I told him what was happening in there. I told him how by indirection they were using the famous party tactics of not openly charging anybody with anything, but indirectly calling them crooks, and that they had these unit meetings and how the party had deteriorated to where they had open meetings, and each one that was left in the party would bring one or two guys, social meetings, and say all kinds of things about those of us that are in the leadership of NMU. And he said he will talk to these people and see that that is stopped ...

But Stone's complaints brought no results; and after Curran's resignation from the CMU the Party seemed to let go with full force.

> ... the party came out and announced over a heading 'Fascists and Trotskyites' and so on, roaming the waterfront, ... that all seamen should be careful not to associate with these people.

Then they had a list of names, and my name was among them, that I was dropped. Again by inference and indirection it appeared as if I was either a fascist or a trotskyite or whatever you call it.[45]

A vice-president of the NMU during this period was Frederick (Blackie) Myers, called by William Z. Foster "one of the finest elements of our party," and "one of the best builders of the party on the waterfront."[46] His position in the union was a key one; he was in charge of the organizational department and had full authority to place organizers on the union staff. The secretary, Ferdinand Smith, was also in the group as was Howard McKenzie, another of the vice-presidents. McKenzie never openly professed Party membership, but Bridges considered him a Communist and Stone mentions a union convention at which McKenzie first professed his Communist membership but then withdrew the statement.[47] The Party also controlled the editorial policy of the NMU paper, the *Pilot*, through the influence of Secretary Smith and its editor, Chamberlain.

The Communists, therefore, were in a good position, from within the union as well as from without, to deal with Curran's rebellion when it began in 1946. They set about recruiting new membership for the Communist party on the waterfront. A headline in the *Daily Worker* during the period[48] read, "Recruit 1,000 seamen, Now Seek 1,500 More." The story went on, "New waterfront members are being grounded in Communist principles immediately. Every maritime recruit in New York is expected to take a five day course in Communist fundamentals. Longer courses are given men who have more time ashore."

All this was in preparation for the 1946 referendum election for officers in the NMU. Myers hired new union organizers to travel among the membership and campaign for the election of pro-Communists. Curran alleged that this was the case in the union's drive to organize the Isthmian Line, where the NMU was contending for NLRB representation rights against the AFL Seafarers International Union.[49]

Myers proceeded to appoint only those organizers who were members of the Communist Party . . . some of whom did not even have the qualification of two years at sea.

To meet the Communist onslaught, Curran decided to carry the issue to the membership. He demanded and received the right to be heard in full in the *Pilot* and there wrote lengthy articles describing the nature of his fight within the union and his opposition to Communist control. He personally travelled with his story to as many ports as he could reach, or sent his lieutenants. Wherever they went, they insisted that the NMU membership was not Communist and that there were only about 500 party members among the 70,000–80,000 union members, Party members, however, were well placed, and controlled "approximately 107 out of the 150 elected officials" of the NMU, through tactics "no different than those practiced by the Nazis when they destroyed the trade union movement of Germany."[50]

Curran's campaign was indeed an education for the union's members. Having had the benefit of close observation, he proceeded to expose the methods and tactics of the Communist followers within the NMU. He revealed that the Communists had spent $20,000 in the 1946 NMU election, part of which was used to place their members "on the waterfront on a full-time basis in the union halls in the various ports and their specific job was to coordinate the work of the Communists within the union in that port in influencing the members, particularly the new members who knew very few of the officials, into voting for the right ones."[51]

He alleged that the party coordinators also distributed approved slates of candidates and attempted to influence those who did not know how to vote, "and in some cases, these Party members even voted the ballot for the new member. They were also responsible for seeing to it that the proper kind of smear and slander campaign was conducted in the port against those who were non-Communists running for offices."

Curran went on to alert the NMU membership about tactics used by the Communists to control union meetings even when they are in a minority. The Communists, he said:[52]

come to the meetings well organized, having met before the meeting at outside meeting places. All of their members are fully instructed and have their resolutions in their pockets. Their speakers are chosen. They are trained and disciplined and above all are prepared to stay all night at a meeting in order to tire out the non-Communist members, make them disgusted, and leave the meeting, then they have full control of the meeting and are able to pass any resolutions and actions they want.

He warned further that if this tactic doesn't succeed,

they do everything possible to disrupt the meeting, raising points of order . . . and whenever votes are finally taken they make sure their people count the votes and if necessary make a short count on the vote if it is against them.

Once they do get into a union, Curran continued:

Communists make it their business to see to it that they are on every important committee and if you will notice in our union, the same faces, the same ones are on almost every committee. . . . They make it their business to stay on the beach as long as possible, obtain appointments to jobs and ship only enough to keep them in good standing as active seamen.

In the midst of Curran's campaign against the Communists, his descriptions of their tactics were demonstrated to be correct. His first formal charges were made at a closed membership meeting on February 18, 1946 in Manhattan Center, New York. He sought approval of his report recommending the ouster of Communist officials. The meeting lasted until after midnight and was adjourned to the following week. On February 25, the meeting began at 7 p.m. with some 3,000 seamen present. A vote was not taken until 1 a.m. with only 200 members present. Mr. Curran's recommendation was not accepted.[53]

Curran also accused the editor of the *Pilot* and Ferdinand Smith of suppressing news in the interests of the Communist party. He then went on to state that the Communists in the union had not even done their job of handling ship grievances well, and that their party loyalty interfered with their fulfilling of this most important union function effectively. "Beefs are not being properly settled," he said.

Crews are told to tie up ships if they want beefs settled, in spite of the fact that the contract insures the membership of the settlement of beefs without tying ships up. This is done purposely, to disrupt and stampede our membership and to make it appear that they, the Communists, are the only ones who can settle beefs and they can do it by tying up ships.[54]

Curran charged at a closed membership meeting of his union on February 18, 1946 that the New York Port Agent of the NMU, Joseph Stack, kept "a regular FBI set of cards" in his office, implying that most of it was for Communist use. The *New York World Telegram,* in reporting this charge, stated that government agencies discovered that seamen returning on convoys were quizzed about the size of the convoys, their destination, the content of the shipments, the number of the troops transported, and the identification of the troop units. This information was regularly passed on to Communist national headquarters on the ninth floor of 31 East 12th Street, New York.[55]

Finally, Curran charged that the Communists had stuffed union ballot boxes in the 1946 elections:[56]

> . . . the report of the Honest Ballot Association and the handwriting experts used by them prove beyond doubt that ballots were premarked and many forged. It was shown in membership meetings following elections that balloting committeemen had been handpicked in many cases and even sent from one port to another.

His conclusion was that the Communists were "more interested in assuring that the National Maritime Union becomes a stooge union of the Communist Party than they are in keeping it an instrument belonging to the rank and file seamen who built it."[57]

The 1946 election results were a personal victory for Curran since he was elected by three to one, but inconclusive because his opposition maintained strength in the top hierarchy of the union.[58] But the year 1946 brought about one important change. "Blackie" Myers, who had been in difficulty with the federal government authorities, decided to go to sea, and not run for re-election as vice-president. It is significant that when he did retire, a luncheon was held in his honor which was addressed by William Z. Foster, head of the Communist party, Roy Hudson, head of the Party in western Pennsylvania, and Esther Letz, secretary of Local 65, RWDSU.[59]

The balance of power was not changed in the union, however, by Myers' resignation. He was succeeded by Joe Stack, who was promptly welcomed by the Communist party in the following manner: "He's completely scornful of red-baiting, will get up anywhere at any time and explain with great pride that he is a member of the Communist Party. He is, as a matter of fact, a member of the New York State Board of the party."[60]

When the 1946 election returns in the union showed the Curran forces to have a slight edge in some of the newly elected committees, Curran promptly ousted Stack on charges of misfeasance and malfeasance in office directly traceable to his Communist membership and, therefore, his duty to place political interests above the union's interest. The matter was to be decided, until such time as the next convention chose to act on the appeal, by the newly elected appeals committee of the union, a 15 man board. There, the Curran caucus had 10 of the votes with the result that a 10-5 decision was rendered against Stack.[61]

The Communists were now determined to make the Stack ouster one of the issues around which to organize and prepare for the union's 1947 convention. The year was, therefore, one of feverish activity on both sides. The Curran forces formed a "Committee of Correspondence" to tie their group together. The Communists met these moves with characteristic energy. The *Daily Worker* used terms like "renegades," "left opportunists," "Trotskyites," "fascists."[62] The Communist press went on to tie the Curran camp in with Norman Thomas, Lewis Corey, Walter Reuther, "and others in the Social Democratic camp." The *Daily Worker* warned: "NMU members should no more allow themselves to be humbugged by phony socialism than by phony unionism. Nor should they allow themselves to be used as a stepping stone by these 'leftist' servants of reaction." Finally, they cautioned: "As Joseph Stalin said on one occasion when he warned the Soviet Communists not to overlook the damaging power of a few hidden wreckers, it takes thousands to build a bridge, but one person could blow it up."

With all the active union political campaigning, however, the divided national office of the NMU still had the time and energy to continue its political activity on the international and world scene. Furthermore, it seemed as if, in spite of their bitter power struggle for control of the union, there were few fundamental differences dividing the two factions on the wider issues. This can be explained by the fact that the pro-Curran anti-Communist forces within the union were in the main only recent dissenters from the Communist ideology and training and were still somewhat permeated with that outlook and thought pattern. In one real sense, therefore, the upheaval within the NMU differed from the upheaval in the rest of the CIO. Within the NMU, it was differences over union politics which acted as the catalyst for the break, while within the rest of the labor movement generally, the root of the conflict was more ideological.

The NMU in August for example recommended a boycott of all arms cargoes to Indonesia. Their statement read: "Imperialist Dutch interests backed by giant American corporations and an interventionist U.S. foreign policy, are waging murderous warfare against 70 million Indonesian people."[63]

Two other incidents that took place in August were more the activity of specific groups within the NMU than of the national offices. Nevertheless, they are of interest. The first was a vote by the New York Port of the NMU, which remained Communist-controlled, to boycott all ship bound for Greece.[64] The second took place following the ejection of two Egyptians for disturbances during a UN Security Council debate. The Egyptians returned a few days later supported by a group of about 60 NMU members bearing the slogan: "Down with Imperialism, Freedom for the Whole World."[65]

Coming into the 1947 convention of his union, Curran let loose a vigorous blast against his opponents in his *Report to the 6th Biennial Convention.* He charged that the Communist party had "ruined" the union's organizing drive and had "undermined" its ability to defend itself. He invited the convention delegates and union membership to examine the operations of the CP within the union and was confident that such an examination would "dispel all illusions" about the democratic progressive nature of the Communist party.

Specifically, he accused the opposition of having secret meetings with leaders of the Communist party. He said they had expended union funds for party activities; and they had "flooded our office staff and the *Pilot* with their (CP) members to the point where today almost all of our employees are under the party's domination and control." One of their favorite tricks, he alleged, was to call special union meetings in New York when it was necessary for an out-port party officer to report to CP headquarters, which would mean that the union was paying party travel expenses. He claimed that the CP caucus had used machine tactics in union elections.

"The proof of the system's operation," he went on, "is shown, for example, by the many instances where the same resolution, sometimes with the exact wording, had been submitted at membership meetings, all held on the same day, in a dozen different ports, separated by thousands of miles."

In addition to these charges, he accused the Communists of dividing the union by segregating the membership "by race, color, and nationality." He also said: "The Communists have raised the method of smear, slander, and frame-up to a high art."[66]

A crucial debate at the convention centered about the ousting of Joseph Stack, the previous spring, as vice-president, and the 10-5 decision of the union appeals committee to uphold the ouster. Curran, in debating the issue, admitted that "The convention has a right to reverse the decision of the appeals committee, but it must also face the future results of its decision." He then placed the whole issue as one of personal confidence in him. "You will solve nothing by refuting Curran's charges because you know that Curran and Stack cannot work in the same office," he said. He then asserted that the basic issue was one of the Communist party within the NMU and warned: "The Communist Party has only a short time to live in control of this union."[67]

Stack met the issue squarely in addressing the delegates. He admitted his membership in the Communist party but claimed that did not interfere with his work.

> The Communist Party does not and will not dictate how I will conduct myself in this union. . . . I am not a fanatic. I haven't a closed mind. I believe that I can work with Curran. If I can drink with him and talk with him, I can also work with him. If I am reinstated I think I have the ability and the will to work with Curran or anybody else to the best interests of the union.

The convention sided with Curran. Out of a 15 member NMU officers report committee, the Curran "rank and file" slate won 14. Stack's ouster was then upheld by a vote of 353-351. Curran declared: "Communist control of this union is speedily slipping away."[68]

Curran proved correct. The elections of the next two years completely eliminated the Communists from all positions of authority and power in the national office.

In July, 1948, the results of a three month election among the union's 60,000 members showed Curran winning by a margin of nearly three to one. His supporters won every one of the thirty-two posts in the NMU National Council and the port of New York, key left-wing stronghold, passed into anti-Communist hands. Curran stated that the election proved that the members wanted their union to "function as a trade union and not an organization 'stooging' for a political party." He announced that the ousted union officers, his opposition, would be charged with "crimes against the membership" which would subject them to expulsion. Curran's opponent for president had been Frederick (Blackie) Myers, a founder of the union and one of its vice-presidents until 1946. Two vice-presidents, Howard McKenzie and Chester Young, and the union's national secretary, Ferdinand C. Smith, were also defeated.[69]

The NMU convention in September, 1949, by resolution, condemned

> Communism for what it is, a vicious form of totalitarianism carrying with it religious and political persecution of the worst kind, and we call upon our membership to express in no uncertain terms, that we in the National Maritime union will not tolerate Communists nor their philosophy in our union, and will take every step to root it out of our union completely, along with any other subversive group such as the Ku Klux Klan.[70]

Curran assumed a greater degree of personal control over union affairs so much so that there was a serious split within the Curran forces. The split was intensified in April, 1949, when Curran submitted a constitutional amendment which would deny membership to "any individuals, whether present members or future applicants, who subscribe to, support, sponsor or otherwise follow a course of action demonstrating Communist party membership or "adherence." It went on to exclude from membership in the NMU those who adhere to "any other similar subversive or totalitarian doctrine who permit anti-union acts such as, but not limited to, participation in, conspiring, following, writing or distributing untrue and false statements against the NMU, its officers, or membership."

Curran met the revolt by expelling the dissenters. This, in turn, led to an inquiry by the American Civil Liberties Union. The ACLU designated Professor Philip Taft to undertake the investigation and also inquire into the reports of violence within the union. His conclusions took note of Curran's popularity in the NMU as evidenced by his re-election in 1950 by a 6 to 1 margin in an election supervised by the Honest Ballot Association. It accused the "insurgents" of bringing "civil war to the waterfront" and justified Curran's program as being "extreme instances during a union civil war."[71]

The reaction against Communists and other foreign influences grew so great within the union, in fact, that a resolution was passed by the 1950 convention excluding all aliens from membership. Again this was met by protests from the anti-Communist American Civil Liberties Union as being too extreme, "a ridicule of the democratic process," and of serious damage to America internationally. In a letter to Mr. Curran, signed by executive Director Patrick Murphy Malin and General Counsel Arthur Garfield Hays, the ACLU said:[72]

> We feel that the test of true patriotism or nationalism lies in extending the broadest rights and privileges to all people in this country, including aliens . . . As we understand the principle upon which this country was founded, aliens are entitled to most of the rights which citizens enjoy—certainly the right to belong to a labor union upon which their livelihood may depend.

The union, with the passing of time, achieved greater stature and leadership within the CIO. Mr. Curran was highly regarded by CIO President Philip Murray during the latter's life and was, in fact, seriously considered as his successor by many labor leaders who considered him an ideal compromise leader respected by all the CIO international unions. Curran himself, however, probably because of concern over a bad heart condition, did not advance his own cause and supported Walter Reuther for President. Reuther's victory further strengthened Curran who played a vital role in every important CIO decision up to and including the negotiations leading to the merger of the CIO with the AFL in 1955.

[1] *Daily Worker,* December 7, 1946.
[2] *The New York Times,* December 9, 1946.
[3] Avery, "Communist Power in U. S. Industry," *op. cit.*

4 *Ibid.*

5 *Ibid.*; and House Report 1311, 78th Congress, 2nd Session, pp. 122, 123.

6 *Ibid.*, pp. 42, 52.

7 *The Progressive*, September 1, 1947.

8 *The New York Times*, January 9, 1947.

9 *The New York Times*, February 23, 1947.

10 *Ibid.*

11 *Ibid.*

12 Avery, "Comunist Power in U. S. Industry," *op. cit.*

13 Eight large corporations dominate the agricultural implement field: International Harvester, John Deere, J.I. Case, Allis-Chalmers, Oliver, Massey-Harris, Minneapolis Moline, and B. F. Avery. They manufacture a variety of implements for agricultural operations and processes, and tractors and trucks for farm construction and industrial use, employing about 130,000 production workers. The UAW became the dominant union in the field. By 1949, it had 50 locals chartered in the agricultural implement industry, representing more than 90,000 workers, with a membership of 63,000. These figures exclude the UAW membership in feeder plants, manufacturing parts and sub-assemblies for use by the industry. Meanwhile, the over-all average per capita tax payment from the FE to the CIO was for 43,000 members, and the most recent payment in 1948 was on the basis of a little more than 30,000 members. These figures include membership in other than the agricultural implement field, but where the union exercises jurisdiction as well, such as road machinery, cordage and hardware. Pertinent to the story presented by these statistics is the fact that when the CIO-FE Organizing Committee was formed in 1938, the Steelworkers, which had membership in the field, turned over to the FE 11 locals which had a membership of 20,718. For further details, see CIO, *Report of Committee Dealing With UAW-FE Dispute* (mimeographed) April 4, 1949.

14 *Ibid.*

15 Avery, "Communist Power in U. S. Industry," *op. cit.*

16 CIO, *Hearing Before the Committee to Investigate Charges Against International Union of Mine, Mill and Smelter Workers* (Transcript) January 18, 19, and February 6, 1950, Washington, D.C., pp. 261-265.

17 For a further discussion of the Taft-Hartley Act non-Communist affidavit, see Appendix.

18 The following item appeared in *The Guild Reporter*, September 8, 1950:
"Ben Gold, member of the communist party for 30 years, and for 15 years president of the International Fur and Leather Workers Union, announced he resigned from the party in order to be able to sign a non-communist affidavit under the Taft-Hartley Act.
"But Gold made it clear the resignation was merely for the record, that his ideas hadn't changed. 'I have resigned from the communist party, but I do not give up my belief in true democracy,' Gold stated in a 6-page statement.
"The union, in convention, had directed officers to qualify for NLRB services under the Taft-Hartley Act.
"Earlier the Fur and Leather Workers Union had been expelled from the CIO for following the communist party line."

[19] CIO, *Hearings to Investigate Mine, Mill, op. cit.*

[20] *Report of Committee Dealing With UAW-FE Dispute, op. cit.*

[21] *Ibid.*

[22] CIO, "Resolution No. 59," *Daily Proceedings of the Eleventh Constitutional Convention* (Cleveland, Ohio, October 31, November 1-4, 1949) pp. 334-336, 347, 348.

[23] Bruce Minton and John Stuart, *Men Who Lead Labor* (Modern Age: New York, 1937) pp. 108, 215-217.

[24] Harris, *op. cit.,* p. 136.

[25] Association of Catholic Trade Unionists, "Defeat of R. J. Thomas May End UAW Balance of Power," *Wage Earner*, March 29, 1946, p. 5.

[26] This information was supplied to me by Frederick Woltman, staff writer for the *New York World Telegram.*

[27] *Daily Worker*, October 10, 1943.

[28] The Communists, although defeated by the membership, continued to be active in Ford Local 600, the largest local in the UAW, but their influence ceased.

[29] Philip Taft, "Unlicensed Seafaring Unions," *Industrial and Labor Relations Review*, Vol. 3, No. 2, January, 1950, p. 208. King was later convicted of manslaughter in a waterfront brawl.

[30] National Maritime Union of America, *Proceedings of the Fifth National Convention* (New York City, July 2-13, 1945) p. 507.

[31] This technique is by no means the exclusive possession of Communist trade unions. On August 25, 1950, the Atlantic Coast District Council of the AFL International Longshoremen's Association, began a policy of barring the handling of Russian cargoes. Unofficially, union members extended this embargo to satellite cargoes and boycotted such items as Polish hams, and Czechoslovakian shoes, glassware, and burlap. Both President Truman and Secretary of Labor Tobin found it necessary to appeal to the union for an end to the embargo. See *The New York Herald Tribune*, September 19, 1950.

[32] *Daily Worker*, December 1, 1945.

[33] *The New York Times*, November 29, 1945.

[34] *New York World Telegram*, July 14, 1947.

[35] CIO, *Hearings to Investigate ILWU, op. cit.,* pp. 597, 598.

[36] *Ibid.,* p. 629.

[37] *Ibid.,* p. 591.

[38] *Ibid.,* pp. 600-603.

[39] Taft, "Unlicensed Seafaring Unions," *op. cit.,* p. 210.

[40] *Ibid.,* p. 211.

[41] CIO, *Hearings To Investigate ILWU, op. cit.,* pp. 600-603.

[42] Taft, "Unlicensed Seafaring Unions," *op. cit.,* p. 210.

[43] The next meeting of CIO Maritime Unions did not take place until July, 1950, when the unions, led by Curran, joined employers and government representatives in a conference to prevent Communist sabotage on ships. They decided that Communists or those who "notoriously or consistently" carry out the policies of the Communist Party would be classified as bad security risks. See *The New York Times*, August 1, 1950.

[44] CIO, *Hearings to Investigate ILWU, op. cit.*

[45] *Ibid.*

46 *Daily Worker,* July 10, 1946.
47 CIO, *Hearings to Investigate ILWU, op. cit.,* pp. 627, 628.
48 *Daily Worker,* July 28, 1946.
49 Joseph Curran, "Report to the Membership," *Pilot,* July 5, 1946, p. 23.
50 Dubinsky, *op. cit.,* p. 62.
51 *Pilot,* March 28, 1947, p. 2.
52 *Ibid.,* p. 12.
53 *New York World Telegram,* March 7, 1946.
54 *Pilot,* March 28, 1947, p. 12.
55 Frederick Woltman, *New York World Telegram,* March 5-7, 1946.
56 *Pilot,* March 28, 1947, p. 12.
57 Dubinsky, *op. cit.,* p. 62.
58 Taft, "Unlicensed Seafaring Unions," *op. cit.,* p. 211.
59 *Daily Worker,* July 10, 1946.
60 *Daily Worker,* June 7, 1946.
61 *The New York Times,* October 11, 1947.
62 *Daily Worker,* July 7, 9, 1947.
63 *Daily Worker,* August 18, 1947.
64 *Daily Worker,* August 15, 1947.
65 *The New York Times,* August 29, 1947.
66 *The New York Times,* October 1, 1947; *The New Leader,* January 17, 1948, p. 5.
67 *The New York Times,* October 11, 1947.
68 *The New York Times,* October 12, 1947.
69 *The New York Times,* July 27, 1948.
70 *Pilot,* October 6, 1949, p. 1.
71 Philip Taft, "Civil Rights in the National Maritime Union," a report prepared for the American Civil Liberties Union, August, 1950.
72 American Civil Liberties Union, "Feature Press Service" *Weekly Bulletin* No. 1449, August 7, 1950 (mimeogaphed).

6 | DISSENT IN THE UNIONS: CASE HISTORIES

A number of other unions under Communist control were meeting internal difficulties in 1946-1947. Rumblings of dissent were heard in the United Shoe Workers Union, the United Furniture Workers of America, and even the United Office and Professional Workers of America.

Within the United Furniture Workers, Morris Muster, president, who had previously never seemed concerned at being associated with the Communists,[1] suddenly resigned from union office on the ground that "Communist intrigue and chicanery have captured our international" and "My record as a trade unionist will not permit me to remain head of a Communist-controlled organization."[2]

It was beyond question that the Communists were in control of the Executive Board of the U.F.W. and that Max Perlow, the union's secretary-treasurer, had earned the title of "commissar" given him by George Bucher, head of the union's Philadelphia Local 37. Perlow had frequently acted as secretary-treasurer of Communist-sponsored May Day parades, had supported Communist Peter V. Cacchione for New York City Councilman, had been a member of fund raising committees for the *Daily Worker,* and had served on the resolutions committee of the Communist Political Association.[3] On June 5, 1949, Perlow openly admitted his membership in the Communist party and announced he was resigning, not out of any ideological differences but in order to be able to sign the non-Communist affidavit under the Taft-Hartley Act. He asserted that he had never kept his long-standing Communist membership a secret from union members.[4]

It is because of the teachings of this party that I came to the conclusion that there can be no higher privilege, no greater principle, than to serve the working people in their struggle for a higher standard of living, for higher wages, for job security, for greater and greater guarantees for the workers to live decently and bring up their children as free people without fear to face the future ... Marxism is the best expression of the hopes and aspirations of mankind to free itself from the mounting evils which threaten the world today.

The situation within the United Shoe Workers of America was similar, except for the fact that the pro- and anti-Communist factions within the union were more evenly divided. On October 1, 1946, Frank R. McGrath, president of the union and a member of the national CIO Executive Board, resigned on the eve of his union's fifth biennial convention and just a few months following a referendum election. Excerpts from his letter to the union's General Executive Board follow:[5]

Since the USWA has become an important factor in the trade union movement, Communist groups for the past year have tried to use their opposition to me as a screen for trying to seize control of the union and thereby further their cause of Communism.

They would not recognize the majority vote given in the election in March, but since that date, they have constantly harried the work of the organizers and have stymied the growth of the union by disseminating their union-busting material throughout the local unions. ...

I hope you will fight these plans to the last ditch. The great bulk of the membership of the union is bitterly opposed to Communism and will support you in any fight against this vicious political faction. ...

I have become so thoroughly disgusted with the dirty work of the Communists within our union that there is nothing that I can do under the circumstances to preserve my self-respect but, submit my resignation, effective October 2, 1946. By this action, I am free of all responsibilities to the United Shoe Workers of America as its president.

The Board, Communist controlled, accepted McGrath's resignation with the blast that he was a "union-wrecker" and that his act was "nothing but a cover-up for his desertion of the duties entrusted to him by the thousands of shoe workers."[6]

The significance of McGrath's resignation was in his previous very close affiliation with the Communist party. On January 3, 1944 he sent a letter to Louis F. Budenz, editor of the *Daily Worker*, greeting that Communist daily on its 20th anniversary. He said:

> I have been a reader of the *Daily Worker* for several years. I find your paper has been a consistent supporter of organized labor and has devoted itself to the worthy cause of building cooperation and understanding among the people and goverments of the United States, Great Britain, Soviet Union, China, and the other United Nations.
>
> I congratulate you on your Twentieth Anniversary and trust that you will continue your efforts on behalf of the laboring people. I am sure that you will continue to work with the American people who are supporting the efforts of our great President to mobilize our nation for the early victory planned at the historic conference at Teheran.

McGrath was not new to Communist trade union activity. He had formerly been a leader in the Shoe Workers Industrial Union Council, which had been affiliated with the Communist Trade Union Unity League. The *Daily Worker* of October 30, 1933, listed him as a member of a Communist committee of protest to Washington that year. He had also been affiliated with the Friends of the Abraham Lincoln Brigade. In 1940, he had been a member of the Joint Committee on Trade Union Rights, which supported the Communist party leaders of the International Fur and Leather Workers Union when they were serving prison terms.[7]

When the convention met, CIO Secretary-Treasurer James B. Carey, an invited speaker, attempted to throw his weight against the Communists. He recalled, for example, that the Communists had sabotaged FDR's foreign policy in 1940. In reply, the union's vice-presidents, Isidore Rosenberg and Julius Crane, described CIO national officers as "outsiders."[8]

One of the most consistently pro-Communist unions in the CIO was the United Office and Professional Workers, headed by Lewis Merrill. It had originally been the Office Workers Union, a part of the Communist Trade Union Unity League, also led by Merrill. When the TUUL disbanded and the Communists instructed their followers to join the AFL, Merrill and his associates joined the Bookkeepers, Stenographers and Office Workers Local of the AFL. Merrill was a delegate from that union to a number of AFL conventions and according to John P. Frey, president of the AFL Metal Trades Department, who testified before a House Committee on August 13, 1938, "he associated with and voted with the known Communists."[9] When the CIO was formed and the Communists the following year began to move into it, Merrill and his followers joined the CIO.

Merrill had never admitted to membership in the Communist party, but a former president of the AFL Bookkeepers union testified before the Dies Committee on November 28, 1938 that "on two different occasions Lewis Merrill told (him) that he was a member of the Communist Party" and that Merrill "attended a political conference in the headquarters of the Communist Party in New York" as a representative of the party.[10]

In any event, Merrill had been free in his formal associations with Communist activities and political positions for many years. He had been a signer of a declaration in honor of George Dimitrov, former head of the Communist International,[11] and a most active organizer and speaker for the Trade Union Committee and the citizens Committee to Free Earl Browder, then general secretary of the Communist party. On February 13, 1937, the *Daily Worker* carried Merrill's name as the signer of a cable in behalf of Louis Carlos Prestes, imprisoned Brazilean Communist leader and a former member of the Executive Committee of the Communist International.[12] The *Daily Worker* of November 18, 1942 listed Merrill as one of the contributing editors of the *New Masses,* Communist weekly magazine. On April 12, 1942 he was sponsor and speaker at a *New Masses* rally. He also contributed to the March, 1937 issue of *Champion,* published by the Young Communist League. The *Daily Worker* for October 4, 1942 also published in its magazine section a full-length biographical eulogy of him, entitled "Here's Looking at Lewis Merrill." In 1937, when the American League Against War and Fascism came into being through the efforts of the Communists, Merrill was one of the active members, contributed to its official publication,[13] acted as a sponsor of one of its big New York rallies,[14] and spoke in its behalf.[15] When the Communist line changed to one of "collective security of the democracies against the fascist aggressors" and the Communist-front changed its name to the American League for Peace and Democracy, Merrill became a sponsor,[16] a speaker,[17] and a member of its national labor committee.[18] With the Hitler-Stalin Pact, the American Peace Mobilization came into being to denounce the war as "imperialist." Merrill again became a sponsor, a speaker, and a member of its national labor committee.[19]

During this period, Merrill was a candidate for Congress in the 6th Congressional District, Brooklyn, New York, under the auspices of the Progressive Committee to Rebuild the American Labor Party, a Communist sponsored activity. His candidacy was supported by the Communists.[20] He ran as a "peace candidate." Following the election, he issued a press release on behalf of his union on May 30, 1941, in which he declared: "President Roosevelt's address accompanying his declaration of an unlimited national emergency has confirmed the fears of organized labor regarding the course of the administration's program for national defense."[21] Following the Nazi invasion of the Soviet in 1941, Merrill joined the Communist-liners in support of the war and in ardently proclaiming the need for a second front. At the 1941 CIO convention, he called for the production "of every implement necessary to exterminate Hitler."[22]

The second front period was an active one, for the UOPWA. In April, 1942, the union newspaper carried a banner headline reading "For World Victory Open Up a Second Front." The May 1 issue contained a full page exclusively devoted to a demand for an immediate second front. On August 1, 1942, the newspaper said editorially, "You will see that almost every local, every division, has made its major concentration point the campaign to back up the government and get that second front opened NOW." The editorial concluded that the real importance of a union victory in obtaining a contract was that it "magnified and strengthened" the fight for a second front.[23] The UOPWA continued to campaign for a second front throughout 1943. Its intent was made clear in October, 1943 when the union newspaper carried a full page article entitled "Your War, Your Wages and the 2nd Front" which criticized the Anglo-American leaders for not fully accepting partnership with the Soviet Union.

The Teheran agreement ended this period and led to one of

complete cooperation. In February, 1944, Merrill appeared before
a Senate Sub-Committee and announced that salaries must be
raised in order to achieve the goal of Teheran. Those who favored
strikes were called "Trotzkyites and disrupters."[24] This lasted
until June, 1945 when the Communist Party reconstituted itself.
That month, the UOPWA Executive Board began criticizing the
Truman administration and advocating a program of "Getting the
Boys Back Home" and "Get Out of China." Merrill joined the
critics of American foreign policy with the statement: "Apparently
our delegation to the UNO is less interested in peace than in
protecting the interests of American and British big business in
Iranian oil."[25] Merrill also became a member of the board of
the National Committee to Win the Peace, organized in 1946,
to "promote understanding and agreement with our great ally, the
Soviet Union" and committed to the proposition that "We, the
people of the United States, are not interested in Brittania's rule
or even in defending Standard Oil's interests in Iran."[26]

Lewis Merrill's political and trade union biography, therefore,
showed him so close to the Communist party that the Party could
consider it has been cheated out of dues if his claim that he never
joined the party was correct. That claim by Merrill was also well
known. M. Hedley Stone, NMU treasurer and former member of
the party was referring to it when he said of Merrill: "He used to
beat his chest and say: 'You know, I am not a Communist.' The
record is full of it, until one day he got up and said he was
through with the party."[27]

Stone had the events of December, 1946 in mind when he
made his statement. Within a month after the national CIO con-
vention, Merrill suddenly resigned as a contributing editor of the
New Masses and as a trustee of the pro-Communist Jefferson
School of Social Science. The Executive Board of his union,
UOPWA, then announced a new policy consistent with the newly
adopted CIO program. It stated its opposition to efforts to interfere in union affairs by any political party, whether it be the
Communist party, the Socialist party, the Democratic party, the
Republican party, "or any other political party or fraternal society
or religious organization or other outside organization."[28]

These moves by Merrill and UOPWA apparently took the

Communists by surprise. In an editorial entitled "Appeasement of Red-Baiting Never Paid," the *Daily Worker* declared Merrill's acts "must have gladdened the hearts of the red-baiters, for they never expected a voluntary purge." As for the mild UOPWA resolution, "The Declaration of Policy adopted by the UOPWA's board in general reaffirms some of those policies (national CIO policies), but, while doing so, goes far to the right of the CIO convention statement which, as everybody knows, was a compromise."[29]

Following these attacks, Merrill resigned as president of UOPWA because of "ill health." He was succeeded by James H. Durkin, chosen by the union's executive board. One observer commented on the change as follows: "If there was any question of Merrill's loyalty to the Communist party, there is certainly no question of Durkin's."[30]

The lineup of Communist and anti-Communist unions within the CIO was also slightly affected at this time by the entry into the CIO of two other international unions which had left the AFL for jurisdictional reasons. They were the Amalgamated Lithographers of America and the International Union of United Brewery, Flour, Cereal and Soft Drink Workers. Both could be counted in the anti-Communist camp. In fact, during the 1947 power struggle within the Milwaukee and Wisconsin industrial union councils, the Wisconsin section of the Brewery Workers substantially helped in the anti-Communist victory.[31]

At the same time, within one of the international unions, the United Rubber, Cork, Linoleum and Plastic Workers, the see-saw still continued. Its president, L. S. Buckmaster, had supported Murray's 1946 anti-Communist resolution quite wholeheartedly. Yet, the union's executive board had deplored Wallace's removal from the Truman Cabinet and upon its election in late 1946 was welcomed by the *Daily Worker* somewhat hopefully: "The new board is considered an improvement over the present one," the publication said.[32]

---

[1] Muster had been president of the Eastern Seaboard Council of the AFL Upholsterer's Union and had led a left-wing split into the CIO to form the United Furniture Workers of America in 1937. His record of pro-Communist activities was published in 1944 by the House of Repesentatives Special Committee on Un-American Activities, House Report 1311, *In-*

vestigation of Un-American Propaganda Activities In The United States,
pp. 137, 138.
[2] *The New York Times,* July 1, 1946.
[3] Documentation for these facts was provided me by Mr. Frederick Woltman, staff writer for the *New York World Telegram,* whose files were
made available for my examination.
[4] *The New York Times,* June 6, 1949, p. 1; for a further discussion of the
Taft-Hartley Law non-Communist Affidavit see Appendix.
[5] A copy of this letter, dated October 1, 1946, was made available to me
through the courtesy of the national CIO office.
[6] *Daily Worker,* October 3, 1946.
[7] *Daily Worker,* November 11, 1940; and House Report 1311, 78th Congress, 2nd Session, *op. cit.,* pp. 124-125.
[8] *The New York Times,* October 10, 1946.
[9] House Report 1311, 78th Congress, 2nd Session, *op. cit.* p. 126.
[10] *Ibid.*
[11] *The New York Times,* December 22, 1943, p. 40.
[12] House Report 1311, 78th Congress, 2nd Session, *op. cit.,* pp. 126, 127.
[13] *Fight,* October, 1937, p. 15.
[14] *Daily Worker,* January 11, 1937, p. 2.
[15] *Fight,* September, 1937, p. 27.
[16] *Daily Worker,* March 4, 1939, p. 2.
[17] *Daily Worker,* February 18, 1939, p. 2.
[18] House Report 1311, 78th Congress, 2nd Session, *op. cit.* p. 128.
[19] Attorney General Francis Biddle cited all three organizations as subversive: "The American League Against War and Fascism is the first of
three organizations established in the United States in an effort to create
public sentiment on behalf of a foreign policy adopted to the interest of
the Soviet Union. Its successor, The American League for Peace and
Democracy, was established in 1937 and, it, in turn, gave way in 1940
to the American Peace Mobilization." See the *Congressional Record,*
September 24, 1942, p. 7683.
[20] *Sunday Worker,* September 8, 1940, p. 5; *Daily Worker,* September
17, 1940, p. 4.
[21] House Report 1311, 78th Congress, 2nd Session, *op. cit.,* p. 128.
[22] CIO, *Daily Proceedings of the Fourth Constitutional Convention* (Detroit,
Michigan, November 17-22, 1941) p. 153.
[23] CIO, *Report of Executive Board Committee Appointed by President
Murray to Investigate Charges Against the United Office and Professional
Workers of America* (mimeographed), p. 9.
[24] *Ibid.,* p. 10.
[25] *Daily Worker,* March 29, 1946.
[26] Barbash, *op. cit.,* p. 208.
[27] CIO, *Hearings to Investigate ILWU, op. cit.,* p. 610.
[28] *PM,* December 16, 1946.
[29] *Daily Worker,* December 18, 1946.
[30] This statement was made to me in July, 1947 by Nelson Frank, staff
writer for the *New York World Telegram.*
[31] Avery, "Communist Power in U. S. Industry," *op. cit.*
[32] *Ibid.*

7 | 1947: A TURNING POINT IN THE C.I.O.

The year 1947 proved to be a significant year in the national Washington headquarters of the CIO, although its start was not very promising.

In January a national conference of liberals was held in Washington to discuss a strategy and a program. The conference, which was to become Americans for Democratic Action, stated as one of its premises that Communism and liberalism were incompatible and thus excluded Communists and fellow travellers from its deliberations and membership. Those who sponsored and attended the conference represented the well-spring of the American political liberal tradition. Since this organization, on a political level, was representing the ideals and seemed part of the same ferment which created the anti-Communist bloc within the CIO, a number of the CIO leaders were also present, led by representatives of the Textile Workers Union and the UAW. Among them were Emil Rieve, Walter Reuther, and John Green. James Carey, secretary-treasurer, and Allan Haywood, vice-president, attended as personal representatives of Philip Murray. The conference appointed an organizing committee of which Reuther, Green, Carey, and Wolchok were members.

Somewhat earlier the Progressive Citizens of America was organized around the person and ideas of Henry Wallace. The Communists in and out of the CIO were stimulating the organization of PCA as their political vehicle. The pro-Communist and fellow-traveller unions in the CIO began to affiliate with the PCA, thus creating a kind of ADA vs. PCA atmosphere within the CIO Executive Board.

The issue was inevitably raised when the CIO Executive Board met in February, since the name of the CIO and its officers was being linked to and claimed by both organizations. Murray's temporary solution, which was very disappointing to the ADA anti-Communists, was a policy statement of non-affiliation applicable to both organizations adopted by the CIO vice-presidents.[1] The statement deplored the division in the liberal movement as represented by the PCA-ADA split. It urged unity and ignored the ADA insistence that there could be no unity between liberal and Communist-infiltrated organizations. The agreement entered into was for CIO officials and unions in both factions to keep their names formally away from either organization. For a time, this served to handicap the ADA more than the PCA, primarily because of the fact that the pro-ADA CIO officials apparently kept to the agreement more strictly and were anxious not to alienate or estrange Murray. The pro-Communist unions continued to provide much of the manpower and funds for the PCA. This state of affairs lasted for about a year with the pro-PCA faction becoming more brazen in their relationships. Some of the leaders began to speak under PCA auspices. When R. J. Thomas, still a national vice-president though no longer head of the UAW, addressed an open PCA meeting, the anti-Communists no longer considered themselves bound. They again openly identified themselves with the ADA.

In February, 1948, just prior to the Philadelphia convention of ADA, Walter Reuther and Emil Rieve spoke with Murray about their desire to support the organization, and obtained from him agreement that the earlier CIO vice-presidents' resolution was no longer binding. At that, Leon Henderson, chairman of ADA, and James Loeb, executive secretary, invited Murray to address the convention. He replied that he did not feel prepared to take such a step as yet, but agreed to have a delegation of steelworkers present, suggesting the ADA communicate with David McDonald, secretary-treasurer of the steelworkers' union. McDonald, who was said to consider ADA too radical and "socialist," did not attend the convention. During the weekend of the convention, however, a meeting was held between the ADA leadership and an official CIO delegation headed by Allan Haywood. The CIO leaders, speaking for Murray, said the CIO would associate itself with ADA on condition that it could have seven members on the ADA national board,[2] that there would be no fund solicitation from the CIO rank and file, and that Haywood would handle the financial arrangements between the two. Haywood, however, who remained on the ADA board for two years, never took an interest in the organization, was not too friendly, and did not establish a financial relationship. The first CIO union to make a regular monthly contribution was Emil Rieve's Textile Workers Union. Walter Reuther's UAW soon adopted the same arrangement. It wasn't until 1949, when the ADA was under the chairmanship of Senator Hubert H. Humphrey, that the Steelworkers followed suit on a steady basis.

During the 1948 election campaign, the CIO worked very closely with ADA. In fact, it was as a result of CIO interest and persuasion that the ADA, prior to the national convention of the Democratic Party, worked to obtain the nomination for General Eisenhower.

To an observer visiting the national CIO office during the early part of 1947, there was a distinct air of suspicion and instability which had its effect on the morale of the staff. The legal and publicity departments were clearly within the pro-Communist camp. The office of the Secretary-Treasurer, which had the responsibility for most of the administrative operations at the headquarters; the Department of Education and Research; most of the Legislative office; and the office of the Industrial Union Councils were all strongly anti-Communist. Yet all were housed in the 3rd, 4th, and 5th floors at 718 Jackson Pl. N.W. in Washington.

The Legislative Department was one of those most affected by the division. Its head, Nathan Cowan, a former mine worker who sided with Murray against Lewis in the 1941 CIO break, was less active than he had been in his younger years, but most humble, sincere, and dedicated to the labor movement. His influence was clearly against the Communists, but it was his responsibility to direct a committee representative of all the CIO unions. Since a number of the unions under pro-Communist influence had legislative representatives in Washington, they were represented on the committee and present at all the meetings. The UE representa-

tives on the hill, Russ Nixon and Clifford McAvoy,[3] were particularly active, which necessitated Cowan's close attention, lest
CIO policy be undermined. The UAW Washington representative
at the time, Irving Richter, was identified with the pro-Addes
faction of the union and frequently assisted the UE, as did Robert
Lamb, representing the Steelworkers.

Cowan's fear that the UE and UAW representatives might
possibly undermine CIO policy was well founded. We have already seen how they supported military and labor conscription
during the war when the official CIO stand was that of opposition.
During this post-war period, "Every day they are on the hill
undermining."[4] They were trying to prove the Administration evil
and to perpetuate unrest. Cowan claimed, for example, that they
largely absented themselves during the Congressional debate on
the Taft-Hartley Act, but immediately following its veto, they
swarmed around the halls of Congress antagonizing Congressmen
and losing votes. He alleged that they were not at all helpful in
the CIO attempt to gain a 65¢ minimum wage, primarily because
the unions most affected beneficially by the bill would be Textile
and the Amalgamated Clothing Workers, both on the anti-Communist side of the CIO fence. Furthermore, he accused them of
virtual opposition to the Stratton Bill, designed to liberalize our
immigration policy and allow displaced persons to come to our
shores—a bill which the CIO strongly favored. He explained this
opposition on the ground that they realized the bulk of the refugees
were anti-Communist refugees running away from Soviet control.
The pro-Communist legislative representatives, he charged, were
advocating a statutory screening of all refugees to make certain
they were not "fascists"; Cowan's comment to this was: "We'd
better put up a screen against Commies too."[5]

To meet this internal dissension, Cowan frequently met
quietly with John Edelman, Textile's representative, Tom Owens,
representing the Rubber Workers, and Esther Peterson, representing the Amalgamated. Together, they tried to plan strategy and
harness their activities effectively. Cowan also made a serious
effort to undermine Richter's influence in the UAW by discussing
his problems with Reuther. As soon as Reuther was in a position

within his own executive board to do so, Richter was removed and replaced by Donald Montgomery and Paul Sifton, prominent Washington anti-Communist liberals.[6]

The office of the Director of CIO Industrial Union Councils was also quite openly identified with the anti-Communists. John Brophy, who had enjoyed a lengthy and noble career striving for democratic trade unionism within the United Mine Workers, had also sided with Murray in his break with Lewis. A shrewd observer and a labor philosopher in the finest sense, he no longer actively participated in the in-fighting of office politics, but his was indeed a key position following the 1946 convention in maintaining control over Communist activity within the Industrial Union Councils. In this he was aided by Anthony Wayne Smith, an attorney and liberal "philosopher" in his own right, who had been most active in the beginning stages of ADA and whose ideas were permeated with a native American radicalism which rejected all forms of totalitarianism.

Kermit Eby was at this time Director of Education and Research for the CIO. A Brethren minister by training, he had been a teacher who early learned the danger of Communism in the trade union movement in the course of an intra-union struggle within the Chicago American Federation of Teachers. He joined the CIO as assistant to J. Raymond Walsh, who was one of the most anti of anti-Communists on the CIO staff until 1944 when he resigned as Director to act as assistant to Sidney Hillman in the PAC. Eby, a much milder man and a religious pacifist, maintained no ties with the Communists but urged a calmer anti-Communist program than was being planned. Beginning with 1946, furthermore, Eby found his pacifist position leading him to similar conclusions in foreign affairs although from widely different motivations. This had an effect on the intensity of his opposition to them. His assistants at that time, Stanley Ruttenberg, who became his successor, Katherine Pollack Ellickson, and Helen Gould, were all associated as individuals with ADA.

Many of these activities were under the nominal direction of secretary-treasurer James B. Carey, who supplied the pace in the political thinking of the office. It was, therefore, possible for his staff members to be more anti-Communist by word of mouth and in their activities than was called for by the official CIO position.

There was thus a decided lifting of tension at the national headquarters when on June 28, 1947, Philip Murray released to the press a letter of resignation from Len DeCaux, director of publicity, and a letter accepting the resignation. Mr. DeCaux's letter follows:

> For personal reasons, which I have already outlined to you, I wish to resign as CIO Publicity Director and Editor of the *CIO News*.
>
> I would like my resignation to take effect as soon as you can conveniently relieve me of my duties and trust that July 15 will be satisfactory to you as the effective date.
>
> It has been a privilege and an honor to work for the CIO since its inception. This great movement has inspired, and still inspires, my enthusiastic loyalty and devotion and I hope to continue to be of service to it in any way I can.

Mr. Murray's letter of acceptance read:

> This is to acknowledge your communication dealing with the matter which you and I discussed in the course of our meetings during the present week.
>
> You have expressed an anxiety to do some writing and that whilst occupying your present position as publicity director for the CIO you have not had the time and opportunity to devote yourself to this work.
>
> I have an appreciation of the services which you have rendered the Congress of Industrial Organizations and support which you have given the CIO. I am therefore, in accordance with your letter of June 26, accepting your resignation.

Mr. DeCaux's successor was announced as Allan L. (Pete) Swim, a newspaper man from Arkansas, who had joined the Scripps-Howard organization in 1935, become city editor of the *Memphis Press-Scimitar*, and in May, 1946, had become director of public relations for the CIO Organizing Committee in the South. Mr. Swim was clear and unequivocal in his anti-Communism and knew why his predecessor had resigned.

The resignation was interpreted as a clear indication of Mr. Murray's determination to follow through on the CIO resolution and many expected that Lee Pressman would be next. There had been a great deal of opposition to the *CIO News* under DeCaux. In addition to complaints from anti-Communist international unions, there was a steady stream of complaints from staff members, including Nathan Cowan, of unfair or inadequate news coverage and editorializing. A number of the anti-Communist CIO internationals refused to distribute the weekly to their membership.

Earlier that year, for example, the CIO national office had found it necessary publicly to repudiate pro-Communist support of its Southern organizing campaign. Van A. Bittner, an officer of the Steelworkers, had been put in charge of the campaign, which was expected to take a number of years and millions of dollars. The Communists, eager to join the drive, began to publicize the campaign in their press. Suddenly, a rash of organizations not related to the CIO began fund-raising activities to aid the Southern drive. In order to nip these activities in the bud to prevent harassment of what was already a difficult enough task, Van Bittner, on April 18, released a public statement[7] repudiating outside support. It was clear by implication that his attack was against the Communists. He specifically singled out the Southern Conference for Human Welfare as one of the organizations without which the drive would feel happier. The *CIO News* that week, in covering the story, used three short paragraphs limited to the message that the CIO "does not want any 'interference' from organizations outside the CIO."

A comparison of the news treatment given by DeCaux and by *Steel Labor*, published by the Steelworkers Union to other CIO events revealed significant differences. The 1946 resolution on Communism was headlined in the *CIO News* as "CIO Reaffirms Americanism." The headline for that story in *Steel Labor* was "CIO Warns Communists: Don't Meddle in Unions." When the national CIO instructed its industrial union councils with regard to their outside activities, the *CIO News* headline read "Council Rules Amended"; *Steel Labor's* headline read: "Red Activity in Local Councils Barred by CIO."[8]

It was rumored, however, that the proverbial straw which finally broke the camel's back was a full page story in the June

16 issue of the *CIO News*. The story was quite sceptical of the concessions which Great Britain had just made to India. It carried a picture of a Bombay riot over the caption, "British colonial interests, defending their grip on fantastically profitable Indian trade, have long fostered religious dissension to maintain their power." That same week, Murray had signed an ADA sponsored statement praising the British Labor Government "for setting a new standard of democratic statesmanship in granting independence to India."[9]

With DeCaux's departure, the CIO staff members began to speak much more freely and openly of their anti-Communism. One of the first to do so was George Weaver, Director of the CIO's Committee Against Discrimination and an assistant to secretary-treasurer James Carey. In an address before the American Missionary Association's 4th Annual Institute of Race Relations, he said:[10] "Communists today are more reactionary than the Republican Party."

After making it clear that he "resents anyone even classifying a Communist with a liberal or progressive," he related the problem specifically to the labor movement. "But in the labor movement we have had to face this Communist problem in a realistic manner. We have been the ones on the firing line, we and the whole country have suffered at times in finding out that a Communist will subordinate to an outside ideology the policies democratically arrived at in his union. He is a Communist first and then a trade-unionist." Mr. Weaver then proceeded to explain the conflicts between the interests of the Soviet Union and dedication to democracy. After first pointing out: "In the post-war period Communists are sabotaging and perverting our principles because our policies are in opposition to the policies of the Soviet Union," he narrated the wartime experience which frequently found the Communists opposed to progress in racial equality. "There was a time in the war years when Communists sought to sabotage every move toward the integration of Negro workers if they thought it would hamper production."

At the same meeting, Willard S. Townsend, President of the United Transport Service Employees, a member of the CIO Executive Committee and one of the leaders of the Negro community in America, likewise spoke up: "We have learned you just can't run a labor union when certain members follow the policies of the Soviet Union," he said. "Communists destroy freedom in labor unions. . . . We don't want them in the labor movement."[11]

The die seemed cast. At the July meeting of the CIO Executive Board, Murray was quoted as saying: "If Communism is an issue in any of your unions, throw it to hell out." He followed this comment with: ". . . and throw its advocates out along with it. When a man accepts office . . . paid office in a union . . . to render service to workers, and then delivers service to outside interests, that man is nothing but a damned traitor."[12]

To this, the national labor secretary of the Communist Party replied dialectically:[13]

> To those who say, 'If Communism is an issue in your union, throw it out and throw out its advocates with it,' it is necessary to answer that just as the advocates of Christianity could not be thrown out by the Roman emperors, and just as the roar of the Inquisition commanding that Galileo stop proclaiming the earth round could not stop the advance of science, so today the trade union movement cannot turn back the clock of history.

When the CIO vice-presidents met on the eve of the October, 1947 convention in Boston, the anti-Communists, with Murray's energetic support, were clearly on the offensive. Andrei Y. Vishinsky had just attacked U. S. officials as "war mongering" and Murray immediately let the press know he differed sharply from the Russian view.[14]

Van Bittner, as chairman of the pre-convention resolutions committee, and Pressman, as secretary, had prepared a compromise foreign policy resolution which did not specifically support the Marshall Plan by name, but which specifically commended the foreign policies of Roosevelt, and which, in effect, stated that foreign aid by America should not impair national sovereignty. Emil Rieve and James Carey took issue with the suggested resolution and insisted that the CIO should specifically endorse the Marshall Plan.[15] Murray himself supplied the *piece de resistance* when he succeeded in getting Marshall to address the convention in person. The convention overwhelmingly demonstrated its loyalty to Marshall, his Plan, and the Administration's foreign policy with one of the longest and most exuberant demonstrations of welcome in the history of the CIO.[16]

In the course of the debate on the resolution, the Communists were attacked steadily. Walter Reuther recalled to the convention the Communist criticism of Roosevelt in 1940 and compared it to the "war monger" attacks which they were now levelling at Truman.

George Baldanzi, executive vice president of the Textile Workers and considered one of the outstanding labor orators in America, likewise took off against the Communists.[17]

> ... Are we acting unreasonable when we denounce people like the representatives of Russia who have been denouncing every responsible representative of ours, including the President of the United States, and stating that he is another Hitler? He could not be another Hitler, because if he were a Hitler, Russia would work out a pact with him like they did with Hitler.

Murray joined in the fracas. Joseph F. Kehoe, of the American Communications Association, rose to defend the critics of the Administration's foreign policy. He said: "Let us not say that where someone finds one comma wrong that we are then American traitors and unfit for human society. That kind of nationalism is what breeds war, no matter what nation it exists in, and it is absolutely contrary to American tradition."

At this, Murray, who was standing nearby, interjected: "May I interrupt you for a moment? I assume you also believe the heroes of Stalingrad are entitled to take the rostrum and the public platform to expound their views?" Kehoe's reply: "I believe in the American principles of free speech everywhere for everybody," went largely unnoticed as the delegates saw another indication that the die was cast.[18]

The 1947 CIO convention stimulated further anti-Communist activity within the various internationals and industrial union councils. At its 10th annual convention, the New Jersey State CIO Council, which the previous year had passed a strong anti-Communist resolution but had kept UE representative James

McLeish as 3rd vice-president in order to maintain unity, decided by a vote of 964-139 not to re-elect McLeish. This led to a walkout of 85 "left-wing delegates." A new resolution on Communism was passed.[19]

> The State CIO Industrial Union Council believes in a form of government that is the servant of the people, where there is freedom of speech, freedom of worship and a free labor movement.
>   Communist and Fascist forms of goverment are totalitarian in concept and actuality and diametrically opposed to our form of government. Their presence within the council of the CIO is not representative of the feelings and sentiments of the membership majority.

The convention elaborated upon this further by condemning "the presence within the CIO council of Communists and Fascists" whose purpose is to "get control of and subordinate the CIO to their form of government." Another resolution endorsed the Marshall Plan.

In New York, the local chapter of the American Newspaper Guild for the first time elected to office an anti-Communist slate.[20] Earlier in the year, Milton Murray, national president of the Guild, had testified before the House Labor and Education Committee that Communists had "virtual control" of the New York and Los Angeles locals of the Guild. He had specifically named as Communists Jack Ryan, executive vice-president of the New York Guild and William H. Brodie, executive secretary in Los Angeles.[21] *Front Page*, the monthly magazine published by the New York group, had made a practice of publishing advertisements for Communist activities, reviews of pro-Communist books, and had acted as an organ of the Communist point of view. The victory in New York of the Committee for Guild Unity, in the heaviest voting of the Guild's history,[22] was indeed a sign of the times.

Similar changes took place within the CIO in Minnesota too, where the Communists had exercised control for a number of years. The largest CIO union in the State was the pro-Communist UE. The Communists had begun to colonize Minnesota in 1937 and 1938 when the state Farmer-Labor administration of Elmer Benson welcomed them into positions of responsibility.[23] Many of the leading members of the CIO were open members of the Communist party. These included Clarence Hathaway, former editor of the *Daily Worker*, and William Mauseth, both UE business agents. The president of the UE District 11, of which Minnesota was a part (the area also included parts of Illinois and Wisconsin), was Ernest DeMaio, a "secret member of the Communist Party."[24] He was one of three incorporators of the pro-Communist *Chicago Star*, a director of the Abraham Lincoln School in Chicago, a speaker at a March 9, 1941 banquet at the Ashland Auditorium in Chicago honoring William Z. Foster, a sponsor of the American Peace Mobilization, a member of the Chicago Friends of the *New Masses*, and a member of the Joint Anti-Fascist Refugee Committee and other Communist front organizations. His name was also included among those hailing the *Daily Worker* on its 20th Anniversary.[25]

There was evidence that DeMaio used his position as UE business agent to solicit members for the Communist party. Edward Wiggins, business agent for one of the union locals in St. Paul, said that he had been approached by DeMaio in either the fall of 1947 or the spring of 1948 to join the Party. When the two went out for lunch, a third person at the lunch was a man whom Wiggins identified as "a solicitor for the Communist Party."[26] Anthony DeMaio, a brother of Ernest, was also on the UE national staff assigned to Minnesota. He had been an officer in the Abraham Lincoln Brigade during the Spanish Civil War. In testifying before the House Un-American Activities Committee on April 12, 1940, he admitted to membership in the Communist party:

MR. MATTHEWS: Were you ever a member of the Communist Party?
MR. DEMAIO: I was.
MR. MATTHEWS: When did you join the Communist Party?
MR. DEMAIO: I don't recall the exact date. It was when I returned from Spain.

Also on DeMaio's staff as a field organizer for District 11 was John T. Bernard, former Minnesota Congressman. Bernard had been an instructor at the Abraham Lincoln School in Chicago, a sponsor of the American Peace Mobilization and the American League for Peace and Democracy. On August 31, 1937, he had written in the Communist *New Masses*: "Mass organizations like the Workers Alliance . . . and the League Against War and Fascism . . . must learn to act together, in support of their common interests." He identified himself as a Congressman of the "progressive minority which supports the New Deal against the reactionaries in both major parties, but at the same time presses forward beyond the limits set by administration leadership." He was a member of the national committee of the International Labor Defense, cited by the Attorney General as the "legal arm of the Communist Party"; and he introduced excerpts from the *Daily Worker* into the Congressional Record.[27]

An interesting sidelight indicating the extent to which the Communists controlled policy in the Minnesota state CIO was a resolution unanimously adopted by the state convention on September 8, 1944.[28] It was the state CIO's reply to those civil-liberties-oriented organizations and individuals who had protested the Smith "peacetime sedition" act and the federal government's indictment of the eighteen Trotskyite leaders under the law. This law was the same law applied later against the eleven Communist leaders in 1948-1950, but in 1944 it was used against the Communists' bitter enemies. The resolution read:

> WHEREAS, Eighteen members of the Socialist Workers Party have been convicted by the goverment for sedition, and
> WHEREAS, This group and their associates are using the name of the CIO and were prosecuted for bona fide union activities, and
> WHEREAS, The facts are that this group was convicted for seditious statements and activities against our goverment and our war effort and from the very beginning of the organization of the CIO in Minnesota this group bitterly opposed and fought the CIO and its progressive program to organize the thousands of unorganized workers in Minnesota's mass production industries, and
> WHEREAS, Their vicious attacks against our Commander-in-Chief, President Roosevelt, their similar attacks against Phillip Murray and his courageous leadership in the CIO, are nothing but actions of enemies of the labor movement,
> THEREFORE be it resolved, that this Seventh Annual Convention of the Minnesota CIO goes on record condemning the disruptive and seditious activities of the group and condemning their vicious attacks against the CIO and goes on record opposing any aid or comfort to those serving terms in the federal penitentiary. . .

Following the 1946 national convention of the CIO, dissatisfaction was expressed within the Minneapolis Hennepin County
CIO Council. The beginning of the dissatisfaction coincided with
the political organization of anti-Communist liberals within the state
under the leadership of Hubert H. Humphrey, then mayor of
Minneapolis, later a United States Senator. On March 13, 1947,
Robert I. Wishart, president of the Hennepin County CIO Council,
suddenly, without warning, and with only a month of his term
remaining, submitted his resignation. He had been under attack for
several months by the pro-Communist faction, in spite of his previous friendship for them. He had sponsored, been present at, and
cooperated with CIO-UE meetings called to honor national Communist leaders visiting the Twin Cities; he had been one of 144 CIO
leaders who hailed the *Daily Worker* on its twentieth anniversary
in January, 1944;[29] and he had joined a number of their Communist-
front organizations, including the National Federation of Constitutional Liberties, and the Citizens Committee to Free Earl Browder,
officially listed as "subversive" by Attorney General Biddle.[30]
By 1947, however, Wishart became anxious to assert his independence and separate himself from Communist control. In January, he
had withdrawn as a member of the national UE Executive Board;[31]
now he was taking action on the local level. Wishart's role was a
difficult one. Considered by many the shrewdest political leader
of labor in the state, he did not effectively deny press reports that
his resignation resulted from attempts of the Communists to run
union affairs in the council.[32] It was thought that he resented the
pressure brought against him for his efforts to bring CIO support to
Mayor Humphrey's bid for re-election that year. The Communists
were putting forward a candidate of their own, Robert J. Kelly,
whom the CIO "left-wing" wished to support.[33] It was noted,
furthermore, that Wishart had political ambitions of his own and
was a candidate for 8th ward city alderman that year. It was also
considered significant that he joined the Lutheran Church at this
time.[34]

In any event, it seemed clear that Wishart wanted to avoid a
serious split. He attempted to maintain "unity" between the right
and left wings in the CIO, to take the initiative away from the Communists, and to keep himself in the dominant power position. This

was made easier by the fact that his home base was Local 1145 of the UE, of which he was business agent, and the 5,500 members of which constituted approximately one-fourth of the CIO membership in the city. By resigning when he did, and not waiting for his term to expire, Wishart prevented the opposition from nominating a candidate of their own to replace him.

During the next week, repeated efforts were made to get Wishart to reconsider. He made his terms and objectives clearer by announcing, in an ill-concealed jab at the Communist Party: "I want to see the policies of President Phillip Murray and the CIO carried out in Hennepin County now as they have in the past. Unswerving allegiance must be maintained to that program if labor is to benefit."[35] In all of the negotiations, Wishart had the strong support of the local UAW and its representative Carl Boye, who was secretary-treasurer of the council.

On March 19, Wishart withdrew his resignation "in order to maintain the CIO as a united force in the labor movement" and in order to establish "unity behind the national CIO program."[36] To lend further credence to the prevailing view that his return had brought political concessions from the Communists, Wishart called on the CIO to give all-out support to Humphrey's campaign for re-election. "Mayor Humphrey has been endorsed by the CIO and is our candidate," he said. "I feel that *Minnesota Labor* (offical publication of the state CIO) also should be expected to get behind the Mayor."[37]

Wishart remained quite cautious, however, and went to great lengths to avoid an open break with the Communists, thereby leading a number of the anti-Communists to accuse him of riding two horses. At the September convention of the national UE, his delegation voted with the pro-Communists delegation and Wishart reported to the press that the Communist issue "was not involved." The intra-union battle, he said, was "simply a battle for power between the ins and the outs."[38]

It is interesting to note that the state CIO weekly newspaper, *Minnesota Labor*, called the Wishart incident a "normal occurrence."[39] *Minnesota Labor* itself was a source of controversy within the CIO because of its pro-Communist orientation, under its manager, Sam K. Davis, long active in the Communist Party. The newspaper served as a publicity organ not only for the leadership of the Minnesota CIO but also for the Communist Party.

Communist party meetings were publicized in *Minnesota Labor*[40] as were Russian films;[41] articles were written by Communists;[42] Communist sponsored May Day meetings were supported;[43] and editorial opinions always supported the Communist position.[44] In its issues of July, 1946, the weekly paper publicized a new pro-Communist recording organization, People's Songs Incorporated; supported the Civil Rights Congress; praised *The Great Conspiracy*, by Kahn and Sayres, a Communist sponsored book; condemned Victor Kravchenko's *I Chose Freedom;* announced a meeting sponsored by the St. Paul Communist party; assisted the American Youth for Democracy; and attacked Truman's foreign policy. Beginning with Henry Wallace's Madison Square Garden speech on September 12, 1946 in New York, hardly an issue of *Minnesota Labor* was published which did not praise or quote Wallace or attack the United States foreign policy. When the national CIO in August, 1947 supported the Greek-Turkish aid program, no mention of it was made in the paper. Anti-Communists in the CIO determined that one of their first objectives would be to change the management and policies of *Minnesota Labor*.

Meanwhile, efforts were also being made on a state level to thwart continued Communist control of the CIO there. William Mauseth, a member of the Communist party, resigned in January as state CIO Political Action committee head. His resignation was interpreted as a "right-wing" victory.[45]

The State CIO Executive Board was under pro-Communist control. Rodney Jacobson, state secretary-treasurer, and an anti-Communist, found himself in a most precarious political position within the CIO. He had the friendship and support of Wishart and the cooperation of Fullerton Fulton, Phillip Murray's personal representative in the area and national regional director, but Jacobson had no strength or union base of his own. He, therefore, found it quite difficult to spearhead an opposition to the Communists.

But the national trend made its mark in the state and pressure from the headquarters of the various international unions on the state locals had its effect. This was particularly true of the Textile Workers Union, which, although small in numbers, began to throw around whatever weight it did have and became the vigilant anti-Communist of the state CIO. It was also true, however, of the Steel Workers, considered the senior union in the CIO, the Automobile Workers, and the Brewery Workers, together with some of the smaller unions including the Newspaper Guild, which had always opposed and suspected the Communism of the other CIO unions.

When the State CIO Council met in its 10th annual convention at Hibbing in early November, 1947, the anti-Communists for the first time were organized in informal caucus and found themselves with a 14-6 majority in the newly elected executive board. An indication of the change in CIO temper was the fact that, in addition to Wishart, the UE was represented by another anti-Communist at the convention, Howard Fortier, financial secretary of Local 1140, who had replaced Mauseth. But Clarence Hathaway, Local 1139 business agent and former Communist editor, continued to be a UE delegate to the convention.[46]

At the convention, Wishart was able to push through a resolution condemning "outside influences," which was clearly aimed at the Communist party but which didn't mention it and hence fell short of the national objective. This indicated the remaining Communist strength within the organization and the reluctance of the "right wing" to push their position and disrupt "unity." The convention also nearly adjourned without endorsing Humphrey, who was then being urged by national and state labor officials to be a candidate for the Senate against Joseph Ball the following year. At the last minute, Al Esnough, representing the Textile Workers, moved the endorsement, which was quickly, and by the Communists, reluctantly, passed. The Minnesota CIO seemed to be a year and a half behind the national organization.

Minnesota, however, with its 14-6 anti-Communist state council majority was well on its way. Soon after the new executive board saw its way clear, it discharged the pro-Communist manager and editor of *Minnesota Labor*, placed Rodney Jacobson in charge, and then hired as editor, Gervase Love, a former Newspaper Guild editor with anti-Communist leanings. At the 1948 convention of the State CIO Council, the anti-Communists further strengthened themselves.

The internal pressures within the Minnesota CIO, strengthened by the national CIO anti-Communist leadership and developments, succeeded in eliminating communist influence by 1950. Communist leaders remained active within some of the unions in the state but decreasingly so and nearly exclusively within independent unions no longer part of the CIO.

[1] *New York Post*, February 21, 1947.
[2] The seven members were: Haywood, Reuther, Carey, Wolchok, Rieve, Buckmaster (Rubber Workers), and Green (Shipbuilding Workers).
[3] House of Representatives, Committee on Un-American Activities, 81st Congress, 2nd Session, *Hearings Regarding Communist Activities in the Cincinnati, Ohio, Area*, Part 1, July 12-15, 1950, pp. 2750-2752.
[4] Interview with Nathan Cowan, July 15, 1947.
[5] *Ibid.*, July 24, 1947.
[6] *Ibid.*; and interview with John Edelman, July 16, 1947.
[7] *The New York Times*, April 19, 1946.
[8] Avery, "Communist Power in U. S. Industry," *op. cit.*
[9] *Labor Leader*, July 25, 1947.
[10] *The New York Times*, July 11, 1947.
[11] *Ibid.*
[12] This quotation was supplied to me by a member of the CIO staff who was present at the Executive Board meeting.
[13] *Counterattack*, August 8, 1947.
[14] *The New York Times*, October 9, 1947.
[15] *The New York Times*, October 10, 1947.
[16] CIO, *Daily Proceedings of the Ninth Constitutional Convention* (Boston, Massachusetts, October 13-17, 1949) pp. 258-263.
[17] *Ibid.*, p. 279.
[18] *Ibid.*, p. 283.
[19] *The New York Times*, December 8, 1947.
[20] *The New York Times*, December 21, 1947.
[21] *The New York Times*, March 16, 1947.
[22] 5,800 out of 7,500 eligible members cast ballots. The margins of victory ranged from 300 to 500.
[23] Arthur Naftalin, *A History of the Farmer-Labor Party of Minnesota*, a doctoral dissertation (unpublished), University of Minnesota, 1948.
[24] Avery, "Communist Power in U. S. Industry," *op. cit.*
[25] *Ibid.*; and House Report 1311, 78th Congress, 2nd Session. *op. cit.*, p. 66.
[26] *Minneapolis Star*, November 16, 1954.
[27] House Report 1311, 78th Congress, 2nd Session, *op. cit.*, pp. 80-83.
[28] George Morris, *The Trotzkyite 5th Column in the Labor Movement* (New Century Publishers: 1945) pp. 30-31.

[29] House Report 1311, 78th Congress, 2nd Session, *op. cit.* pp. 52, 57, 65.
[30] *Ibid.*, pp. 44-50.
[31] *Minneapolis Star,* March 14, 1947.
[32] *Minneapolis Tribune,* March 14, 1947.
[33] *Minneapolis Star,* March 14, 1947.
[34] *Ibid.,* March 30, 1947.
[35] *Minneapolis Tribune,* March 15, 1947.
[36] *Ibid.,* March 20, 1947.
[37] *Ibid.,* March 24, 1947.
[38] *Ibid.,* September 26, 1947.
[39] *Ibid.,* March 21, 1947.
[40] *Minnesota Labor,* January 11, 1946; January 25, 1946; February 8, 1946.
[41] January 18, 1946.
[42] January 25, 1946; February 8, 1946; March 8, 1946.
[43] May 3, 1946.
[44] May 17, 1946; May 24, 1946.
[45] Kenneth Crouse, "Union Communists," *St. Paul Pioneer Press,* March 9, 1947.
[46] *Minneapolis Tribune,* November 1, 3, 1947.

THE CASE OF
8 | THE UNITED ELECTRICAL WORKERS UNION

The slow change and occasional signs of rebellion within the UE in Minnesota were being duplicated elsewhere in the country. The *Daily Worker* on August 1, 1948, declared: "... the main industrial base of our party is in electrical and that base which is weak and shaky must be guaranteed and strengthened." The stakes were indeed high.

The UE, from the very beginning of its organization within the CIO, was dominated by an organized Communist minority. Its membership came from a number of former company unions which threw off the company union shell during the period of ferment that created the CIO. Most of its early leaders, as a result of this origin, had very little political sophistication or organizational experience. It was therefore, possible for the energetic Communists to take active leadership and, in the words of one labor historian, lead the workers "around from one policy to another regardless of the interests of the union."[1]

James B. Carey, president of the UE, did not come to see the Communist affiliation of his associates and the fact that they were using him until late 1940. Carey was then the youngest national labor leader in America and soon to be the secretary-treasurer of the CIO under John L. Lewis. Benjamin Stolberg tells an interesting tale in this connection. Following an article which Stolberg wrote for the *Saturday Evening Post* in 1939, charging that the UE was Communist dominated, Carey denied the charge and asked for a luncheon date with Stolberg to persuade him of his error. He then asked permission to bring James Matles![2]

Although Matles, the union's director of organization, had

officially denied his Communist party membership, he had been quoted in the *Daily Worker* of November 6, 1933 as saying: "Only the Communist party as the party of the working class represents the interests of the entire working population." On this basis, and on the basis of other material available to him, Frederick Woltman in the *New York World Telegram* of October 29, 1946, called him "a veteran Communist party member as long ago as November 1933" and Woltman has never been asked to answer the accusation in any court of law.

Matles and Julius Emspak, secretary-treasurer of the UE, came to the UE from the Steel and Metal Workers Industrial Union, an affiliate of the Trade Union Unity League. Matles had originally been a grand lodge master of the International Association of Machinists and was instrumental in leading 10,000 members out of the IAM into the TUUL. He then became secretary of that union's metal and machinery division. When the TUUL dissolved, he led his union back to the IAM, but in 1937, when the Communists began to operate in the CIO he led his union into the UE.[3]

Carey, who started work as a boy, took a job in 1929 as an inspector in a radio manufacturing plant. In 1933, he assisted in organizing his fellow employees into an AFL federal labor union; and in 1934 was appointed an AFL general organizer. He helped lead his and other similarly dissatisfied AFL and small independent unions into the CIO and became president of the United Electrical and Radio Workers in 1936.[4] His experience in the CIO led Carey to take an interest in related social, political, and economic problems of the community. A religiously motivated Catholic, eager to formulate a social philosophy, he was soon exposed by his sophisticated associates to a number of Communist-front organizations. He became a delegate to the American Congress for Peace and Democracy, during the collective security phase of the Communist line, and then a member of the national labor committee of the American League for Peace and Democracy, which was formed at that Congress.[5] He also became a national officer of the American Youth Congress. When the Communist line began to change to an isolationist one, however, following the Hitler-Stalin Pact, Communists in his union had succeeded in developing a political machine which had control over the union's decision-making process.

A news item in the *Daily Worker* of February 5, 1937, illustrated the type of personnel which joined and became active in the UE:

> James Lewis, 22, vice-president of District 12 of the United Electrical and Radio Workers and a member of the Communist Party, died late Wednesday night following a pneumonia attack. Lewis, who was a member of the Young Communist League for 5 years before joining the Communist Party, was an outstanding leader in the Electrical Union.

The 1940 convention of the UE, meeting at the Hotel Hollenden in Cleveland, heard the war denounced as "imperialist" and as a struggle between two thieves. The officers' report, signed by Julius Emspak, secretary-treasurer, declared that the Second World War began as the result of "rivalries and national ambitions that had been ripening for more than a score of years in Europe." The 700 delegates to the convention were called upon to cooperate with the forthcoming meeting of the Emergency Peace Mobilization in Chicago.[6] The convention officially notified President Roosevelt that conscription "involves a very definite departure from the basic principles of the Constitution of the United States and the Declaration of Independence."[7]

The UE locals proceeded to put this program into operation. Emspak became a sponsor of the Committee to Defend America by Keeping Out of War, and later a member of the national council of the American Peace Mobilization. Simon Gerson, reporter for the *Daily Worker*, estimated that 100 locals of the UE were represented at the American Peoples Meeting on April 5, 6, 1941, in New York the national convention of the American Peace Mobilization.[8]

The UE, of course, was in a very strategic position affecting our national defense before and during the war. It has been estimated that three-fourth of its membership was employed in defense industries, manufacturing aircraft and marine equipment, gauges, aerial cameras, motors, and cartridges. During the war, in 1943, the union claimed 970 collective bargaining agreements with Westinghouse Electric covering 75,000 employees, with General Electric covering 120,000 employees, with General Motors 30,000 employees, with RCA with 12,000 employees, and with other defense plants including Fairchild Aerial Camera Co., Liquidometer Corp., Colt

Patent Fire Arms, Phelps Dodge Copper Products, Remington-Rand, Babcock and Wilcox, Electric Dynamic, National Radio Tube, Union Switch and Signal, and U.S. Cartridge Co.[9] It was, therefore, quite significant when the UE set in motion a general strike campaign throughout the industry in October, 1940, a month after the meeting of the American Peace Mobilization. A few of the strikes did take place and their political character became evident from the fact that members of the American Peace Mobilization in New York joined in supporting them.[10]

The 1941 UE convention was held in September in Camden, New Jersey, after Hitler's attack on the Soviet Union. The Communist-line had changed and the Matles-Emspak leadership now supported the war effort wholeheartedly. Emspak's officers' report demanded that the union take "every step necessary to crush Hitlerism" and announced that the disagreements within the union on foreign policy had now all disappeared.[11] Carey, however, thoroughly awakened to the Communist danger, was not prepared to let the issue drop and began what turned out to be a nine-year effort to break the union's Communist control. He presented a resolution to the General Executive Board which would have permitted local unions to exclude Communists, Nazis, and Fascists from holding union office. He was charged with "red-baiting" and received the support of only two members of the board. When he refused to back down on the issue, he was defeated for the presidency. The convention then adopted, by a vote of 789 to 377, a motion to bar only those found guilty of "acts against the nation or against the union."[12] Carey's supporters characterized this resolution as a meaningless "straddle."[13] Carey's supporters also charged the *UE News* with being "Communist." Emspak, its editor, vigorously defended the paper and was elected as secretary-treasurer. Matles was chosen as national organizational director and Albert J. Fitzgerald was chosen president.[14]

With Carey's ouster, the lines between the Communists and the anti-Communists were sharply drawn and the Communist control became stronger. Carey continued to come to most of the union conventions as a delegate from one of the local unions, but he spent less time on UE affairs and practically all of his time carrying out his duties as secretary-treasurer of the CIO. The anti-Communist forces, therefore, without an on-the-spot leader became weaker and were demoralized. Some activity continued, however, and at the 1942 convention, Local 113, District 1, submitted a resolution "to go on record that no Communists, Nazi, or Fascists be employed the UER & MWA." Local 101 proposed a similar constitutional amendment: "No proven Communist, Nazi, or Fascist shall be eligible to hold office in the United Electrical and Machine Workers of America."[15] Both moves were defeated.

At the ninth convention of the UE, held at the Hotel New Yorker in New York, in September, 1943, Emspak's officers' report called for the "opening of a western front."[16] He became a member of the President's Labor Victory Committee and led his union in support of the Communist position that "for the duration" wage demands and other "normal" trade union activities were to be suspended. He declared that UE "members are willing to abstain from their just demand for a general cost-of-living wage rise at this time."[17]

The UE also adopted the Browder Communist position of eliminating the "class struggle" and stressing employer-worker cooperation. Their 1944 election pamphlet, *Guide to Political Action*, referred to "Enlightened, win-the-war managements will agree that a win-the-war Congress helps production." In discussing the problem of transition to production for peace, the publication continued: "The best guarantee of such an orderly and rapid transition is political action of employees and employers alike."[18] The new popular front, many employers were probably amused to learn, included them.

To prove their loyalty to the "status quo" and UE's abandonment of the "class struggle," Emspak even urged UE members to go through a picket line during a strike. The "salaried workers" at Westinghouse in Springfield, Massachusetts, were out on strike, when Emspak in a letter to his Local 202's business agent said:[19]

As you know, the (UE Westinghouse) Conference Board authorized the issuance of an appeal to the salaried workers to abandon their strike and their phony leadership, to go back to work and join with UE. We will do everything in our power to expose the misleadership given to these people, and we will do everything in our power to see to it that our workers are not deprived of the right to work.

If the strike continues and it becomes necessary, we will engage in cross picketing, and in exposing in every possible way the connivings of the company union leadership with the Company to deprive the salaried workers of what was and what is justly due them. We will not worry about charges of strike-breaking from Bollens, because as a mouth-piece of the Company he has been busy for years in undercutting the standards of the white collar workers and working against the interests of the UE membership.

The *UE News*, under Emspak, remained quite loyal to the Communist position. A Report of the House Un-American Activities Committee charged; "Almost every issue carries some laudatory article dealing with the Soviet Union."[20]

All during this time, Communist leaders openly carried on their activities within the union. Local 448 of the UE, Union City, New Jersey, endorsed the *Daily Worker* on November 8 and 28, 1943, as "the best labor paper in the country." The UE stated that the Communist press had given the union 367 inches of space during the seven days of the 1943 convention. Similar treatment was afforded in 1942 when the UE adopted a resolution condemning "red-baiting" as the "chief instrument of Nazi oppression and of the Pro-Fascist fifth column of America."[21]

At that same 1942 Cleveland convention, one of the delegates, Louis Torre, representing Local 1114, addressed himself as follows to one of the resolutions which he and the union leadership opposed:[22]

> ...The difference between Communism and Facism is the difference between freedom and slavery.
>
> We are fighting for freedom—and in my opinion the Communist Party today is fighting for victory; that is the reason President Roosevelt freed Earl Browder.
>
> In my opinion, if we stop Red-baiting, follow the policy of this union as we have been going along, we will not only build the union but we will give a contribution to our nation which will give leadership to the labor movement, and once and for all stamp out Red-baiting from the labor movement and build a democratic organization.
>
> Certainly any Nazi or Fascist should be expelled—not only expelled; he should be shot! I, for one will expose such Nazi and

Fascists in our organization! (applause) But, brothers, I believe we should continue the progress in this convention and end it up by rejecting this Nazi, Red-baiting amendment to the Constitution.

District Council 4 of the UE, representing the New York-New Jersey area was particularly active in behalf of the Communist cause. In 1945, when the *Daily Worker* began a $100,000 fund raising campaign, the Council Executive Board went on record in its support and authorized James McLeish, president, and Ruth Young, secretary, to join a committee of sponsors.[23] That same year, which was an election year in New York City, the council supported Benjamin Davis, a Communist Party member, for the City Council and urged his nomination by the New York American Labor Party.[24]

The *New Leader*[25] published a few "pocket-size biographies" of some of the UE leaders with Communist affiliations. This list went as follows:

WILLIAM SENTNER, president of District 8, in the November, 1943, issue of *Fortune*, boasted of being a CP member. In 1935, Sentner was the secretary of the East St. Louis section of the CP. In 1939, he became a member of the City Committee of the CP of St. Louis.

JAMES LUSTIG, in 1931, ran for position of Alderman in the 25th District on the CP ticket (*Daily Worker*,11/3/31). In an article in the *Daily Worker* (11/6/33) Lustig was revealed to have endorsed the CP.

JAMES MATLES, organization director of UE, was quoted by *DW* (11/6/33): 'Only the Communist Party as the party of the working class represents the interests of the entire working population.' He has been a CP member for more than a decade.

JULES EMSPAK, according to a bulletin issued by Local 475, was a member of the National Council of the American Peace Mobilization, a CP-Front organization which dissolved when Russia was attacked. Emspak was an official along with Matles and Lustig, of the Steel and Metal Workers Union which was affiliated with the Trade Union Unity League organized by the CP.

RUTH YOUNG, secretary of District 4, publicly admitted being a member of the CP at the 1941 convention of the UE.

THOMAS F. DWYER, business representative of Local 475, in 1940 ran on the Communist ticket for Congress in the sixth Congressional District (*Daily Worker*, 10/21/40).

LOGAN BURKHARDT, vice-president of UE Local 601, pledged himself to help 'roll up a big Communist vote,' according to the *Daily Worker* (11/1/40).

HERBERT MORATS (also known as RICHARD ENMALE), is at present the assistant research director on James Matles' staff. He is a teacher at the Jefferson School, the successor to the CP Worker's School.

JAMES MACLEISH, president of District 4, admitted reluctantly at the 1941 convention of UE that he was a member of the CP.

DAVE DAVIS, business agent of Local 155, was elected to the National Committee of the CP in 1945.

SIDNEY MASON, assistant business manager of Local 475, is a member of Peter V. Cacchione branch of CP.

SAMUEL KANTER, business representative of Local 475, is a member of the Brighton Club of the CP. He sponsored the testimonial dinner to William Z. Foster at Hotel Granada, Brooklyn (*DW*, 5/15/45).

NAT COHEN, executive board member of Local 475, was elected to the National Committee of the CP in July, 1945.

ROBERT PAGNOTTA, business agent of Local 475, is a member of the Utica Club of the 11th AD of the CP. He was a member of the Young Communist League and its successor, the American Youth for Democracy.

MERCEDES REID, business representative of Local 475, was delegate to the CP convention in July, 1945 (*DW*, August 8, 1945). He was a member of the Citizens Committee to re-elect (CP) Councilman Peter V. Cacchione.

The House Un-American Activities Committee, of course, listed others.[26] In discussing Ruth Young, it added the information that in February, 1938, she had signed a public manifesto which read in part as follows:[27]

> The growth of the party depends upon our own efforts and will. We pledge to make the slogan 'Build the Party,' the center of discussions and action among our members and among the broad masses of our sympathizers.
> Forward to build a strong and powerful Communist Party!
> Forward for a strong people's front to defeat fascism and war!
> Forward to the American October!

When confronted at the 1941 UE convention with her signature on the manifesto and its reference to the October Bolshevik revolution in Russia, she replied only that she was "not aware that it is illegal in the United States for anyone to hold any political or religious belief."

With the deterioration of American-Soviet relations in 1946 and the consequent change of the Communist party line, the UE General Executive Board began to attack the Truman administration's foreign policy as shaped by "monopolists" and "imperialists" and as one seeking to provoke another war. It wanted American foreign policy to be more cooperative with Russia and less cooperative with "the slave-masters of the British Empire."

In 1946 opposition to the pro-Communist leadership in the union was resumed, coinciding with the growing differences over American foreign policy and with similar anti-Communist activity throughout the CIO. Within UE it remained quite weak for a time. At the 1946 UE convention in September, the Fitzpatrick-Matles-Emspak slate received a 6 to 1 majority and the convention, by a vote of 2,827–679, condemned "red baiters." At this convention, Murray, anxious to maintain unity and remembering the war years, said, much to the disappointment of the anti-Communists:[28]

> I am particularly proud this morning to place on this record the following remarks, that no one could be more pleased or more deeply appreciative of the splendid support that has been given them by your organization and its officers. They have done so royally, sustained and maintained and fought for all national policies, and supported the president of this organization in the furtherance of these policies.

In the July prior to the convention, Murray had also appointed Emspak as one of a five-man board to control the activities of the CIO Political Action Committee after Sidney Hillman's death.

On the eve of the 1946 national convention, John A. Metcalfe, president of UE Local 601 with 17,000 members and the largest local in the UE, resigned, charging that the union was Communist controlled.[29] "At the bottom of the trouble in Local 601 are the activities of a small number of Communists whose plans for control and domination of our local are deeply resented by an enormous majority of Catholics, Republicans, Democrats, and all good labor men," he said. Referring to a recent decision by the local membership, he continued: "Our membership refuses to increase the per capita to the international because they believe the money will be spent on political propaganda to extend Joe Stalin's empire or to entrench a formidable fifth column to weaken our national defenses."

He said the Communists had tried to control the local for ten years and they had finally succeeded. During the period of 1944 and 1945, a Communist political machine was firmly established. He charged that expenses of the local increased tremendously, and that unconstitutional election expenses jumped from around $4,000 to $16,500.

In a letter to Emspak, as editor of the *UE News,* Carey on January 8, 1947, served notice of increased anti-Communist activity within the union and explained his position to the union membership. "The issue between me and the present UE leadership goes solely to the proposition that our great International Union has become known as a transmission belt for the American Communist Party."[30]

By 1947, the anti-Communist leaders in the UE had formed an organization called the UE Members for Democratic Action. They began acting as an informal committee of correspondence, calling strategy meetings and looking for recruits preparatory to the forthcoming union convention. To meet this threat, the UE General Executive Board issued a statement implying that the existence and activities of the UEMDA were anti-labor and threatening sanctions if they did not disband and cease activities. In reply, the officers of UEMDA—Harry Block chairman, James V. Click secretary, and Bart Enright treasurer—issued a statement defending themselves which they, in turn, distributed as widely as they could.[31]

Carey was considered the titular head of the UEMDA because of his prior presidency and position of national CIO leadership, but he did not take an active day to day leadership role in the new organization. Block, its president, was former president of the UE District in Philadelphia; Click, secretary, was chief steward of Local 1102 in St. Louis where the anti-Communists were gaining ground. Another active leader was Earl T. McGrew of Chicago who had left UE to act as a business agent for the CIO Textile Workers but who continued as a part-time business agent for UE Local 1121.

One of the first successes of the UEMDA came in St. Louis when under the leadership of Local 1102, they succeeded in defeating William Sentner and thus took control of District 8. A letter to the membership by John J. Burns, Local 1102 president, explained their objectives:[32]

Your Local Union has taken a leading part in the battle to make the UE a truly American trade union and in opposing those National and District officers who would operate it in the interests of the American Communist Party. Officers of Local 1102 have taken a leading part in the establishment and operation of the UE Members for Democratic Action, a group within UE dedicated to freeing our Union from Communist bonds.

In May, 1947, UEMDA began publishing a newspaper to assemble the news of anti-administration activity within the UE. It was called *The Real UE*. Its first issue reported the fact that Seymour Linfield, associate general counsel of the UE, had represented the Communist Party prior to 1941 as a branch organizer on the waterfront. The article stated that during the war his application for Officers' Training School had been rejected because of his Communist Party record. They also pointed to the fact that another of the UE's counsel, Morton Friedman, had been dismissed from his post as chief of the classification division of the War Manpower Commission because of his pro-Communist tendencies. One of the first items of news published was the fact that Local 1237 in New York, a local of about 800 members employed by typewriter companies, had accused the *UE News* of being a "political journal expounding the foreign policies of the Soviet Union" and of pursuing a "pro-Soviet, anti-American policy . . . justifying every action of the Soviet Union rather than . . . promoting more bread and butter for the membership." The first issue also told the UE members about the anti-Communist activity in the National Maritime Union under Curran and printed one of Curran's articles on Communism as well.

The theme of *The Real UE* seemed to be expressed in its masthead quote from Philip Murray: "If Communism is an issue in any of your unions, throw it to hell out, and throw its advocates out along with it. When a man accepts office—paid office in a union—to render service to workers, and then delivers that service to other outside interests, that man is nothing but a damned traitor."

The Real UE had referred to the anti-administration activity of New York Local 1237. The following month that local publicly charged the UE General Executive Board with misusing union funds by contributing $1,000 to the Civil Rights Congress, "a well-known

Communist front organization which has assumed full responsibility for the defense of Gerhardt Eisler," one of the international leaders of the Comintern.[33]

In July, James J. Conroy, business agent of the local, testified before the House Un-American Activities Committee and repeated the same charges.[34]

The growth and intensity of the opposition did not stop the UE leaders from continuing with their activities, and with their plans for the 1947 12th annual convention. The special guest at the convention was Henry Wallace, whose speech the UE later reprinted in pamphlet form for distribution to its 600,000 members.[35] Another guest was Carl Marzani, former State Department employee who had been convicted for falsely denying his Communist affiliations.[36] The convention turned out to be an overwhelming victory for the pro-Communist administration. A proposal submitted by the UEMDA delegates calling for the indorsement of the 1946 national CIO convention resolution "rejecting and resenting" Communist interference in union affairs was decisively defeated. All other UEMDA resolutions against the union leadership, which were listed in the convention resolutions handbook supplied all delegates under the heading, "Red Baiting" were likewise defeated. Instead, a resolution which was listed in the convention handbook under the heading "Carey-Block Group and Disruptive Tactics," was passed. This resolution ordered the UEMDA to dissolve or face the threat of expulsion from the international. To this resolution, Carey replied: "I am in this fight, and I will remain, in the face of any action to purge the UEMDA. I think that ultimately we will win, and get the Communists out of this union."

The UE convention, of course, did not ignore foreign policy. It adopted a resolution stating that "Wall Street" controlled the Truman administration to "suppress and exploit the people of the world." Commenting on these sentiments, a delegate, William Drohan of Local 1102, spoke in opposition because the resolution made it appear that all the troubles of the world could be cured if only the Soviet army were "called over here to rescue us from the hole we were in."[37]

The administration candidates were re-elected by margins of 8 to 1. It was in commenting on this convention, incidentally, that

Robert Wishart, president of the Hennepin County CIO Council who "went along" with the administration, stated:[38] "The Communist issue was not involved." As for Fitzgerald, UE president, under whose supervision the union had been run since 1941, Wishart said: "By no stretch of the imagination can Albert Fitzgerald . . . be called a Communist or extreme leftist." He said Fitzgerald was a "staunch Catholic" who had replaced Carey in 1941, "largely through the efforts of General Electric Co. employees who are members of the union."[39]

But UE locals were slowly changing to an anti-Communist leadership. The great stimulus seemed to be the Taft-Hartley Act and its anti-Communist affidavit requirement. The UE leadership, for obvious as well as perhaps principled reasons, refused to sign the affidavits. This meant that the UE could not participate in representation or unfair labor practice proceedings before the National Labor Relations Board and thus exposed the union's flank to attacks from other unions and from aggressive companies.[40]

Immediately, local unions within the UE, up until now satisfied with the economic benefits and grievance settlements produced by the leadership, began to fear for their economic gains. Anti-Communists were now able to strengthen their political and ideological arguments, against the leadership, with frank economic appeals.

The RCA-Victor local in Camden, New Jersey, which had sent staunch administration supporters as delegates to the Boston convention in September, now in December, overwhelmingly voted to repudiate the UE-NLRB boycott policy. The local ordered its executive board to file non-Communist affidavits and further ordered an investigation of all the executive board members "both for their communistic tendencies and also for their financial records in the union." In the course of the union's membership meeting debate, shouts were heard of "Go back to Russia" and "Speak up, you commies."[41]

The national UE officers also had further difficulty with the 800-member Local 1237. James Conroy, the local's business agent, had first announced that the local's officers were willing to sign affidavits and then asked the national UE officers to do the same.[42] The NLRB soon ruled, however, that a local union could not qualify under the Taft-Hartley Act even if its union officers took the oath so long as the national officers did not. Since Remington Rand and other employers were taking full advantage of this interpretation and refusing to bargain, Local 1237 and other locals were caught in an impasse. Conroy, in evaluating the dilemma, concluded: "This is developing into a situation in which non-Communists may find themselves obliged to leave the UE as a means of protecting their wages and working conditions." He recognized the difficulty of such a step and its effect upon the success of the internal anti-Communist efforts by concluding: "Getting them out is exactly what the Communists want."[43] In reply, James McLeish, UE district president, accused the local officers of "secretly plotting ... to destroy Local 1237.[44] Finally, in February, 1948, Local 1237 withdrew from the UE.[45]

> The UE has followed every twist and turn of the Communist party since 1940 and its decision against compliance with the Taft-Hartley law has left us high and dry. We will not remain affiliated with a union whose Communist leadership attempts to deal with out employers without our knowledge and consent.

In the course of the next year, a survey undertaken by *Fortune*[46] estimated that more than 70,000 UE members had ousted their party-line leadership, and a number of local unions, like Local 1237, had left the international to join the CIO-UAW, or the AFL-IBEW, or to remain independent. In addition, the union had lost a number of strikes and contracts as a result of the Taft-Hartley handicap under which it was operating. Strikes at Dayton and Evansville, to prevent loss of union contracts under Taft-Hartley decertification proceedings, were among those which failed. Organizational strikes at the new Beaver, Pennsylvania, Westinghouse plant and the Mine Safety Appliance Co. at Pittsburgh had fizzled badly. It was estimated that about 25,000 UE members had seceded to the anti-Communist United Automobile Workers. Unemployment was rising in the industry with an estimated 80,000 UE members jobless by early 1949.

The UE leadership had also lost a great deal of prestige in the course of the 1948 Henry Wallace campaign for president. The union had thrown itself wholeheartedly into the campaign, with funds, personnel, and energies, and had thereby further alienated itself from the rest of CIO leadership. Wallace's repudiation by organized labor, was considered a repudiation of the UE leadership.

Nevertheless, the leadership seemed well entrenched constitutionally through a system of controls from the top down. At Schenectady, New York, for example, the anti-Communists captured seven out of ten officers' posts. But a month later, after the top machine had come to the local scene to exert its influence, the "party-liners" won 22 out of the 29 posts in the Executive Board elections and were then in a position to surround and stifle the new officers. The explanation for the difference in the two elections was that in the earlier one, the entire membership had voted, while in the second only the "general committee," a group of about 400, was eligible to vote.[47]

Top leadership power was great. Matles, as organization director, had a staff of about 150 field representatives personally responsible to him. Many of these were, in a sense, "patronage" positions. Personnel exchange between the Communist party, the Progressive party, and the UE was a common practice. Many union officials expelled from other unions for their pro-Communist activities found a haven in the UE, as did a number of ex-public officials now ineligible to hold public office. With this experienced and large personnel, Matles could and did move into local situations to support wavering pro-administration leadership.[48] The international leadership was also aided by an intensive public relations program both in and out of the union. UE sponsored a weekly national radio program; produced four 16 mm. sound films; made extensive use of educational materials; and distributed literature profusely. In 1948, UE printed more than three million copies of twenty pamphlets[49]

But the opposition trend spread to the three largest locals. We have already taken note of the opposition's half-victory in the GE unit at Schenectady. There were anti-Communist victories in the Westinghouse local at Pittsburgh and even in the Lynn, Massachusetts local, the home base of President Fitzgerald. In Pittsburgh, as in a number of other communities, the opposition UEMDA group was spearheaded by a branch of the Association of Catholic Trade Unionists. ACTU'S chaplain, Father Charles Rice, was a friend of both Philip Murray and James Carey and was thoroughly sophisticated in the operation of the labor and radical movements. To aid the anti-Communists, Father Rice had written a tactical manual on *How to Decontrol Your Union of Communists.* An illustration of its hard-headedness and usefulness is the following specific advice:[50]

> Place your people carefully in the meeting hall. Try to have a good-sized bunch down front... Place others on each side and place a nice contingent in the back. This is called the Diamond, the oldest meeting strategy in the world. It makes it look as if the entire meeting is filled with your people.

The full story of Communist activities within Pittsburgh's Local 601 was revealed in 1949 in testimony before the House Un-American Activities Committee.[51] Edward Copeland, business agent of the local, testified that he had been a member of the Communist party from 1943 to 1945 and that the local had been the scene of a great deal of Communist activity. He thus corroborated the charges brought in 1946 by Local 601's president when he resigned.[52] Copeland identified Frank Nestler, editor of the local union paper, Thomas J. Fitzpatrick, chief steward, Frank Panzino, assistant chief steward, and Robert Whisner, subdivision steward of the union, as having attended Communist meetings with him. Another witness, William Henry Peeler, a member of the union, gave evidence of Communist recruiting within the union. He described how Dorothy Faraday, secretary of UE district Council 6, had solicited him for membership in the Communist party. Similar efforts were made by Nathan Alberts, a member of the union staff, who proudly referred to Fitzpatrick and Panzino as fellow Communists. Blair Seese, another member of the union, reported that Fitzpatrick had privately admitted party membership to him. Seese had also been asked to join the Communist party by an officer of the union, Marshall Docherty. Stanley Glass, recording secretary of Local 601, testified the Fitzpatrick had personally solicited him to join and had also described to him the glories of the Soviet Union.

There was also evidence that Local 601 officers had used the union office for the circulation of petitions in behalf of the twelve Communist leaders on trial in New York and also for the solicitation of subscriptions to the *Daily Worker*. Union mailing lists were also reportedly used to circulate Communist literature.

When Fitzpatrick, Panzino, and Whisner were given an opportunity to reply to the charges levelled against them before the Committee, they used the Fifth Amendment against self-incrimination to refuse to answer questions about their Communist party membership. Whisner, however, did admit to a trip to the Soviet Union in 1934, followed by speaking engagements for the Friends of the Soviet Union and a letter to the January, 1935, issue of the magazine, *Soviet Russia Today*, captioned "USSR Points Way for American Workers."

The UE national leadership faced further difficulty in holding on to its membership from government officials responsible for defense operations. The Atomic Energy Commission, for example, instructed General Electric not to recognize the UE at the new Knolls Atomic Power Laboratory in Schenectady, New York. Oscar Smith, Deputy Director of Organization and Personnel for the AEC, defended this policy by stating that the AEC could not afford to have work interrupted at atomic energy installations by union officials who worked for a foreign power rather than for the best interests of union members.[53]

For a short time in 1948, it also looked as if Fitzgerald, UE president, would break away from the Matles-Emspak group. It was known that Philip Murray had discussed the problem with him and was hoping for such a split finally to cleanse the UE and forestall any more drastic action by the national CIO. Fitzgerald went so far as to attack Vishinsky and Molotov as "saber-rattlers and war-mongers."[54] But that was the last rustle. Fitzgerald finally cast his lot for good with the Emspak-Matles faction, come what may.

The anti-Communists within the UE prepared for a final effort at the 1949 UE convention. A large meeting was held in Dayton, Ohio in May 1949 to prepare for the convention. As a result of local resolutions and instructions, the Carey forces felt they had an even chance to win in spite of the fact that the administration controlled the convention machinery. The seriousness of their effort was evident from the fact that Carey brought with him technical aides from the national CIO office, and borrowed from Emil Rieve for the convention Textile's general counsel, Isadore Katz.

This time the UE convention was fairly evenly divided and tension was high. Prior to the convention, Carey and his associates stated privately that the ability of the UE administration to control the credentials and voting procedures would require the anti-Communists to capture 60 percent of the convention strength to insure victory. This was certainly not obtained and the UE convention showed the pro-Communist administration forces winning all the top elections by a vote of about 2,393 to 1,477. Many observers saw evidence from these results that the anti-Communists indeed represented a majority of the membership.

An analysis of the convention voting showed that convention delegates of eight locals casting 419 votes had been instructed by their membership to vote right-wing, but had disregarded these instructions. Further, the convention credentials committee disqualified one instructed delegation casting 38 votes and seated a left-wing delegation in its place. This, claimed the Carey forces, would have elected their candidate for UE president, Kelley, with a vote of 1,957, to 1,878 for Fitzgerald, and would have by a similar margin defeated Emspak and Matles as well.

On November 2, at the national CIO convention, the UE leaders were charged with "disloyalty to the CIO," and "dedication to the purposes and program of the Communist Party, contrary to the overwhelming sentiment of the rank-and-file membership who are loyal Americans and loyal CIO members." The union was then expelled as "the Communist Party masquerading as a labor union." The convention also directed the CIO executive Board to charter a new union.[55]

The following day, Philip Murray formally presented the charter for a new International Union of Electrical, Radio and Machine Workers to Carey. The union was seated at the convention. On November 28, the union held its organizational convention in Philadelphia and announced a membership of more than 200,000. The following year, in December, 1950, the IUE held its Second Annual Convention in Milwaukee, and with it became the dominant industrial union in the electrical industry. It reported itself to be the collective bargaining agent of more than 300,000 workers and an actual membership of 250,000.[56]

The expulsion of the UE from the CIO proved to be a quite

decisive blow to the Communist party's efforts to influence American labor. The UE, in a great many states, had been the medium through which the Communist voice was heard in State and local industrial union councils. In addition, the union's large membership steadily decreased as it lost the cloak of legitimate union respectability which the CIO had provided. CIO and AFL unions organized constant "raiding" drives against the UE, the great bulk of which were successful. By 1955, the merger of the CIO with the AFL, the UE was by far the smallest of the unions in the electrical field and was reported to have less than 80,000 members compared to more than 300,000 for the IUE, and about 500,000 for the AFL International Brotherhood of Electrical Workers.

[1] Taft, *Economics and Problems of Labor, op. cit.,* p. 478.
[2] *The Shield,* July, 1947.
[3] *Daily Worker,* July 12, 1947.
[4] C. Wright Mills, "The Trade Union Leader: A Collective Portrait," *Public Opinion Quarterly,* Summer, 1945, pp. 158-175.
[5] House Report 1311, 78th Congress, 2nd Session, *op. cit.,* p. 105.
[6] *Ibid.,* pp. 105, 106.
[7] *Daily Worker,* September 4 and 5, 1940.
[8] *Sunday Worker,* April 13, 1941, Section 2, p. 1.
[9] House Report 1311, 78th Congress, 2nd Session, *op. cit.,* p. 103.
[10] *Ibid.,* p. 106.
[11] *The New York Times,* September 2, 1941, p. 1.
[12] House Report 1311, 78th Congress, 2nd Session, *op. cit.* p. 103.
[13] *The New York Times,* September 6, 1941, p. 16.
[14] *The New York Times,* September 5, 1941, pp. 1, 23.
[15] UERMWA Eighth Constitutional Convention, *op. cit.,* p. 208.
[16] *Daily Worker,* September 14, 1943, p. 1.
[17] *Washington Post,* February 25, 1943, p. 16.
[18] Joseph Rosenfarb, "Labor's Role in the Election," *The Public Opinion Quarterly,* Fall, 1944, p. 387.
[19] Letter dated September 21, 1945, quoted in Barbash, *op. cit.* pp. 216, 217.
[20] House Report 1311, 78th Congress, 2nd Session, *op. cit.,* p. 107.
[21] *Ibid.,* pp. 104, 105.
[22] UERMWA Eighth Constitutional Convention, *op. cit.,* p. 215.
[23] *Daily Worker,* April 8, 1945.
[24] *Ibid.,* July 3, 1945.
[25] *The New Leader,* November 16, 1946, p. 5.
[26] House Report 1311, 78th Congress, 2nd Session, *op. cit.,* pp. 88-90, 104.
[27] *Ibid.,* p. 183.
[28] *Sunday Worker,* September 29, 1946.
[29] *The New York Times,* November 17, 1946.
[30] *The New Leader,* March 1, 1947.
[31] *Local Review,* published by UE Local 1102, St. Louis, May, 1947.

32 *Local Review,* June, 1947.
33 *New York World Telegram,* May 29, 1947.
34 *The New York Times,* December 15, 1947.
35 *The New York Times,* September 27, 1947.
36 *The Socialist Call,* October 10, 1947.
37 *The New York Times,* September 27, 1947.
38 *Supra,* p. 116 above.
39 *Minneapolis Tribune,* September 26, 1947.
40 For a further study of the Taft-Hartley non-Communist Affidavit and its effect on Communists within the trade union movement, see Appendix.
41 *The New York Times,* December 11, 1947.
42 *Ibid.*
43 *Ibid.*
44 *The New York Times,* December 15, 1947.
45 *The New York Times,* February 9, 1948.
46 *Fortune,* March, 1949, pp. 175-177.
47 *Ibid.*
48 Committee on Un-American Activities, *Hearings Regarding Cincinnati, op. cit.,* pp. 2730-2758.
49 *Fortune,* March, 1949, p. 175.
50 *Ibid.,* p. 176.
51 Committee on Un-American Activities, House of Representatives, 81st Congress, 1st Session, *Annual Report for the Year 1949,* March 15, 1950, pp. 8-10.
52 *Supra,* p. 129.
53 Committee on Un-American Activities, *1949 Annual Report, op. cit.,* p. 9.
54 A. H. Raskin, "Drive on Communists Gains Momentum in CIO," *The New York Times,* December 12, 1948.
55 *Report of the Administrative Committee to the Second Annual Convention of The International Union of Electrical, Radio and Machine Workers,* December 4-9, 1950, pp. 7-10.
56 The UE at its September, 1950, convention adopted a 5-point foreign policy resolution criticizing "big business" control of American policy, calling for U.S.-Soviet meetings, opposing "totalitarian and corrupt regimes everywhere," and supporting the United Nations. In his opening address, President Albert J. Fitzgerald supported U.S. fighting in Korea, but the union resolution did not mention Korea. The Truman administration was criticized for using the Korean crisis to "cut welfare programs to the bone."

9 | THE PROGRESSIVE PARTY AND HENRY WALLACE

Following the 1947 national CIO convention, the big issue dividing the pro- and anti-Communists was the campaign of Henry Wallace and the formation of the Progressive party. This was closely related to the question of Marshall Plan support. Walter Reuther was one of the first national leaders to crystallize the issue. Speaking at a National Press Club luncheon in Washington in December, 1947, in reply to a question from a reporter with regard to Wallace's candidacy, he said: "... the answer to him is no. We will not go along with the new fellow." He further elaborated:[1]

> I think Henry is a lost soul. He is a great disappointment to many decent people in America. People who are not sympathetic with democracy in America are influencing him. Communists perform the most complete valet service in the world. They write your speeches, they do your thinking for you, they provide you with applause and they inflate your ego as often as necessary.
> I'm afraid that's the trouble with Henry Wallace.

At the January, 1948 meeting of the CIO Executive Board, Philip Murray and Harry Bridges got into a serious argument with regard to the Marshall Plan. Murray asserted that our government's eleven billion dollar defense budget was the result of the "propaganda of Soviet leaders like Andrei Y. Vishinsky." To this Bridges angrily retorted that the defense budget was primarily due to the desire of big business for big profits. This in turn led Murray to charge the existence of Soviet atrocities in Europe with specific reference to Hungary. He said that Bridges seemed to have an answer to all questions except those relating to Russia. He finally turned to Bridges and said were he in Russia criticizing

Stalin as he was now criticizing Truman, he would be liquidated. "I am not so sure that's so," retorted Bridges.[2]

It is interesting that Michael Quill, head of the Transport Workers Union, later reported that the Communists had attempted to prepare for this Executive Board meeting by caucusing prior to the meeting. Specifically, he said, ". . . the Communist Party, again under the leadership of John Williamson, called a meeting the night before the CIO Board meeting in January, 1948 in a room at the Hay-Adams Hotel."[3] Present at the meeting besides Quill were Bridges, Flaxer of the Public Workers, Matles of the UE, Gold and Potash of the Fur Workers, Henderson of the Food and Tobacco Workers, Selly of the American Communications Association, and Santo of the Transport Workers. At the meeting, "there again Williamson tightened the line that we have got to come out of the CIO Board meeting and fight for a resolution supporting Henry Wallace and do everything possible to carry out that program of the Communist Party behind Wallace."

That resolution, of course, never came. Instead, very shortly thereafter, Murray, who eighteen months before had taken Southern California out of Bridges' jurisdiction as CIO regional director, now discharged him from that office.[4]

The Communist character of the Wallace movement became more and more evident to the trade union leaders until it became clear that this was the issue by which to distinguish the anti-Communists from the pro-Communists and their fellow travellers. This polarization was further crystallized by the Communist party, which insisted on energetic Wallace support from all of its trade union associates. In fact, Eugene Dennis, general secretary of the CP, early in 1948 criticized many of the trade union leaders who were not as militant as they might have been and not too eager to embrace Wallace and thus clearly identify their affiliation. "During the first two years of the post-war period when we pursued—and correctly so—the tactic of left-center coalition of the CIO, we failed to consistently develop an independent position," Dennis said. He went on:[5]

> We were much too slow and tolerant in combatting erroneous views of a part of the national leadership of certain district organizations and many of our trade union cadres who up to the time

of the announcement of the Wallace candidacy expressed doubts
as to the advisability of an independent Presidential ticket, and
confused the maneuverings and treacherous position of most of
labor's top officials as being the position of the rank and file of labor.

It became apparent, therefore, that the decision to urge Wallace's
independent candidacy was more a decision of the Communist
party professionals than the trade union leaders who feared the
risk involved.

Obviously certain of his corroborative facts, but unwilling
publicly to state his source, Philip Murray, speaking at the fifth
biennial Textile Workers Union convention, stated that the Progressive party "was inaugurated at a Communist Party meeting
in the City of New York in October of 1947." He went on:[6]

> There can be no question about that. The Third Party was created
> by people who are not in the labor movement. It was thrust upon
> the American people by organizations that have no interest in the
> labor movement, and its creation was deliberate in the sense that
> its propagators and its creators sought to impose the Third Party
> idea on the American people for the deliberate purpose of creating
> confusion and division in the country.

Murray did not state his source of information about the
October, 1947 meeting, but within the CIO it was clear that the
information had come from Michael J. Quill, international president of the Transport Workers Union and member of the New
York City Council. Quill, who had succeeded Curran as president
of the Greater New York CIO Council, had just resigned from his
council post asserting that the New York CIO Council's political
decision in favor of Wallace was splitting the CIO and he would
side with the national CIO.[7] He made it clear at first that his
differences were primarily "trade union" and not "political." Quill
described his "trade union" policy as "wages before Wallace." His
conversion was halting, for he said that he was still opposed to the
Marshall Plan and remained sympathetic to Wallace. "I'm still for
Wallace if being for him will not split the CIO unions. If being
for Wallace will split the CIO, the price is too great. I am a trade
unionist first." Even this meant an open break, however, and in a
few days—by March 26—Quill was criticizing "the crackpots of the
Communist Party."[8]

Quill, who had been close to the Communist party, if not actually a member, ever since he had been in the labor movement, knew whereof he spoke when he discussed Communist meeting decisions, because he had participated in those meetings. He told Murray of a meeting he attended on Saturday, October 18, 1947, the day following the close of the CIO convention in Boston. It was held at the headquarters of the International Workers Order on Fifth Avenue in New York. Present were Eugene Dennis, general secretary of the Communist Party, John Williamson, CP labor secretary, Robert Thompson, New York State chairman of the Communist Party, James Matles and Julius Emspak of the UE, James Durkin of the United Office and Professional Workers, Joseph P. Selly, the American Communications Association, Hal Simon, "another representative of the Communist Party. ... He was from the UE," Arthur Osman, Local 65 of the United Retail, Wholesale and Department Store Employees of America, Herbert March, head of District 1 of the United Packinghouse Workers,[9] "that fellow who screwed up the strike in the packinghouse," Harry Bridges, ILWU, and Ben Gold and Irving Potash, International Fur and Leather Workers Union.[10] Quill reported: "Eugene Dennis told us in very blunt language to disregard everything that happened at the CIO convention in Boston, and he especially said to disregard the Political Action resolution." The reason for this admonition was very clear. Dennis continued, said Quill: "the national leaders ... of the Communist Party have decided to form a Third Party led by Henry Wallace and that Wallace would come out in the next few weeks and announce that he was a candidate for President of the United States on the Third Party ticket." The union leaders were then told that the "Communist Party was asking all the left-wing controlled unions to start to petition and campaign now, to start the publicity, to line up endorsements for Wallace as soon as he announced himself on the radio."

Quill reportedly questioned the widom of the decision, but made no issue of it. "I thought that running Wallace was a pressure campaign in order to get a better ticket at the Democratic convention, and that it was a straw in the wind that would be hauled back as soon as the Democrats would show some sign of loosening up on the ticket." By December, 1947 when it became clear that Wallace's candidacy would split the labor movement and the New Deal vote to the advantage of the Republicans and Dewey—"and I had some real fears about Dewey becoming President of the United States"—Quill tried to reason with Dennis without success. "So I discussed it with Gerhart Eisler, and Eisler told me it was in the best interests of the Soviet bloc that the Third Party should be headed ... by Wallace and made it very clear to me that that was the only reason why the Third Party ticket was gotten up."[11]

This question was next discussed by Quill at the Communist caucus of CIO leaders at the Hay-Adams Hotel the night before the January 22 meeting of the CIO Executive Board. Again, however, he failed to make an impression.[12] Immediately following the meeting, therefore, he went to see William Z. Foster, national chairman of the Communist Party.

> I expressed to him fear that this move will split the unions, and weaken our position locally and nationally against the employers. He said the Communist Party ... decided that all the unions that it can influence within CIO are to go down the line behind Wallace, if it splits the last union down the middle, but he said, 'We have also decided to form a Third Federation of Labor in the United States carved out of the AF of L and the CIO in order to implement the Henry Wallace movement.'[13]

Quill's last attempt, before breaking with the party, was to speak with Wallace himself.[14]

> I made a trip through the country and found our own locals splitting at the seams because of the Wallace situation. Then I came back and spoke to Henry Wallace, on Sunday, I believe it would be February 24th. I can check that, because it was at a mass meeting I spoke to him. I asked him why he didn't discuss this matter with Phil Murray since Phil was speaking for 6,000,000 members. Wallace told me that he hadn't time, that Phil was busy and he was busy and there was no time to discuss it with Murray.

The very next month, Quill took to the public platform to announce he was through with Communists. At a meeting in Manhattan Center in New York before two thousand of his members, at the climax of his speech, he seized a copy of the *Daily*

Worker and raising his hands high over his head, he tore it into shreds. "That's what I think of them!"[15]

The conversation between Quill and Wallace, and Quill's reaction to it, symbolized the sharp differences that developed between Wallace and the CIO leadership headed by Murray. During the 1948 presidential campaign, the CIO spent as much energy attacking Wallace and his candidacy as they did attacking Dewey and the Republican Party. It became clear that Murray considered the support of Henry Wallace irreconcilable with loyalty to the CIO.

One of the earliest evidences of this was the announcement by Philip Murray on February 6, 1948, that Lee Pressman had resigned as CIO general counsel. This spelled the end of a very long and effective period of Communist activity within the brain trust of the national CIO, a period which had started at the very beginning of the CIO's history. All Communist influence within the CIO legal department disappeared when Murray appointed, as Pressman's successor, Arthur Goldberg, prominent and brilliant labor lawyer from Chicago. Goldberg's influence grew steadily in the CIO until he became one of the organization's most effective leaders and spokesmen. His presence was a source of great strength to Murray in the continued drive against the Communists.

Pressman actively joined the Wallace movement soon after he left the CIO, and ran for Congress in New York on the Progressive party ticket. He continued his association with the Progressive party and with the Communists until August, 1950, when he resigned from the American Labor Party, and in the same month appeared before the House Un-American Activities Committee and admitted to membership in the Communist Party. Today he is practicing law and has but minimum contact with the labor movement.

Pressman's letter of August 11, 1950 resigning from the American Labor Party read as follows:

> In the approaching political campaign which will bring the various parties and their candidates before the public, it is my judgment that the American Labor Party cannot enlist the support or the confidence of any important segment of the voters.
> It is crucial for any progressive political parties to have the

full and energetic support of organized labor. This, the American
Labor Party does not enjoy. The basic reason is the outstanding
conviction that the policies, activity and political direction of the
American Labor Party do not represent or reflect the democratic
or progressive interests or aspirations of the American people
but rather the Communist Party.

I feel that the service which every peace-loving American
wishes to perform in relation to the important tasks confronting
humanity today cannot be accomplished within the American
Labor Party. I am, therefore, submitting my resignation as a member
of the American Labor Party.

[1] *The New York Times,* December 19, 1949.
[2] *The New York Times,* January 24, 1948.
[3] CIO, *Hearings to Investigate ILWU, op. cit.,* p. 74.
[4] *The New York Times,* March 6, 1948.
[5] *The New York Times,* February 13, 1948.
[6] *The New York Times,* April 29, 1948.
[7] *The New York Times,* March 27, 1948.
[8] Textile Workers Union, "General Office Bulletin," April 1948.
[9] The United Packinghouse Workers of America is the largest union in the
meat-packing industry. District 1 includes most of Illinois, Wisconsin, and
Indiana, taking in Chicago, the packinghouse center of the United
States. Herbert March was an organizer for the Young Communist League
and a member of the Communist National Committee. (See Avery,
"Communist Power in U. S. Industry," *op. cit*). March was also head of
the Chicago Industrial Union Council. The UPWA was always heavily
influenced by Communists and was, in fact, in 1944, accused by the
House Un-American Activities Committee of being "dominated by Com-
munist leadership." (House Report 1311, 78th Congress, 2nd Session,
op. cit., p. 123).
There was a strong anti-Communist bloc from the beginning which
shared in the control of the union, although mostly as a minority.
At its national convention in 1947, the union adopted a resolution which
March declared to be "excellent" denouncing "Red-baiting." (*Daily Worker,*
May 8, 1947) It called for the formation of a third party "at the proper
time" since the Republican and Democratic parties offered the voters
nothing more than a "tweedledee and tweedledum" choice. The union
urged that the third party should be formed by groups in the community
"interested in the objective of the peoples' welfare" who would "join
together for the purpose of establishing an independent political party so
as to give voters an opportunity to vote for representatives that will act
in their interests." (*The New York Times,* May 7, 1947.)
[10] CIO, *Hearings to Investigate ILWU, op. cit.,* pp. 66, 67, 99.
[11] *Ibid.*
[12] Victor Riesel, "Inside Labor," *New York Post,* May 7, 1948.
[13] CIO, *Hearings to Investigate ILWU, op. cit.,* pp. 71, 72.
[14] *Ibid.,* pp. 74, 75.
[15] Jules Weinberg, "Priests, Workers and Communists," *Harper's* November,
1948, p. 49.

10 MIKE QUILL AND THE TRANSPORT WORKERS UNION

Quill's defection proved to be a crucial defeat for the Communists and equally an important victory for the anti-Communists. Control of New York's sprawling transportation system was a vital prize. The Communists had spent much money and energy in capturing it. On May 1, 1934, Communist John Santo, later to be secretary of the union, wrote in the *Daily Worker*:[1]

> If the transit workers of New York should strike for six hours, the life of the whole city would be upside down. . . . The taxi strike might have turned into a gigantic battle the like of which New York has never seen and which would knock a number of bricks off the capitalist structure.

There was much truth in Mr. Santo's boast.

In July, 1933, the Communist Party held an Extraordinary Conference in New York at which a policy of "concentration" was decided on. Charles Krumbein, New York State Secretary of the Party, defined the policy when he stated: "Transport in all big cities plays a very important political role. I think it is a field we must concentrate on."[2] The Communist Party began to organize "concentration units" carefully selected to help build the union and control it.

One of the key figures in the Transport Workers Union and in the Communist control of that union was John Santo, who became TWU general secretary-treasurer although he had never been a transport worker himself. Santo came to New York in 1933 from Cleveland, where he had edited *Vi Elore,* the official national newspaper of the Hungarian branch of the Communist party. He opened the TWU headquarters early in 1934 and began to edit its bulletin. He came to have an extremely powerful influence in the New York CIO and his wife, Mary Santo, became chairman of the New York State CIO Auxiliary Council.

In 1934, Santo, Quill, and a handful of transport workers began meeting quietly. There is reason to believe that they early affiliated with the Trade Union Unity League. The Transport Workers Union came into being and Quill was elected its president in December, 1935.

Quill's career was an active and fiery one. Born in Ireland in 1905, he had grown up during the repressions and saw members of his family carried off to British jails by the Black and Tans. When he reached the age of fifteen it is reported that he carried a rifle in a brigade of the Irish Republican Army. In 1926, he came to the United States. In 1930, he was employed as a station agent and a gateman on the Interborough Rapid Transit system, working twelve hours a day for seven days a week. By 1937, the union which he helped organize and of which he was head, was all-powerful in New York and received a charter from the national CIO.

Quill never admitted to membership in the Communist party, although there was much testimony that he was a member. Whether he held a card or not, however, it is irrefutable that many Communists considered him a member; that the Communists always supported him; and that he fell within the definition of "Communist" established some years ago by the U.S. Civil Service Commission when they said "a Communist is a person who has followed the party line through one or more changes."[3]

The House Un-American Activities Committee heard testimony to the effect that Quill had become TWU president after the Communists had instructed his opponent to withdraw so as to make the election unanimous. Former members of the Communist party testified that they had sat in Communist meetings with him, unit 19-S, and had collected his party dues from him. There was also evidence that he had solicited others to join the party.[4] On September 23, 1937, speaking to the Rubber Workers Convention, Quill said, "I would rather be called a Red by the rats than a rat by the Reds."[5]

There was no doubt but that Quill had contributed to Communist publications; that he had supported Communist-front organizations; and that his foreign policy position had followed the Communists through collective security and the American League for Peace and Democracy, on to the isolationist American Peace Mobilization, and then on to the transformation of the imperialist struggle into a "people's war for freedom."[6]

In fact, in a very interesting colloquy at recent private CIO hearings in Washington on Communism, M. Hedley Stone of the NMU, a former member of the Communist party, in a reply to a series of questions from Harry Bridges, admitted that in his judgment Quill had, before his break, also been a member of the party. In trying to prove Bridges a Communist, Stone had referred to a number of CP meetings at which Quill had also been present, dating from 1937 or 1938. Finally, while hedging "I don't know whether Quill has been proven here a member of the party or not," Stone exclaimed:[7]

> At any time anyone attends a meeting under the directions the same as I attended it, and they were there, I believe them to be a full-fledged Party member that got there by a direct invitation by a top functionary.

Again, after a question as to what further proof he had:

> A. I couldn't prove a duck was a duck, except it looks like a duck and the whole world says 'That is a duck,' and it quacks like a duck, and that is what I was taught, that it was a duck, and I was raised that way, so until my dying day, until they change a duck to another name, I am going to answer when people point at it that that is a duck.
> Q. (Bridges) And you are referring to Quill as well as me?
> A. (Stone) I am referring to you and anyone else you want to name that I have mentioned.
> Q. Including Quill?
> A. It includes Quill.

The Transport Workers Union was indeed a strange place for the Communists to gain a position of control since more than eighty percent of the union's members were Catholics and most of them Irish or of Irish descent. However, as Irish Catholics, many were more concerned with the politics of Irish repression than with the issue of Communism. "A man's stand on communism was less important than his opinion on the partition of Eire."[8] The IRT Subway in New York was once called the "Irish Republican Training School" and there was no doubt that transport workers considered Quill's claim to service in the Irish Republic Army of more significance than his left-wing "party-line" activities. Mike Quill, therefore, and Austin Hogan, pro-Communist head of TWU's largest Local, 100, were very crucial to Communist control of the union.

Quill testified to the fact that the Communists had controlled many of the inner operations of his union. Their interference went beyond the political realm; it extended to trade union policies as well. During the first year of the war, the Communists opposed Quill's new organizing efforts among airline mechanics. When he proceeded to organize airlines over Communist objections, he faced a great deal of difficulty, even within his union.

When asked, sometime later, by one of the CIO Executive Board members whether he, as TWU president, had ever obeyed Communist orders not to go into a local situation, he recalled that he had called off a powerhouse strike in New York when the New York City government was planning to sell a public power project to the Consolidated Edison Company. "The national unity was still on," he explained.[9] In reply to a question whether "the Party has been able to stop organizational activities or the granting of charters," Quill said:[10]

> The Party had that power; wherever they control an organization, they can either make or break it. They will remove charters, ask you to withdraw, they will make deals, they will do anything to keep their grip.

The general counsel of the Transport Workers Union during this period was Harry Sacher. He had been closely associated with the Communist sponsored Workers School, with the International Labor Defense, and with the *New Masses*, among many other Communist activities. Testimony was presented to the House Un-American Activities Committee that he was a member of the Communist party and a "trusted insider."[11]

Opposition to Quill and to the Communists remained quite weak, unorganized, and sporadic during most of 1937-1947. It began to develop somewhat in 1945 and 1946 and centered primarily at first in the members working for the New York Omnibus Company, controlling much of New York's bus transportation. It was inevitable in this situation that the Catholic Church should have some part in the drive.

We have already noted the existence of the Association of Catholic Trade Unionists as well as the activities of Father Rice in Pittsburgh. The ACTU was founded in 1937 as an offshoot of The Catholic Worker movement led by Dorothy Day. Papal Encyclicals promulgated by Leo XIII, Pius XI, Pius XII, had outlined a program which became for many Catholics a Catholic labor philosophy. It recognized the right of working men to organize trade unions for purposes of collective bargaining, and it called for a more equitable distribution of property among those who labored for a livelihood.

Responding to this philosophy, many priests had taken up the cause of organized labor and many others had written expertly on it.[12] This proved to be very important to the CIO, because the cities in which it is strongest contain a high percentage of Catholics. These include the Irish in most of the cities in the north and in the prairie states; Italians in New York and New England; Poles in Chicago, Detroit, Cleveland, Pittsburgh, New York and Connecticut; and Mexicans in the southwest.

In the early days of the CIO organizing drive, Catholic clergy were of significant assistance, particularly to Philip Murray and the Steel Workers Organizing Committee. In August, 1936, Bishop Boyle told the Catholic steel workers of Pittsburgh: "I have known (Murray) for the past thirty years and he's a good sound Catholic and labor leader." He encouraged the priests in his diocese to help the unions and a Catholic Radical Alliance was formed to do picket duty, speak, and help organize.

In Buffalo, on the Sunday prior to a significant SWOC organizing election, Bishop Duffy instructed the priests in his diocese to read from the social encyclicals. He wrote a letter for the CIO to use in its pamphlets, excerpts of which read:

> Not only the Bishops and priests of the Catholic Church, but the Popes, in a long series of encyclicals, emphasized that the working-man has the right and duty to unionize... The Catholic Church of the diocese of Buffalo has maintained this principle and will support it as the right of free men in the face of any difficulty.

In Cleveland, Msgr. Joseph Smith gave $25 weekly to a SWOC strike fund; and in South Chicago, Bishop Sheil appeared at CIO packinghouse workers mass meetings. In New Orleans,

Father James Drolet had a hand in organizing most of the CIO locals in that city.[13] The names of Cardinals Mooney, Stritch, and Mundelein; Bishops Sheil, Boyle, Duffy, and Haas; Monsignors John A. Ryan, Joseph Smith, and Ligutti; Fathers Boland, Rice, Monahan, Drolet, Masse, Corridan, Clancy, Higgins, Shortell, Carey, Smith, and Hammond—all bring to the minds of many labor leaders the concept of a "labor priest."[14]

As a general rule, these priests considered their role to be an educational one, of translating Church teachings into action. Labor schools have been, therefore, established all over the country in every large industrial city. One hundred such permanent schools have been established: twenty-four directed by the Jesuits; thirty-two by diocesan authorities; and the rest sponsored by Catholic fraternal organizations, colleges, and the Association of Catholic Trade Unionists. It is estimated that 7,500 men and women are "graduated" each year.

One such school was the Xavier Labor School, at the Church of St. Francis Xavier in New York, directed by the Reverend Philip A. Carey, a Jesuit. Its course of study, like that of most of the schools, was intensely practical. It included: labor law, trade union methods (organizing, contract negotiation, handling grievances), parliamentary procedure, economics, public speaking, labor history, and labor ethics. Many of the instructors were experienced trade union officials. A number of its graduates assumed important trade union roles, like Joe Fisher, president of the CIO Utility Workers Union. Among its students, too, were some who became anti-Communist leaders in the UE.[15]

Two of the Xavier Labor School's graduates were Raymond Westcott and John Brooks, officials of Section 505 of Local 100 of the TWU, who were very instrumental in taking control of the New York Omnibus Company local away from the Communists. As clerical workers for the company, they saw the need to organize themselves and their fellow clerical workers into a union, but hesitated to join the red-tinged TWU. When they went to their parish priest for help, they were referred to the Xavier School. When they finally led their group into the TWU, they did so in the knowledge that they and a stream of their co-workers had attended the Xavier School. Every officer of their unit was a graduate.

Practical experience added to their training. One such experience provides additional insight into Communist methods. A few months after they joined TWU in 1946, a call came from "CIO Headquarters" for two representatives from each local and section to march on Washington to protest the repeal of OPA. Since the union members considered the cause to be valid, Westcott and Brooks arrived in Washington. But they were met at the train not by representatives of the CIO, but by a committee wearing American Labor Party tags. Mimeographed sheets were given to each delegate asking that he register for a function of the ALP. "Every man on the committee," said Brooks, "sounded like a ranking member of the politburo, and where the hell was the official representation of the CIO?" They had been tricked into a "party-line" activity.

By 1947 the anti-administration forces of the TWU were in a much more cohesive position than they had ever been before. They had representation on the union's executive board and they had defeated the union leadership in a membership referendum concerning the five-cent fare for New York. While the union leadership defended the five-cent fare, the membership decided a higher fare would permit wage increases.[16]

The anti-Communists were also assisted by the fact that the Immigration Service of the United States Department of Justice in September, 1947, charged John Santo, who had been the union's secretary, with being an undesirable alien, with illegal entry, false citizenship, and with being a Communist.[17] M. Hedley Stone later testified that Santo was the "Party leader" at a Communist fraction meeting which Stone attended in 1942 to discuss strengthening Bridges' longshoremen's union on the East Coast.[18]

It was Quill's "conversion," however, which took the Transport Workers Union out of the Communist orbit. There was evidence in 1947 that he was tiring of the Communists. But he admitted in personal conversations that his decision to split from them was slowed by fear for his family's welfare should the Communists retaliate with violence as they were capable of doing. With growing pressure from anti-Communists within his union, however, and the Communist attempt to split the CIO by supporting Wallace, Quill first broke with the American Labor Party, then resigned from the Greater New York Council, and finally publically repudiated the Communists.[19] Within a year, he was successful in driving them from positions of influence in the union. The TWU convention in December, 1948 ousted all left-wingers from the union's international executive board.[20] With this decision, Quill declared:[21] "We are now back alongside of Philip Murray and alongside CIO." Quill defeated Hogan for president by a three to one roll-call vote. Gustav Faber was elected secretary-treasurer. Santo's post as organization director was abolished. Immediately following the convention, Harry Sacher was dismissed as general counsel and replaced by John F. O'Donnell.

In October, 1950, Douglas MacMahon, former secretary-treasurer of TWU, wrote Quill admitting his previous Communist party membership. MacMahon, one of the first six members of the union, became secretary-treasurer in 1942. He was ousted as union officer at the 1948 convention, along with Austin Hogan, John Santo, and others. His letter was released by the union and quoted in the *CIO News* for October 30, 1950. Excerpts follow:

I am writing to tell you that I was wrong and you were right. I quit the Communist Party well over a year ago, having come to realize their policy was one of disrupting the labor movement.

If they could not rule then they would ruin. It is indeed fortunate that the CIO has the able leadership of men like Phil Murray or the damage might have been a great deal more than it was.

The plan was to discredit any and all gains made and to try and make the workers feel that they were sold out. If the union was wrecked and the men took it on the chin, that would be just too bad. Disrupt was the slogan. Wreck was the goal.

Several months after the Chicago convention it was clear to me that such a program offended every trade union principle. I therefore quit the Communist Party. Since then as I watched from the side-lines, the continued gains of the union have done my heart good.

When you take a good look at the Communist policy as I have finally done, you can see that in every instance it dovetails with that of the worst reactionaries in the country.

As one who started with you to build TWU in the face of the full opposition of the reactionary transit companies, I can therefore appreciate the full impact of the gains achieved. I know TWU will keep up the good work and continue the militant fight.

[1] *New York World Telegram,* January 21, 1946.

[2] Frederick Woltman, *New York World Telegram,* July 11, 1941.

[3] House Report 1311, 78th Congress, 2nd Session, *op. cit.,* p. 151.

[4] *Ibid.,* pp. 151, 152.

[5] *New York World Telgram,* June 16, 1941.

[6] House Report 1311, 78th Congress, 2nd Session, *op. cit.* pp. 151-157.

[7] CIO, *Hearings to Investigate ILWU, op. cit.,* pp. 628, 629, 640, 641, 644, 645.

[8] Weinberg, *op. cit.,* pp. 50, 51.

[9] CIO, *Hearings to Investigate ILWU, op. cit.,* pp. 160, 161.

[10] *Ibid.,* pp. 163, 164.

[11] House Report 1311, 78th Congress, 2nd Session, *op. cit.* pp. 168, 169.

[12] See Reverend Jerome L. Toner, *The Closed Shop* (American Council on Public Affairs: Washington, D. C., 1942), Foreword by Right Reverend John A. Ryan.

[13] *Catholic Worker,* January, 1937—August, 1937; and Philip Taft, "The Association of Catholic Trade Unionists," *Industrial and Labor Relations Review,* January, 1949, pp. 210-218.

[14] A prayer used by the ACTU to open and close union and other labor meetings received the official Catholic imprimatur on December 22, 1937 from Patrick Cardinal Hayes, Archbishop of New York:

PRAYER OF THE WORKER

LORD JESUS, Carpenter of Nazareth, You were a worker as I am, give to me and all the workers of the world the privilege to work as You did, so that everything we do may be to the benefit of our fellowmen and the greater glory of God the Father. Thy Kingdom come into the factories and into the shops, into our homes and into our streets. Give us this day our daily bread. May we receive it without envy or injustice. To us who labor and are heavily burdened send speedily the refreshment of Thy love. May we never sin against Thee. Show us Thy way to work, and when it is done, may we with all our fellow-workers rest in peace. Amen.

[15] Weinberg, *op. cit.,* pp. 51-53.

[16] *Ibid.,* pp. 49-56.

[17] *The New York Times,* September 7, 1947.

[18] *Supra,* p. 78. The U. S. Immigration Service ordered Santo's deportation on October 12, 1948. He voluntarily left the U. S. for Rumania on June 10, 1949.
"A news report from Vienna following the Hungarian revolt against the Soviet Union reported that Santo, who had become in 1949 one of the top governmental officials of communist Hungary, escaped that country and announced his plans to ask for readmission to the United States as a reformed communist. His statement indicated that he had decided some six years ago that communism as 'an economic method' was a 'complete farce and failure' . . . I feel now that with or without war the so-called communist political, economic and moral system must collapse. . . . I have not only 'modified' my opinion of communism, I have changed it." *The Washington Post & Times Herald,* November 24, 1956.

[19] Weinberg, *op. cit.,* p. 56.

[20] A. H. Raskin, "Drive on Communists Gains Momemtum in CIO," *The New York Times,* December 12, 1948.

[21] *CIO News,* December 13, 1948.

11 | C.I.O. EXPELS COMMUNIST-DOMINATED UNIONS

By the end of 1948, and the national CIO convention in Portland, Oregon, the drive against the Communists was gaining momentum within the CIO. In November, Philip Murray had revoked the charter of the Greater New York Industrial Union Council under the authority given him in 1946. At that time new rules had been promulgated for local industrial union councils. The CIO president was given authority to institute proceedings through the CIO Executive Board for the removal of council officers and seizure of council property and funds, if he had reason to believe that CIO council officers were not complying with the rules.[1] Under this provision, the California State CIO Council's charter was revoked later that year, after hearings held in December, and a new council was formed in June, 1949. The Los Angeles Council was reorganized in April, 1949 without having its charter lifted. In August, 1950, the charters of the San Diego, Alameda, and Contra Costa councils were revoked.[2]

In the two years since Murray had begun associating himself with the move against Communists in the CIO, the unions in which Communist influence was strong had decreased to about 15 percent of the CIO membership, as compared to the earlier 25 percent. The only large union still in pro-Communist hands was the UE with its 500,000 members.

The Portland convention turned out to be a costly one for the Communists. "We either have a policy in this movement or we do not have a policy," Murray asserted as he criticized the "ideological dive-bombers," "pouting people," "small cliques," "degraded thinkers," "dry-rot leaders," "afflictions on mankind." Walter Reuther just as explicit but milder, put it this way: "... either get clear in the CIO or get clear out."[3]

The convention ordered a settlement of the UAW-FE juris-dictional dispute[4] by ordering the FE to merge its 65,000 members into the UAW where, of course, its pro-Communist leaders would be suffocated, within sixty days.

Murray also took severely to task the pro-Communist United Office and Professional Workers. He pointed out that they had a membership of 34,000 members out of a potential 6,000,000 and were failing in their primary responsibility. The United Public Workers with 54,000 members, and the Food and Tobacco Workers with 24,000 members, likewise heard Murray state that the na-tional CIO would take steps to interfere with their internal opera-tion but he did not specify what these steps would be.[5]

Nevertheless, in spite of protests from Reuther and other anti-Communists, Albert J. Fitzgerald, UE president, who was also chairman of the Progressive Party convention, which nominated Henry Wallace, retained his post as one of the nine CIO vice-presidents.

A resumé of the 1948 convention shows that in spite of the fiery invective, the Communists were still in the CIO and in one piece. They had suffered a severe shock and an acute loss of prestige, but remained alive and kicking. Murray had directed most of his fire against the smaller of the pro-Communist unions, rather than the larger ones, such as the UE, the Fur Workers, or the Longshoremen; and even in the cases of the smaller unions, the charge against them was based on poor union organization, rather than ideology.

Nevertheless, summarizing the year, A. H. Raskin, skilled labor reporter for *The New York Times,* said: "Eliminating Com-munist influence is an essential preliminary to building a sound labor movement, in the opinion of Mr. Murray and the rest of the CIO high command."[6]

Textile Labor, organ of the aggressively anti-Communist Tex-tile Workers Union, in its issue of December 4, 1948, following the convention, faced the future with confidence as it evaluated editorially the convention happenings:

For the first time in history a CIO convention has openly and officially denounced the lunatic fringe of communists within the organization. The delegates were delighted, and the newspapers ate it up.

Unfortunately this welcome move had one bad effect—the importance of the communists in CIO was exaggerated in most news stories. Not enough stress was placed on the fact that the party-liners were never able to produce as many as 50 votes in a convention of nearly 800 . . .

The following year, 1949, was spent establishing a basis for the final elimination of Communist influence within the CIO. By the time the national CIO convention met in November, 1949, the leaders were ready to deal with the communist problem directly. A resolution was passed expelling the UE as "the Communist Party masquerading as a labor union" and chartering a successor union in its jurisdiction. The resolution's significance merits partial presentation of its text here:[7]

Resolution No. 58

ON THE EXPULSION OF THE UERMWA

We can no longer tolerate within the family of CIO the Communist Party masquerading as a labor union. The time has come when the CIO must strip the mask from these false leaders whose only purpose is to deceive and betray the workers. So long as the agents of the Communist Party in the labor movement enjoy the benefits of affiliation with the CIO, they will continue to carry on this betrayal under the protection of the good name of the CIO . . .

The certificate of affiliation of the CIO is a symbol of trust, democracy, brotherhood and loyalty in the never-ending struggle of working men and women for a better life. There is no place in the CIO for any organization whose leaders pervert its certificate of affiliation into an instrument that would betray the American workers into totalitarian bondage.

By the actions of its leadership, by their disloyalty to the CIO, and their dedication to the purposes and program of the Communist Party, contrary to the overwhelming sentiment of the rank and file membership who are loyal Americans and loyal CIO members, the leadership of the United Electrial, Radio and Machine Workers of America have rendered their union unworthy of and unqualified for this certificate of affiliation.

The UERMWA has been selected by the Communist Party as its labor base from which it can operate to betray the economic, political, and social welfare of the CIO, its affiliates and general membership. The program of the UERMWA leadership that has gradually unfolded is but an echo of the Cominform. At the signal of the Cominform, the Communist Party threw off its mask and assumed its true role as a fifth column. Its agents in the labor unions followed the Communist Party line. The UERMWA leadership abandoned any pretense of loyalty to the CIO and its program. The record is clear that wherever the needs of the Communist Party in the Soviet Union dictated, the leadership of the UERMWA was always willing to sacrifice the needs of the workers. The evidence, known to every CIO member, is overwhelming . . .

The 1949 Convention also voted to expel the FE. It amended the CIO Constitution[8] to empower the CIO Executive Board:

> . . . upon a two-thirds vote to revoke the Certificate of Affiliation of or to expel or to take any other appropriate action against any national or international union or organizing committee the policies and activities of which are consistently directed toward the achievement of the program or purposes of the Communist Party, any fascist organization, or any totalitarian movement, rather than objectives and policies set forth in the constitution of the CIO.[9]

In accordance with the new amendment, William Steinberg, president of the recently chartered American Radio Association, and a member of the CIO Executive Board, brought charges against ten CIO international unions and alleged that they were "consistently directed toward the achievement of the program or the purposes of the Communist Party rather than the objectives and policies set forth in the Constitution of the CIO." He asked that their charters be revoked by the Executive Board.[10] The ten unions were:

The American Communications Association
Food, Tobacco, Agricultural and Allied Workers Union of America
International Fisherman and Allied Workers of America
International Fur and Leather Workers Union
International Longshoremen's and Warehousemen's Union
International Union of Mine, Mill & Smelter Workers
National Union of Marine Cooks, and Stewards
United Furniture Workers of America
United Office and Professional Workers of America
United Public Workers of America

Murray named the committees to hear the charges, evidence, and testimony against the accused unions. Amalgamated Clothing Workers' Jacob Potofsky was made chairman of a committee to hear charges against Food and Tobacco, Furniture, and Mine, Mill and Smelter. Other members of the committee were Joseph Curran and UAW secretary-treasurer, Emil Mazey.

Emil Rieve, chairman, Harry Sayre, head of the Paper Workers Union, and Joseph Beirne, head of the newly admitted Communication Workers of America, were appointed a committee to hear the case of the Public Workers. Martin Wagner, head of the Gas, Coke, and Chemical Workers, replaced Beirne on the committee to hear UOPWA.

Oil Workers' president, O. A. Knight, chairman, Joseph A. Fisher of the Utility Workers, and vice-president J. J. Moran of the Communication Workers, were appointed the committee to hear charges against the Longshoremen, Fishermen, and Marine Cooks.

Members of the committee to hear the case against the American Communications Association were David J. McDonald, of the Steelworkers, as chairman, Harry Sayre and Joseph Froesch. McDonald was also chairman of the committee to hear charges against the International Fur and Leather Workers; serving with him were Jack Moran and Martin Wagner.

The charges against the United Furniture Workers were soon dismissed as a result of a change within the union. Morris Pizer, president, decided to break away from the pro-Communist majority on his executive board, which was led by secretary-treasurer Max Perlow and organizational director Ernest Marsh. At the union's June, 1950 convention in Chicago, the left-wing officers were defeated and Pizer was re-elected by a vote of 24,108 to 7,234. He carried with him the entire 27 member executive board. Perlow was defeated for secretary-treasurer by Fred Fulford by a vote of 7,043 to 19,476. Furthermore, the convention by a vote of 25,524 to 6,307 approved a resolution supporting the CIO program.[11] This was the culmination of an anti-Communist move within the union which had begun in June, 1946, when a major revolt against Communist control had nearly split the union wide open. A large group of furniture workers appealed at that time to Philip Murray to help them in a "fight for economic and political freedom from a group whose interests are subservient to a foreign country." The block was led by George Bucher, president of the Furniture Workers Philadelphia Local 37. The immediate stimulus for this revolt came from a convention of the union held in Detroit that year, when Morris Muster, international president, was re-elected on an "anti-Red" platform, but as a result of a system of block voting found that no one else on his slate was victorious. Muster, who had been head of the UFW since its inception in 1937, resigned as president and as a member of the CIO national Executive Board. In his resignation he declared that of the 42,000 members of the union not more than 1,000 were Communists but that this small minority dominated the union.

> In this particular situation, of the 130 delegates at the convention in Detroit, there were 10 or 12 who never saw the inside of a furniture factory but wormed their way into locals and by political intrigue became delegates to perpetuate an individual (Perlow) in office despite the fact the majority did not want the man.

By 1948, when the Taft-Hartley non-Communist affidavit had become an important issue in many unions, the rebellion flamed anew. One local, Local 335 at Tell City and Jasper, Indiana, unanimously voted to disaffiliate and became independent.[12] When Pizer, in late 1949, decided to break with Perlow and take the union away from Communist control, he was able to capitalize on the earlier discontent and, with that support, prevail.

In December, 1949, the CIO committees began hearing the cases dealing with the Mine, Mill and Smelter Workers, United Office and Professional Workers, Food and Tobacco, and the United Public Workers. On February 15, 1950, the committees made their recommendations to the CIO Executive Board, which acted immediately. The Mine, Mill and Smelter Workers were expelled that very day, effective at once; the United Office, and Professional Workers, the United Public Workers, and the Food, Tobacco and Agricultural Workers were expelled effective March 1st.[13] The four unions had fewer than 100,000 members. The same CIO Executive Board meeting ratified Murray's withdrawal of a charter from the California CIO Council on the grounds that it was Communist-dominated.

The cause of the unions' expulsions was clearly stated:

> . . . the Communist movement, from its inception, purported to be a movement of working people. Its basic thesis was that a new order of society must be created by revolution of the working classes and that the 'dictatorship of the proletariat' must be established. Because of this basic thesis, Communist philosophy has always been predicated upon the use of trade unions as an instrument of Communist policy and as a weapon by which the Party would emerge. . . . The Communist movement has thus always sought to operate through trade unions, to speak in the language of labor and as a spokesman and leader of labor, and thus, by trickery and strategem, to direct labor toward the goals of Communism.

Communist activity, the report added,

> . . . is based upon one fundamental objective—the support of the Soviet Union, the country in which the Communist Party first achieved its goal of dictatorshop. . . . The policies which the Party adopts are stated to be policies for the achievements of the goals of American labor—not for the advancement of the cause of the Soviet Union. But over a period of years, it is clear that the goals of American labor, as stated by the Party, are always found to be those policies which will aid the Soviet Union. As the tactical position of the Soviet Union in the world has changed, the program of the American Communist Party 'for American labor' has accommodated itself. And, when it seemed in the interests of the Soviet Union for American labor to forsake its heritage and to adopt policies contradictory to the whole fabric of the labor movement, the Communist Party adopted such policies.

The four committee reports on which the final expulsions were predicated, followed a generally similar pattern. They reviewed the charges filed against each union; reviewed Communist Party policies of recent years; reviewed the particular union's policies and activities during the same period; and concluded with specific findings and recommendations.[14]

1 *The New York Times,* November 16, 1946.
2 *CIO News,* September 25, 1950.
3 Robert Bendiner, "Politics and People," *The Nation,* December 18, 1948.
4 *Supra,* p. 67.
5 Raskin, *The New York Times,* December 12, 1948, *op. cit.*
6 *Ibid.*

[7] CIO Eleventh Constitutional Convention, *op. cit.*, pp. 302-305.

[8] *Ibid.*, pp. 347, 348.

[9] *Ibid.*, p. 288.

[10] CIO, *Hearings to Investigate ILWU, op. cit.*, pp. 4, 5.

[11] CIO, *Report of the Committee to Investigate Charges Against the United Furniture Workers of America* (mimeographed).

[12] *The New York Times*, February 25, 1948.

[13] *CIO News*, February 20, 1950.

[14] Subsequently, all of the reports of the CIO Executive Board committees to investigate charges of Communism against international unions within the CIO were published by the Sub-committee on Labor and Labor-Management Relations of the Senate Labor and Public Welfare Committee. These reports were presented to the Senate by Senator Hubert H. Humphrey on October 1, 1951 as Senate Document No. 89, 82nd Congress, 1st session.

PART III

Chapter 12-13

THE FORMAL CASES AGAINST
COMMUNIST-DOMINATED UNIONS

12 | THE FORMAL CASES AGAINST THE COMMUNIST-DOMINATED UNIONS · I

UNITED OFFICE AND PROFESSIONAL WORKERS

The CIO investigating committee, after examining the publications, officers' reports, and convention proceedings of the United Office and Professional Workers of America, formally found that[1]

> ...the policies and activities of the UOPWA followed and continue to follow exactly, without deviation, the program of the Communist Party.... Never in the history of the UOPWA has any policy ever been adopted which in any way runs counter to the policies of the Communist Party or to the interests of the Soviet Union as those interests are reflected in the program of the Communist Party.
>
> If the Communist Party program had been a consistent one, this absence of conflict might not be significant. But, in view of the fact that in a period of ten years the Communist Party has taken almost every conceivable position on every issue of public importance in the United States, the absence of any conflict between the position of the Party and the position of this union is of great significance...

By following "the twists and turns, the zigs and zags of the Communist Party line," the UOPWA lost membership, the CIO committee reported. In 1946-47, UOPWA reported to the CIO an average dues-paying membership of approximately 45,000, but by November 1949, this membership had dropped to the "pitiable" figure of about 12,000.

We have already examined[2] in some detail the internal pro-Communist operation of UOPWA. The committee report took further note of the union's allegiance to Communist doctrine by tracing its foreign policy. Prior to 1938, UOPWA "...expressed

fervent support for Roosevelt's anti-aggression program" but after
the Stalin-Hitler pact, the union "sharply reversed its field."

> The union not only opposed involvement in the war, it opposed
> lend-lease, it opposed aid to Britain, and in general, took the
> position that American labor's problems were at home and that
> what happened abroad was of no significance.

But after the invasion of Russia by the Nazi military machine,
"UOPWA again shifted its field. Through its newspaper, it called
briskly and with no uncertainty for 'full aid to Britain and Soviet
Russia.'" By the spring of 1942, UOPWA had opened a "full-
fledged, all-out propaganda demand for the immediate opening
up of a second front." Following the Teheran Conference, UOPWA
"was most vociferous in denouncing any signs of labor militancy."
Its president, the CIO committee recalled, "commented favorably
on Harry Bridges' proposal that labor continue its no-strike pledge
into the post-war period."

By 1946, however, the union had decided that "America's
foreign policy was just a reflection of the fact that 'big business is
driving toward war.'" "The union's general post-war position was
the same as that of the Communist Party and it remains the same
today," the CIO committee said. "The union's position at the
present time, as regards the CIO, is, as is the Communist Party's,
one of violent and destructive opposition."

The Committee then took note of the fact that UOPWA's
attitude toward the CIO and the trial was noticeably ambivalent.
On the one hand it launched a "vitriolic attack upon the CIO."
The CIO was accused of "selling out" the fight against the Taft-
Hartley Act and its policies were denounced as the "program of
the reactionary employers and their political agents." It was described as a "government-dominated and regimented organization"
which was "serving the purposes of those international financiers
and reactionary politicians who are fomenting a third world war."[3]
On the other hand, it apparently had a "desire to remain within
the CIO." The committee explained the inconsistency by referring
to a series of articles[4] by John Williamson, the Communist Party
labor director, which criticized the ousted UE for having "abandoned the fight against the CIO." The articles urged other CIO

left-wing unions to use the hearings to attack the national CIO.
The committee concluded:

> The history of this union, when compared with the history of
> the Communist Party ... shows beyond a doubt that the present
> coincidence of the program of the Communist Party and of the
> UOPWA is ... the result of devotion by this union to the over-
> all purposes of the Communist Party rather than the objectives
> of the CIO.

UNITED PUBLIC WORKERS OF AMERICA

The committee's report on the United Public Workers of
America described the union as the product of a merger in 1946
of the State, County and Municipal Workers of America and the
United Federal Workers. On the basis of various union statistics,
it estimated that at the time of merger the SCMWA had nearly
three times as many members as the UFWA; and it estimated
that the percentage of federal workers in the UPW "may now
well be less than 11 per cent."[5]

The committee found that the prewar and wartime "history
of UFWA policy ... does not exhibit the shifts and contortions
that SCMWA policy does. ... The union's record during this period
is straightforward. In the post-war period, however, it clearly
took positions identical with those taken at that time by SCMWA."
The CIO committee had apparently decided to defend the early
policies of the UFWA because it had at that time been under the
nominal administrative direction of the national CIO office, with
first John L. Lewis and then Philip Murray choosing the union's
presidents. In fact, however, as we shall see, Communist influence
was very great in the organization throughout its entire history,
since the national CIO headquarters paid very little day to day
attention to the operation of the union. After the merger, the
leadership of the new UPWA was nearly identical to that of
SCMWA.

After an examination of the evidence the committee found
that because of its position as a union of government workers
UPWA's public pronouncements were "less blatantly and less
openly" pro-Soviet than those of other pro-Communist unions.
But the committee was also conscious of the fact that the union

never publicly adopted any policy which in any way ran counter to the policies of the Communist party or the interests of the Soviet Union. In support of its conclusions, the committee traced the activities of SCMWA and UPWA, comparing them with the positions of the Communist party. One interesting bit of evidence presented by the committee was an editorial in the union newspaper in 1946 to the effect that the housing shortage was due to the production of atom bombs.

With regard to the first convention resolution passed by the new UPWA after the merger in 1946, which criticized American foreign policy for being anti-Soviet, the committee referred to a story by Jerry Klutz, *Washington Post* columnist, to the effect that the resolution was adopted out of order at the suggestion of George Morris, *Daily Worker* reporter, who wanted a story to offset the criticisms directed against Russian foreign policy at the Textile Workers Union convention that day. According to Klutz, opponents of the resolution were called "reactionaries and Red-baiters" and a suggestion by a delegate that a line be added to the resolution recommending the withdrawal of Russian troops from Poland, Czechoslovakia, Estonia and other countries was voted down.[6] The committee then went on to state,[7]

> ...on the basis of all the evidence presented to it, the Committee unanimously concludes that the policies and activities of the UPWA are consistently directed toward the achievement of the program and the purposes of the Communist Party rather than the objectives and policies set forth in the CIO Constitution.

The report on the United Public Workers concluded with a special statement in view of the fact that "the members of the UPWA are, in the main, government employees."

> Although the persistent Communist Party line tactics of its leadership have driven out of the UPW the major portion of its American membership, the Committee has no doubt that there still remain within the union, members who are fooled by the pseudo-unionism and the false militancy of the UPW leadership. And there are undoubtedly others who have opposed that leadership but have remained within the union. The Committee has here necessarily measured the union by its leadership, by those who control the organization and speak for it.

But the Committee wishes to make it crystal clear that its condemnation of that leadership, and of the union, does not necessarily reflect a condemnation of each individual member. The CIO is putting its house in order. But, in doing so, it does not condemn each member of the union which it finds to be Communist-dominated, and, the Committee feels, this point should be emphasized in the case of a union, the jobs of many of whose members would be endangered by a fallacious translation of the Committee's findings as to the union's leadership into a condemnation of each of its individual members.

The president of the United Public Workers was Abram Flaxer. He had been the president of the State, County, and Municipal Workers of America since it was organized in 1937. Before that, he was general manager of the New York local of the AFL American Federation of Government Employees, where a number of the AFL leaders considered him to be a Communist, according to the testimony of John P. Frey, head of the AFL Metal Trades Department.[8] There was additional evidence that Flaxer had been a leader at Communist party fraction meetings at which SCMWA policies were determined.[9]

It was apparent long before the CIO committee report that there was no question of Flaxer's allegiance to the Communist program, nor any question of his union's allegiance. During the "collective security" phase of the "party-line," they participated in "Stop Hitler" parades and many activities of the American League for Peace and Democracy. With the signing of the Stalin-Hitler Pact, Flaxer became strongly anti-war, and became a leader in the American Peace Mobilization. The SCMWA wholeheartedly advanced the cause of the "Yanks Are Not Coming" and energetically threw itself into APM activities.[10]

Following Hitler's invasion of the Soviet, Flaxer at the 1941 convention of the CIO, said:[11]

The object of our foreign policy is the defeat of Fascism and we are going to take every step that is necessary to bring about this defeat ... It is a policy which requires the revision of our Neutrality Act ... and requires that our seamen stand ready at their stations and be ready to shoot at sight.... It is a policy that recognizes that this war is our war ... The struggle that the Red Army, the people of the Soviet Union, are conducting against Hitler has served to inspire the World.

During the war period, the SCMWA editor was Helen Kay. In the August 6, 1932 issue of the *Daily Worker* she contributed an article entitled "The Power of the Daily Worker" which dates her Communist activities to an early period. In 1933, she was editor of the *New Pioneer,* the Communist Party's official publication for children, and had over the years contributed to *Soviet Russia Today* and other Communist publications.[12]

Another indication of SCMWA's pro-Communist loyalties was the fact that it had hired former UAW official Wyndham Mortimer for its staff after he had been forced to leave that union because of his Communist activities.[13]

The United Federal Workers, as the committee noted, was a small union when it joined with SCMWA to form the United Public Workers, and as a result, had never reached full bloom on its own. Both Lewis and Murray had placed the union under non-Communist receivership, first under Jacob Baker and then under CIO vice-president Allan Haywood, both of whom served as union presidents. During this period, however, the secretary-treasurer of the union was Eleanor Nelson, who had helped form the UFWA in 1937 when a group of federal workers split from the AFL American Federation of Government Employees.

Eleanor Nelson, like the leaders of SCMWA, had been a member of the American League for Peace and Democracy during the "collective security" period. Following the August 23, 1939 Pact, she and many of the UFWA leaders opposed the war. It was necessary for President Allan Haywood specifically to prohibit UFWA locals from sending delegates to the American Peace Mobilization. Yet, following the Nazi invasion of Russia, Miss Nelson made this statement at the 1941 national CIO convention.[14]

> Our organization was very well pleased when the convention took the action it did supporting the foreign policy of the President . . . We feel Hitler must be defeated and we are doing all we can to see he is . . .

The October, 1942 convention of the UFWA favored an immediate opening of a second front; passage of the teen-age draft; and a declaration of war on Finland.[15]

The 1946 amalgamation of SCMWA and UFWA had indeed

been a suitable marriage based on mutual interests. They were two of a kind.

FOOD, TOBACCO, AGRICULTURAL AND ALLIED WORKERS UNION

The committee set up to investigate the charges against the Food, Tobacco, Agricultural and Allied Workers of America found that "it is abundantly clear that the FTA consistently follows the Communist party line. The record is plain that wherever the needs of the Communist party and the Soviet Union dictate, the leadership of the FTA is always willing to sacrifice the needs of the workers in that industry and organized labor in America as a whole."[16]

> It is equally clear that the Certificate of Affiliation granted to the FTA by the CIO has fallen into the control of a group devoted primarily to the principles of the Communist Party and opposed to the Constitution and democratic objectives of the CIO.

The committee noted that Donald Henderson, former FTA president, who had "concealed his membership in the Communist Party from the membership of his union and from the CIO," resigned that Communist affiliation in order to qualify for signing Taft-Hartley non-Communist affidavits.[17]

"The slavish adherence by the FTA leadership to the program and policies of the Communist Party has resulted in a steadily declining membership," the committee said. For the fiscal years ending September 30, it offered these FTA membership figures: 1947—46,700, 1948—29,370, 1949—22,590.

"By the action of its leadership," the committee added, "by their disloyalty to the CIO, and their dedication to the purpose and program of the Communist Party, the leadership of the FTA have rendered their union unworthy and unqualified for their Certificate of Affiliation with the CIO."

To prove their conclusion, the committee traced the parallel between Communist Party policy and that of the union and found "the most glaring evidences of FTA endorsement of the Communist Party line." At one point, the committee report compared the union's support during the war of national service legislation, which the CIO opposed, with the union's later accusation that CIO support of the Marshall Plan would prepare a war machine in the United States which would eventually include forced labor for workers.[18]

Donald Henderson's affiliations with Communist causes dated back to 1932. In that year he became executive secretary of the American Committee for Struggle Against War, American branch of the World Congress Against War, a Communist-International sponsored meeting at Amsterdam which called upon the proletariat of the world to prepare to "turn imperialist war into civil war." He also was very active in the Student Congress Against War, formed at Christmas of that year; and became executive secretary of the United States Congress Against War, which met in New York on September 29, 1933. Earl Browder, in his report to the Communist International, later said: "The Congress from the beginning was led by our Party quite openly."[19] The American League Against War and Fascism grew out of the Congress, and Henderson became its executive secretary, until he transferred to the agricultural field.

In the spring of 1933, Henderson was dropped from the faculty of Columbia University; for a time he became a Communist *cause celebre*. In September, 1935, he wrote an article for *The Communist* entitled "The Rural Masses and the Work of Our Party," which began in this fashion:[20]

> ... during the past 2 years our party has been successful in developing policies and organization which are rapidly achieving a successful turn to mass revolutionary work and influence in the cities and among the industrial urban proletariat.

The article went on to point out the necessity for the Communist party to "carry through" its ideas of "Soviet power ... in the small cities, towns, and villages, and on the farms." It was following these articles and activities that he became active in the agricultural field.

The CIO investigating committee did not formally take note of these early activities of Henderson in evaluating the charges against the union. The committee's report, however, did discuss some of his more recent activities as they related to the charges.

The 1948 convention of the CIO authorized the executive board to withdraw from the World Federation of Trade Unions because of its Soviet domination. In spite of that, Henderson, who was still president of the FTA, attended the Paris WFTU meeting in April, 1949.[21]

One other interesting event took place involving Donald Henderson. The union, in 1949, for reasons of self-interest, decided to comply with the Taft-Hartley Act and have its officers sign the non-Communist affidavit. Henderson, who was faced with the choice of resigning his Communist party membership or his union position, decided to do the latter. He, therefore, resigned as president in "protest" against the signing of the affidavit which he asserted to be unconstitutional and a matter of principle to him. He was then immediately appointed the union's National Administrative Director. When the NLRB, however, questioned the authenticity of Henderson's resignation and refused to recognize the union's having qualified under the law, Henderson was forced openly to admit his membership in and resignation from the Communist party as he signed the affidavit. This was the first time that the fact of Henderson's membership in the Communist Party was admitted to his union's membership. Today (1956) he is not active in the labor movement; and the union he led is likewise out of the picture.

INTERNATIONAL UNION OF MINE, MILL AND SMELTER WORKERS

The national CIO committee found in its investigation of the International Union of Mine, Mill and Smelter Workers, that testimony presented at the hearings demonstrated conclusively that the policies and activities of the union "are directed toward the achievement of the program and the purposes of the Communist Party rather than the objectives set forth in the CIO Constitution. This conclusion is inescapable both from an analysis of the policies adopted by Mine, Mill, as shown by documentary exhibits ... and by direct and uncontradicted testimony by former officers of the union that the Communist Party directs the affairs of the union."[22] The committee said that "the shocking character of the direct control by the Communist Party of the leadership of this union, and through them, of the union itself, was further brought home to the committee by direct testimony showing in detail the exact manner in which the policies of the union are dictated by the Communist Party." It cited in particular the testimony of Homer Wilson and Kenneth Eckert, former Mine, Mill officers.

> Both Wilson and Eckert made it perfectly clear to the Committee that the fact that this union followed the Communist Party line was not accidental. It was the result of complete domination of the union's leadership by the Party. The Party group within the union had a systematic working apparatus for making its decisions and for translating those decisions into union policy.

The committee cited testimony that a four-man Communist steering committee—of which both witness Eckert and Maurice Travis, now secretary-treasurer of the union, were members—"determined Communist policy within the union. They did this in consultation with the leaders of the Communist Party. Meetings were frequently held with Communist Party leaders such as William Z. Foster, the chairman of the party; Eugene Dennis, its general secretary; John Williamson, its labor secretary; and Gil Green, its Illinois director. In addition, there was a regular envoy from the Communist Party who was designated as liason man between Mine, Mill and the Party."

Eckert, who had been a former Communist party secretary in Toledo[23] and a member of the union's executive board, testified specifically to the secret meetings he and other union leaders had attended with leading Communists.[24]

> On several occasions Maurice Travis and I had meetings with the top leaders of the Communist Party of the U. S., John Williamson, William Z. Foster, Eugene Dennis, and Maurice Travis and I and at other times other members of the leaders of the Mine-Mill attended Party meetings together with the leaders of certain other CIO unions, United Electrical Workers, Fur and Leather Workers, National Maritime Union, in some instances.

Eckert told of one meeting, for example, at Denver's Shirley-Savoy Hotel in February, 1947, at which the "party representative" agreed to "request of some of the other Left Wing unions to help Mine-Mill out financially."[25]

The committee said that directives moved from the party and the steering committee—sometimes enlarged for special purposes to a so-called Progressive Caucus within the union; and that this mechanism served as a "transmission belt" for the adoption of "Communist-inspired policies."

Thus, although the membership had a theoretical veto power, the Communist party's control over the union newspaper, organizational staff, and leadership, gave to the party the decision-making power. It was the party, therefore, which decided that Reid Robinson should resign as president—and for party reasons. Similarly, the membership had no control over the appointment of Maurice Travis, a newcomer to the union, as executive assistant to the President; which, in turn, led him to the vice-presidency and presidency following Robinson's 1947 resignation. Travis, incidentally, had joined the staff of the Mine, Mill and Smelter Workers after being expelled from a local of the United Steelworkers for Communist activities. It was the party, too, which later decided that in view of the difficulties facing the union, Travis' Communist affiliations were too well known for him to function effectively. A Communist steering committee, therefore, had Travis assume the position of secretary-treasurer and gave the presidency to John Clark, less known but just as reliable.

"The testimony of Eckert and Wilson was not contradicted," the committee said, adding that the committee was "shocked and outraged by the direct testimony that the union's policies were determined in secret meetings with high officials of the Communist Party prior to their submission to the union's governing body and to the membership...."

The committee further said that in 1948 the union rejected warnings from the CIO that its devotion to the Communist Party was imperilling its status in the CIO.

The difficulty of proving Communist affiliation is always great. Eckert pointed to one of the problems when he said, "Reid Robinson did not carry a Party membership card insofar as I know." But he went on to explain, "... most of the people, as well as myself in this union and other unions that I know of did not attend branch meetings like other Party members. They were protected. The membership was not to be known..." "But the Party policy was carried out by Reid," he said. "I know of no instance where he ever deviated from it."[26]

Reid Robinson's pro-Communist affiliation dated back at least to the American League Against War and Fascism. In this militant period, the Communist party called for general strikes against "imperialist war." Robinson was president of Butte Local 1 of the International Mine, Mill and Smelter Workers, affiliated with the AFL, and permanent chairman of the Second Northwest Congress Against War and Fascism. At the 1935 convention of the AFL, Robinson, a delegate, introduced two resolutions on the general strike. One, "Resolved, That in the future the American Federation of Labor instead of discouraging these general industrial strikes use every means in carrying them to a successful conclusion...." The second, "Resolved, That in the event that this Nation becomes involved in any imperialistic war, we call upon President William Green to immediately call a general strike of all workers affiliated with the American Federation of Labor."[27]

When the Communists adopted a collective security foreign policy and the American League Against War and Fascism became the American League for Peace and Democracy, Robinson became a member of the national executive committee and of its national labor committee. This policy called for revision of the Neutrality Act and for the boycott of Japanese, Italian and German goods.[28]

The IUMMSWA, which joined the CIO in 1937, adopted the following resolution at its August, 1938, convention:[29]

> Whereas: At the present time the chief threat to the peace of the world and therefore the United States as well as the greatest threat to the welfare and security of the International Trade Union Movement arises from the activities of the Fascist aggressor nations.
>
> ...Resolved: that the International Mine, Mill and Smelter Workers go on record in support of Peace Act, H. J. 527 introduced into Congress by Rep. Jerry J. O'Connell, which would provide for quarantining the aggressor by prohibiting the exportation of arms and munitions to such aggressor nations.

At that same convention, the union adopted a resolution calling
for a boycott of Japanese, German and Italian goods and supporting President Roosevelt's October 5, 1937 "Quarantine of the
Aggressor" Chicago speech.[30]

The following year, just a few days prior to the Nazi-Soviet
Pact, the union's 1939 convention met in August and adopted a
resolution urging a revision of the Neutrality Act as "absolutely
necessary if we are to stop aiding the aggressor nations and
punishing their victims."[31]

Soon after the signing of the Hitler-Stalin Pact, Robinson
served as vice-chairman of the Committee to Defend America
by Keeping Out of War, vice-chairman of the Emergency Peace
Mobilization, and vice-chairman of the American Peace Mobilization. At an organization meeting of the APM in Chicago on
September 1, 1940, he said: "We hate war because we go into the
bowels of the earth to mine the copper and the zinc for the bullets
which find their resting place in the bowels of other workers."[32]

In August, at the union's 1940 convention, Robinson took note
of his APM activities:[33] "It will be a marvelous thing to impress
upon the people of the United States, especially those boys in
Washington who are trying to create war, that the American
people are opposed to war." He declared:[34]

> The American people have been people who have always gone
> to the front to protect Democracy, but the American people
> refuse to go to some foreign land to make profits for some of the
> great industrialists such as the Anaconda Copper Company and
> the American Smelting and Refining Company, as we did in the
> last war.

A few months later, Robinson wrote a letter to the Senate
in which he said that the Lend-Lease bill (H.R. 1776) was "the
most dangerous piece of legislation affecting the workers of America, that has ever been presented to the Congress of the United
States."[35] He wrote in his union's February 17 publication that
the bill "would empower the President of the United States to
wipe out trade unions with one sweep of his pen." In the later
March 17 issue of the paper, he said, "The Tory bill 1776 would

enable these corporate interests to drag America more deeply into this war."[36]

Robinson thus made use of the union's newspaper, which was a special edition of the national *CIO News,* to reach the union members with his views on foreign policy. He attempted to develop the fact that the U.S. had nothing to fear from a Hitler victory. "We have a problem in America which is more serious than any problem of invasion of Hitler or any other nation." He claimed that Hitler could not possibly attack the United States.[37]

This series of messages continued in the union newspaper until Hitler attacked the Soviet Union in June 1941. In fact, it continued a day after the attack and thereby proved an embarrassment to the union and a source of amusement to its critics. The attack took place on June 21st and 22nd, which was a Saturday and a Sunday. The union paper for that week was dated and appeared on June 23rd, the Monday following the attack. The paper was printed and closed, however, on the previous Friday, a day prior to the attack. The June 23rd issue, therefore, carried a large picture of Robinson addressing a Butte Miners Day meeting and saying: "There are two main jobs for the members of Butte Miners Union 1. The first is to support the movement to keep America from being taken deeper into the war."[38]

A month later, Robinson attempted to explain the sudden shift in his foreign policy. His column in the union newspaper for July 21, 1941 said:[39]

> So long as the international conflict remained partially localized and such vast areas and great peoples as the United States, all of the Pan-American nations and the powerful Soviet Union were outside the conflict, we sought to remain at peace because we recognized the danger from those enemies of democracy—those native Fascists—who would use the emergency to further their own anti-democratic ends under the guise of a great effort for democracy and against international Fascism.
>
> Now Hitler has made unmistakable his thirst for world domination by launching war upon another sixth of the globe, the vast territory of the USSR. In so doing, he has disposed of the hope that powerful nations remaining out of the war might be the instrumentalities for bringing about a real people's peace. . . .

In the war years that followed, these explanations were put aside and forgotten so that at the 1943 convention of the union, Reid Robinson was able to make the following statement:[40] "Labor correctly estimated the character of this war as a people's war, a war for the liberation of millions, a war to keep civilization from going backwards, a war to protect our families and our unions."

Immediately following the invasion of the Soviet, the union began an active pro-war campaign. At the August, 1941 convention, Robinson declared: "It seems clear that continued military victories for Hitler means our inevitable involvement in this war, regardless of our desire for peace."[41]

When the national CIO convention took place in 1941, Robinson forgot his 1940 speech: "We have a problem here in America which is more serious than any problem of invasion of Hitler." Instead he said: "The CIO must decide in Convention assembled that the business of defeating Adolf Hitler is the most serious task it has met . . . every other problem we have passes into insignificance when posed against this central duty of supporting every conceivable step that will bring Hitler to his downfall."[42]

The parallel between the Communist Party position and that of Mine, Mill continued when the pendulum swung again in 1945. Early in 1946, the union carried a news story accusing Great Britain and the U.S. of an atom bomb "conspiracy."[43] The May 27, 1946 issue of the union paper carried a cartoon of a conference table around which were a Molotov-like figure representing "Russia" and two angry appearing people representing "Britain" and "USA." In the background are two soldiers, one Russian and the other American. "GI Joe" is quoted as saying: "Remember when we joined hands at Torgau, Ivan? In those days we knew who were our friends."[44]

The 1946 convention of the union rejected a resolution criticizing the USSR as well as Great Britain and the USA for maintaining armed forces outside of their borders. The executive board of the union in 1947 passed a foreign policy resolution criticizing the US but not Russia, and opposing the Truman Doctrine. The union newspaper "had only praise for the Communist coup in Czechoslovakia."[45]

The union also opposed the Marshall Plan as "in danger of

being transformed into a weapon of economic oppression. It is difficult to maintain confidence in the Marshall Plan ... when we see it used at the same time as a means of rebuilding Germany, the home of Nazism, at the expense of its victim nations."[46]

In 1948, the union supported Henry Wallace for President. "Its newspaper was practically converted into a Progressive Party organ and trade union news was subordinated to Progressive Party propaganda," concluded the national CIO committee investigating the union.[47]

With the 1946 shift in foreign policy, the union began to meet increased internal difficulties very similar to those met by other pro-Communist internationals in the CIO. Opposition to Robinson, and Communist domination, received encouragement from the fact that the national CIO was becoming increasingly concerned about Communist activities.

The union's internal problems became particularly vexing because of Robinson's personal difficulties and indiscretions. One of Robinson's former associates, Homer Wilson, a member of the Mine, Mill Executive Board, described the embarrassment this caused the Communist caucus within the union:[48]

> President Robinson had started indulging in excessive alcoholic beverages, and he had become so irresponsible that he ran his financial standing into a shape that he had to approach a company to raise money. He approached Mr. Pack of the Doehler-Jarvis Die Casting Corporation.

Word of Robinson's request for a loan spread through the union and was used by the opposition. Wilson reported a conversation he had with one of the Communist leaders in the union, Chase Powers, a member of the executive board from California. He reported Powers as saying to him: "The guy is guilty, but if we throw him out the Party will lose some of their connections and it is better to keep him in here than to let Rasmussen have it, and we will work out a deal on it." The deal was for the Communist party to pay Robinson's debts in return for an agreement from him to appoint an assistant to look after the union business. Travis was appointed the assistant and rapidly became the leading Communist spokesman in the union.

The 1946 convention of the union at Cleveland found opposition to the union's leadership at a high peak. A resolution to bar Communists from union office was defeated by the narrow margin of 439-401.[49]

Under the union's constitution, officers were not elected at the convention, but by a referendum. The candidates were Robinson vs. James J. Leary for president and Maurice Travis vs. Ralph Rasmussen for vice-president. The convention designated a canvassing committee of one member from each district, a total of nine, to tally the referendum vote.

When it came time to announce the referendum results, the committee split. A majority of six declared Robinson and Travis elected. The minority declared Leary and Rasmussen the victors. In protest against the decision of the majority of the canvassing committee, a significant group of about 40 to 50 local unions with a membership of about 30,000 to 35,000, a fourth of the total, withdrew from the Mine, Mill and Smelter Workers within a few weeks. Those wishing to remain in the CIO joined the International Union of Marine and Shipbuilding Workers.

Robinson resigned shortly thereafter and was succeeded by Travis.

To meet the crisis caused by the protests against the election results, the national CIO, in March, 1947, through its Executive Board, adopted a motion that a special committee of three be designated to ascertain the facts and "offer the good offices" of the CIO in arranging a peaceful solution. Jacob S. Potofsky, president of the Amalgamated Clothing Workers; Van A. Bittner, vice-president of the United Steelworkers; and L. S. Buckmaster, president of the United Rubber Workers, were appointed.

The CIO committee found irregularities in the voting, criticized the secessionists—and the Shipbuilding Union for taking them in —and severely took Robinson to task for his conduct and resignation.[50] The most significant aspect of the committee's final report, however, related to "outside interference" into the union's affairs by the Communist party. Charles Moyer had resigned about this time as secretary-treasurer of the union, alleging Communist control of the union through Travis, thereby stimulating the committee's interest in the problem. The committee uncovered photostatic copies of letters proving beyond question that Travis consulted with the Communist party in shaping the union's policies. A letter from Phil Wilkes, organizer for the Communist party, to Travis, dated May 13, 1946, read:

> ... you could do a lot in organizing the good people prior to nominations and elections ... I'm not clear how the question on candidates will be handled in Mine, Mill. Perhaps a delay is necessary, but if that is so, we should be advised immediately on who is to be supported and why. I'm sure you are the proper candidate for the office discussed. . . .

The CIO committee, therefore, recommended to the national Executive Board that they urge the Mine, Mill and Smelter Workers to request Travis' resignation or remove him as president. They also recommended that an administrator be appointed for six months by Murray to conduct the union's affairs until they were stabilized.

The report was accepted by Murray and a majority of the CIO Executive Board, but openly rejected by the union. Murray, deciding not to attempt interference with the internal "autonomy" of the union, merely referred the committtee report to the naional CIO convention for its information and declared this "ends the dispute so far as the CIO is concerned."[51]

In 1947 the union held its convention in St. Paul. This convention differed quite markedly from the 1946 convention, where the anti-Communists came close to winning a majority and taking over the organization. This time the Communists had easier sailing. In the course of the past year, more than a quarter of the union's membership had seceded from the union because of opposition to the union's pro-Communist leadership. This drastically weakened the anti-administration forces at the convention and left the Communists in complete control. It was at this convention that Travis, responding to a decision of the union's Communist caucus, decided to give up the presidency of the union and became secretary-treasurer. John Clark became the new president and Reid Robinson one of the vice-presidents.[52] This spelled the end of an effective anti-Communist bloc within the union. Communist influence and control over the policies and internal operations of the union became more and more obvious until, in 1949, Travis openly admitted to Communist membership.

The announcement came in connection with a decision by the union's officers to sign the Taft Hartley non-Communist affidavit. The Mine, Mill and Smelter Workers was one of the unions which found it necessary to utilize the operations of the NLRB if it was to maintain its position against competing unions. It was this which forced the officers' decision to sign the affidavit. Travis, in order to sign, publicly resigned from membership in the Communist party.

> This has not been an easy step for me to take. Membership in the Communist Party has always meant to me, as a member and officer of the International Union, that I could be a better trade unionist; it has meant to me a call to greater effort in behalf of the union as a solemn pledge to my fellow-members that I would fight for their interests above all other interests.

In his open explanation to the union's members on August 15, 1949, Travis said:[53]

> Since the interest of the International Union is uppermost in my mind, I have been confronted with the problem of resigning from the Communist Party, of which I have been a member, in order to make it possible for me to sign the Taft-Hartley affidavit. I have decided, with the utmost reluctance and with a great sense of indignation, to take such a step. My resignation has now taken place, and, as a result, I have signed the affidavit.

In a joint statement commenting on Travis' resignation, officers Clark, Robinson and Orville Larson said: "We regret that this action is necessary, but we commend him for his forthright and courageous stand, and we are happy that the International Union is thus assured of his continued leadership."

From 1947 to 1949 the International Union of Mine, Mill and Smelter Workers prepared its members for the coming estrangement from the CIO. This was highlighted during the Progressive party campaign in 1948. Later, when the CIO decided to abandon the Communist-dominated World Federation of Trade Unions, Mine, Mill denounced the plan as a service to Wall Street. It also accused the CIO of "selling out" in connection with the Taft-Hartley Act. After the CIO 1949 convention, Mine, Mill supported the expelled

UE and attacked the CIO program as a "boss-inspired invasion."[54] All this hurt the union's strength. In the fiscal year 1946-1947, for example, the union reported and paid a per capita tax to the CIO on an average dues-paying employed membership of more than 100,000. In 1948-1949, the average dropped to 65,000. By October, 1949, the figure reported to the CIO was 44,000.

When the union was notified that it was to be brought up on charges before a committee of the national CIO, it was ready with a provocative reply. A letter signed by the union's officers to Philip Murray, dated December 1, 1949, charged the proceedings were "illegal and improper,"[55] and in violation of democratic principles "that all of our people have the right to think and speak freely and have the right to their own opinions on the issues of the day.... A democracy in which beliefs are dictated from the top is no longer a democracy; a labor organization which says, 'agree with me or get out,' is doomed." It went on to attack the CIO committee members, Potofsky, Curran and Murray, and Murray himself, accusing him and the United Steelworkers of racial bias. They asked for a hearing "by a panel of distinguished and interested Americans" at an "open public hearing . . . not in Washington but in Montana, Utah, or in some other area where there is a large section of our membership." The issue, the letter continued, was "not whether Mine, Mill follows the Communist Party line but whether the CIO Constitution requires every autonomous international union to give up its rights to determine its policies for itself."

Travis elaborated this point further during the course of the hearings: "I would like to know where in these objectives in the Constitution of the CIO it says that we have to support the Marshall Plan or oppose Lend-Lease or conform to the foreign policy of the Democratic Administration or any other administration."[56] The union also charged that the CIO was just as "guilty" as it was of following the Communist Party line from 1939 to 1947.[57]

The union's defense was later added to the evidence against them when the Potofsky committee showed the similarity of the defense to the reasoning in a series of articles which appeared in the *Daily Worker* from December 6 to 9, 1949. The committee then charged that the union's December 1st letter to Murray followed Communist party suggestions:[58]

In fact, the headings in the Union's mimeographed statement, presented on February 6 are almost a recapitulation of the points raised in the *Daily Worker* articles; 'The charge is phony'; 'The trial is a sham'; 'The amendment is illegal'; 'The trial committee is biased'; 'The trial is part of a plot to destroy Mine-Mill'; 'Red-baiting is the weapon of reaction'; 'Autonomy-cornerstone of CIO policy'; 'Mine-Mill has organized its industry'; 'Who is really violating CIO policy'; 'Preserving the autonomy and democracy of Mine-Mill.' In its very defense, therefore, the Union faithfully parrots the dictates of the Communist Party.

Following the expulsion of the union, the Steelworkers set out to undermine its strength. Philip Murray expected that the task would not be too difficult, but the efforts to take away the IUMMSW membership met with disappointment. The Mine, Mill and Smelterworkers Union leadership had signed the non-Communist affidavit under the Taft-Hartley Law and thus qualified to be placed on the ballot of National Labor Relations Board elections. An intensive drive was made by the Steelworkers union to defeat the expelled union in their largest local in Butte, Montana. An election held in 1954, however, gave a majority to the independent union and thus set the Steelworkers back sharply. Another key election in 1956 also favored Mine, Mill against the Steelworkers.

The future of the union, however, still remained uncertain. Late in 1954, a National Labor Relations Board examiner ruled specifically that when Maurice Travis, Secretary-Treasurer of the union since 1948, signed the Taft-Hartley non-Communist affidavit he had done so falsely, and that the union was in non-compliance because the members knew of its falsity. The examiner based his ruling largely on a union newspaper article over Travis' signature in 1949, soon after Travis signed his first non-communist affidavit. at that time Travis stated that he "had resigned from the Communist Party to make it possible for him to execute his affidavit ... but he nevertheless continued to believe in the principles of Communism and the Communist Party." The examiner stated: "There is no evidence that Travis has since altered his allegiance to the Communist Party or his loyalty to beliefs in Communism."

The National Labor Relations Board supported its examiner but was overruled in this case and in another case affecting Ben Gold of the Fur Workers Union by the United States Supreme

Court, which held that the NLRB could not disqualify a union from having its name on an election ballot if its officers falsely filed affidavits. Had the NLRB position been upheld, the union would have been in grave difficulty in the competition for membership.[59]

Before leaving the story of the relationship between the CIO and the International Union of Mine, Mill and Smelter Workers, it is important to examine briefly the activities of two former union officials who testified at hearings before the Potofsky-Curran-Mazey Committee. Their lives reveal something of the operations of the Communist party within a union and the impact of those operations on the individuals caught in the net.

First is Homer Wilson, who lived in Strawberry Plains, Tennessee. He became a member of the Mine, Mill and Smelter Workers Union in October, 1934, when that union was affiliated with the AFL. His fellow members and mine workers elected him to serve first as union committeeman and then as local union president. As a local president, he became acquainted with staff members of the union. They told him that they belonged to the Communist party and discussed party activities in his presence. They were men of superior education who impressed him. In 1941, they invited him to become an international organizer. In 1942, he was elected to represent the Southern District as a member of the international Executive Board. He assumed office in January, 1943, working out of the Alabama office.

> As quick as I got down there, Mrs. Franz and Alton Laurence invited me to lunch with them along with Mr. Rob Hall, who was an organizer for the Communist Party. I had lunch with them, and we discussed problems then facing the Mine, Mill and Smelter Workers in that area, and they also pointed out to me their contacts throughout the International Union.[60]

Wilson was impressed with the fact that the party had a great deal of influence within the union and that "it would be to my advantage to join the Party." He apparently did not formally join, but "I give it a lot of consideration." The Communist Party at this time strongly supported the war and was thoroughly patriotic. There was, therefore, no reason for Wilson to see any conflict between his American loyalties and his friendship for the Communist party.

One other factor impressed him. "This Mr. Hall that was the party organizer was a very highly educated man, and I liked to associate with him at that time. In fact, I got him to help me with a report I had to draw up for a district conference, and he did a very good job on it." Mr. Hall seemed accustomed to these chores for the unions as part of his party activities: "he said he done that for all of the Mine-Mill organizers, and some other CIO unions in that area."

When Mr. Wilson became a member of the union's Executive Board in January, 1943, he joined the pro-Communist caucus, since it seemed to be the pattern and it brought him prestige, influence, and the satisfaction of associating with better educated people. Nor did it begin to embarrass him before 1946, for his union's policies were strongly in support of his government's policies.

The life of our second man, Kenneth Eckert, tells a more sophisticated and interesting story.[61] Eckert was born and raised in Toledo, Ohio. He worked on a railroad until 1930 but during the depression was laid off along with thousands of others. He joined an organization called the Unemployment Councils in Toledo, which he later found was organized by the Communist party to promote the interests of the unemployed. Its announced aims seemed worthy. The councils wanted to obtain unemployment relief, and sought to find homes for the evicted.

> I found out later, however, when I came to learn more about these things, that the misery and grief of the unemployed, and the organizations created to capitalize on that, that the intention was merely to use those organizations as a transmission belt, as has often been said, and said originally by Lenin, in order to carry out the policies of the Communist Party, and extend them to a broader mass of people who could be brought into such an organization but would not be ready to accept the program of the Communist Party as such.

Eckert soon became head of the organization and led many of its demonstrations. He organized a camp of unemployed on the Toledo courthouse lawn at the time of an American Legion convention. Later, in his own township of Washington, where relief had been cut off, he helped organize about a thousand people who walked into the largest store of a food market chain in Toledo "and cleaned it out."

Following these activities, early in 1932, Eckert accepted an invitation to join the Communist party, although he had "very little or no knowledge of what it stood for, its principles, or (knew) very much about it." He had, however, some knowledge "of the broad concept of socialism, my former father-in-law having been a member of the Socialist party during the first World War and after that for some time."

Within a few months, he was approached by the District Organizer of the Communist party in Toledo, B. D. Amos, who informed him that he had been selected by the party to attend a party school. Eckert welcomed the opportunity, although he did not know the school's location. It developed that the school was the International Lenin School at Moscow, "located on Vorofskaya Street, the former palace of one of the favorites of Catherine the Great, who had had it built for one of her lovers, Pushkin."

Eckert spent fourteen months at the Lenin School. When he returned, Communist leader, John Williamson, told him to resume his activities in the unemployed movement. In Toledo, however, he was assigned to become an organizer for the Trade Union Unity League in the automobile industry. He also organized a local in Toledo and participated in other labor disputes. In 1934, the *Literary Digest* accused Eckert and Louis Budenz of leading the violent Electric Auto Lite strike.

His next assignment was as secretary of the Communist party in Toledo where he stayed until the Trotskyite trials in Russia, when he was removed from his post for alleged Trotskyite tendencies then went to the west coast and to sea. Later he returned to Michigan where he became an organizer for the National Associattion of Die Casting Workers, and then Chicago regional director for that union.

Within a few years, a controversy arose within the union on the question of affiliation with the CIO United Mine, Mill and Smelter Workers Union. The Communist party "was very desirous of seeing this merger effected," and it tentatively took place in 1942. Eckert explained the reason for the Communist position in these words:

... the leader of the Mine, Mill and Smelter Workers, Reid Robinson, whom they regarded as a very progressive leader, was in danger of losing the leadership of that Union because of a very large opposition which had developed in the Union, and that by merging the Die Casters with the Mine, Mill and Smelter Workers—the staff of the Die Casters was almost exclusively members of the Party, therefore exercised a great deal of influence on the locals of the Die Casters—thereby bringing the Die Casters into the Mine, Mill and Smelter Workers and make it possible for Reid Robinson and others in the leadership of Mine, Mill to keep that union in the column of those unions which could be counted on to carry out the line of the Communist party ...

The merger was difficult to complete as opposition to it developed from within the Die Casters. Eckert, a staff member, when asked his opinion, wired a Die Casters merger meeting expressing opposition to the merger, in spite of the Communist position. He was, therefore, kept from the meeting, which decided to go ahead with the merger.

Shortly after this occurred, Eckert entered the army and spent a year overseas. His service brought him in contact with a large number of Russian displaced persons. This, he said, helped cause him to break intellectually with the Communist Party, even though the organizational break didn't come until later. He queried, with his "smattering of Russian and a few words in German," all Russians he could meet "to find out pretty much just what things were like" since he had been in Russia in 1933.[62]

Eckert also seemed to be bothered by Earl Browder's expulsion from the Communist Party. All of this caused him to be

... very, very dubious if the Communist Party would ever or could ever with its structure establish any kind of a socialistic society. These feelings also were intensified by the terrific hostility manifested by the Communist Party toward any other organization which might also have social objectives but believed that they should be obtained by evolutionary methods instead of revolutionary methods, if it can be put that way, the British Labor Party, for example, the Socialist Party in this country, and so on.

Following the war, the Communist Party again made overtures to Eckert, who was reinstated to membership and became active.

I never actively took a positive step, but more or less I did in fact become a member again, a very active one, so active, in fact, that I was one of the committee of four which was the Party steering committee in the Mine, Mill and Smelter Workers. The committee was Maurice Travis, Al Skinner, who was International Representative of Mine, Mill, and Chase Powers, who was the Board member of District 7 from the West Coast. This Party steering committee was the committee that brought the Party decisions on major matters which affected Party policy to the caucus, known as the Progressive Caucus inside the Mine, Mill and Smelter Workers.

Eckert's final summary to the CIO investigating committee is likewise worth quoting from for a further understanding of the operations of Communist control within labor unons.[63]

To summarize what I have said here, gentlemen of the Committee, I have tried to show here insofar as I have personal knowledge of these events, and insofar as I have been personally involved in them, that the allegations made against the union are correct, are absolutely true. The Communist Party, through having counseled the leadership, through its influence in the leadership of this union, first of all through the top leadership, and secondly, this leadership, who hired the staff members—these staff members, who are in almost every instance members of the Communist Party, are the people who negotiate the contracts for the rank and file, for the local unions, who are the people who are able to influence the people in the local unions. It is this machine set up, top leaders of the organization down through the staff members, who are able to transmit the decisions from these people outside the union to the union itself, and to make it the policy of this Mine-Mill and Smelter Workers. It is by that method, followed over a considerable number of years in Mine-Mill, that builds the record, as I stated in my opening remarks, for anyone to see where the policy of the Mine, Mill and Smelter Workers deviates not one iota from the position of the Communist Party, although as I said previously, many people sincerely believe that they are following the correct policy.

[1] CIO, *The Report of the Executive Board Committee Appointed by President Murray to Investigate Charges Against the United Office and Professional Workers of America* (mimeographed).
[2] *Supra*, pp. 96-100.
[3] CIO, *Report of Committee to Investigate UOPWA, op. cit.*, pp. 12-14.
[4] *Daily Worker*, December 6-9, 1949.

[5] CIO, *Report of Executive Board Committee Appointed by President Murray to Conduct Hearings on United Public Workers of America* (mimeographed), p. 10.
[6] *Ibid.*, pp. 13-16.
[7] *Ibid.*, p. 29.
[8] House Report 1311, 78th Congress, 2nd Session, *op. cit.*, pp. 108-112.
[9] Testimony of Charles Rindone before CIO committee investigating charges against UOPWA, *op. cit.*, p. 19.
[10] House Report 1311, 78th Congress, 2nd Session, *op. cit.*, pp. 110-111.
[11] CIO Fourth Constitutional Convention, *op. cit.*, p. 157.
[12] House Report 1311, 78th Congress, 2nd Session, *op. cit.*, p. 121.
[13] *Supra*, p. 25.
[14] CIO Fourth Constitutional Convention, *op. cit.*, p. 237.
[15] House Report 1311, 78th Congress, 2nd Session, *op. cit.*, pp. 141-143.
[16] CIO, *Report of the Committee to Investigate Charges Against The Food, Tobacco, Agricultural and Allied Workers of America* (mimeographed), p. 13.
[17] *Ibid.*, p. 11.
[18] *Ibid.*, p. 8.
[19] Earl Browder, *Communism in the United States* (International Publishers: New York, 1935), p. 184.
[20] House Report 1311, 78th Congress, 2nd Session, *op. cit.*, p. 118.
[21] See p. 239 below.
[22] CIO, *Report of the Committee to Investigate Charges Against the International Union of Mine, Mill and Smelter Workers* (mimeographed).
[23] Avery, "Communist Power in U. S. Industry," *op. cit.*
[24] CIO, *Hearings to Investigate Mine, Mill. op. cit.*, pp. 182, 183.
[25] *Ibid.*, pp. 196, 197.
[26] *Ibid.*, pp. 186, 187.
[27] House Report 1311, 78th Congress, 2nd Session, *op. cit.*, pp. 162, 163.
[28] CIO, *Report of Committee to Investigate IUMMSWA, op. cit.*, p. 6.
[29] CIO, *Hearings to Investigate IUMMSWA, op. cit.*, pp. 68, 69.
[30] *Ibid.*, pp. 70, 71.
[31] *Ibid.*, pp. 72, 73.
[32] *Daily Worker*, September 2, 1940.
[33] CIO, *Hearings to Investigate IUMMSWA, op. cit.*, p. 77.
[34] *Ibid.*, pp. 73-76.
[35] *Daily Worker*, February 28, 1941.
[36] CIO, *Hearings to Investigate IUMMSWA, op. cit.*, pp. 82, 83.
[37] *Ibid.*, pp. 73-75, 80, 81.
[38] *Ibid.*, pp. 84, 85.
[39] *Ibid.*, pp. 88-90.
[40] *Daily Worker*, June 11, 1943.
[41] CIO, *Hearings to Investigate IUMMSWA, op. cit.*, pp. 92-95.
[42] *Ibid.*, pp. 102, 103.
[43] CIO, *Report of Committee to Investigate IUMMSWA, op. cit.*, p. 8.
[44] CIO, *Hearings to Investigate IUMMSWA, op. cit.*, pp. 106, 107.
[45] CIO, *Report of Committee to Investigate IUMMSWA, op. cit.*, p. 8.
[46] CIO, *Hearings to Investigate IUMMSWA, op. cit.*, p. 114.
[47] CIO, *Report of Committee to Investigate IUMMSWA, op. cit.*, p. 8.
[48] CIO, *Hearings to Investigate IUMMSWA, op. cit.*, p. 144.

[49] Samuel Romer, "Disruption in CIO," *The New Leader,* September 6, 1947.

[50] CIO Committee Appointed to Investigate Break Within the International Union of Mine, Mill and Smelter Workers, *Report to President Murray,* May 16, 17, 1947, pp. 8, 9, 10, 14, 15.

[51] *The New York Times,* October 11, 1947.

[52] Romer, *op. cit.*

[53] CIO, *Hearings to Investigate IUMMSWA, op. cit.,* pp. 127, 128.

[54] CIO, *Report of Committee to Investigate IUMMSWA, op. cit.,* p. 8.

[55] CIO, *Hearings to Investigate IUMMSWA, op. cit.,* pp. 12-19.

[56] *Ibid.,* p. 353.

[57] CIO, *Report of Committee to Investigate IUMMSWA, op. cit.,* p. 14.

[58] *Ibid.,* p. 15.

[59] *The New York Times,* December 11, 1956.

[60] CIO, *Hearings before Committee to Investigate IUMMSWA, op. cit.,* pp. 139-143.

[61] *Ibid.,* pp. 168-181, 210-211.

[62] *Ibid.,* pp. 178-180.

[63] *Ibid.,* pp. 210, 211.

13

THE FORMAL CASES AGAINST THE COMMUNIST-DOMINATED UNIONS · II

Following the expulsion of the four unions just discussed, a second series of hearings began.

AMERICAN COMMUNICATIONS ASSOCIATION

On April 11th and 12th, 1950, the committee appointed to investigate the American Communications Association opened its formal hearings. The history of the American Communications Association, and its political activities, paralleled those of the other pro-Communist unions in the CIO. Its predecessor organizations had been the Radio Telegraphists Association, which was captured by Communist leadership very early. The first president of the CIO union was Mervyn Rathborne, whose career in the union was a puzzling but revealing one.

Rathborne joined the Radio Telegraphists Association when it was first organized in 1931. In October, 1932, he resigned from the organization, expressing dissatisfaction with its methods and policies. Thereafter he rejoined the Association and then became a candidate for the post of secretary-treasurer on an anti-Communist ticket. In a letter dated November 9, 1934, he charged the Communists within the union with sabotaging and disrupting the organization; in another letter of December 11, 1934, he said, "the nature of the Communist obliges him to carry on underhanded intrigues, plots, and plans in any other non-Communistic organization." Rathborne charged that the ARTA was "in danger of being dominated and run by a small but powerful group of Communists" and supported his charge by referring to some of the union's resolutions endorsing the Congress Against War and Fascism.

Suddenly, Rathborne declared that he had been advised by his opponents that his "well-being and health would continue to be good" only if he withdrew from the race for secretary-treasurer. His magazine, *C.Q.*, which had been a severe critic of the Communists, ceased its criticism and in 1935 began to support them. Soon thereafter, Hoyt Haddock,[1] retiring president of the union and a spokesman for the pro-Communist position, recommended Rathborne for the presidency. There was evidence that Rathborne became a member of the Communist party and an important Communist maritime figure. It is clear that he joined the gamut of "front organizations," including the American League Against War and Fascism, which he had earlier attacked.[2]

Rathborne became an associate of Harry Bridges on the west coast, and secretary of District No. 2 of the Maritime Federation of the Pacific, dominated by Bridges. He came to New York in 1937, where he served as president of the ARTA and as president of the New York Maritime Council. When the ACA succeeded the ARTA in August, 1937, Rathborne continued as president until October, 1940, when he resigned, claiming illness. He later appeared again as secretary-treasurer of the California State CIO, at a time when that Council was under pro-Communist leadership.

Joseph P. Selly succeeded Rathborne as international president of the American Communications Association. He had not been either a telegraph or a radio operator, but had come to the union from the Federation of Architects, Engineers, Chemists, and Technicians. He had taken a course in architecture at Cornell University and thus qualified for membership in the union as a draftsman. In 1937, he was appointed an organizer in the ARTA. He served as vice-president of its successor, the ACA, for a while and then became president.

The link between the ACA and the Communist party was referred to by a number of the union's members and ex-members over the years. Benjamin Stolberg referred to the union as "under the complete control—without any effective opposition of Stalinist officers."[3] Joseph Zack, former member of the Communist Party central executive committee, likewise testified to that effect.[4]

The ACA, under both Rathborne and Selly, followed the

Communist party line. At its 1938 convention, it supported Roosevelt's speech calling for quarantining the aggressors and wanted to amend the Neutrality Act. Following the Russo-German Pact, it became isolationist and in April, 1940, when the Nazi armies were seizing Denmark and Norway, Rathborne asserted the war "is being fought for nothing but profit."[5] When Selly assumed office, he likewise reported: ". . . We hear a lot of words spoken about 'necessary sacrifices' and 'national unity'. . . .But we want to know what for."[6]

During this period, the union found itself in some difficulty because of legislative efforts to prevent sabotage on board American vessels. One bill was introduced authorizing the Federal Communications Commission to suspend the license of any radio officer who might be suspected of membership in the Communist party, the German American Bund, or any organization "subject to foreign control." Another bill would have prohibited the distribution of subversive literature on merchant vessels and also establish citizenship requirements for seamen aboard American vessels. The FCC proposed to photograph and fingerprint all employees of communication companies actually engaged in the communication process. The union opposed all these proposals.

The Congress, however, did enact Public Law 351 in 1941, providing for the elimination of subversive radio operators from the merchant marine. This led the FCC to remove from ships about 40 ACA members as subversive. Following severe criticism by a number of CIO unions, however, and following the change in the Communist line so that the ACA wholeheartedly supported the war effort, the FCC reinstated in 1942 a number of those suspended.[7]

The shift in the union's position was striking after the June 22, 1941 invasion of Russia by Germany. The ACA Executive Board had met on June 16 and 17 and reaffirmed its opposition to war and Roosevelt's foreign policy. On June 22, the invasion took place. On June 28, a special meeting of the executive board was called which asserted, "Our union has always opposed fascism"; called upon the administration "to give full aid to the Soviet Union, Great Britain, and all other nations opposing Hitlerism"; and condemned those "who are still flirting with the idea of appeasing Hitler."[8]

From that point to the end of the war, the pattern was the same: "second front," "Teheran," "the enlightened section of capital." This was then followed, after V-J Day, with criticisms of the United States, praise of "democratic Chinese forces," excoriation of "big business... American imperialism," praise for Henry Wallace. The "Hell-bent-for war paragraph-troopers of the newspaper industry and the get-tough-with-Russia-at-any-cost swivel chair political generals" were blamed for the international tensions.

At the national CIO conventions, Selly and secretary-treasurer Kehoe began to take public issue with the national CIO leadership. At the 1948 Portland convention, Selly spoke against the Marshall Plan and against aid to China and Greece. Soon after that convention, the union, sensing the future, began to demand "respect" for the "autonomy" of the affiliated unions and, in fact, supported the Farm Equipment Workers Union in its refusal to comply with the CIO's directive to merge with the UAW. The ACA also strongly protested the CIO's withdrawal from the World Federation of Trade Unions.

With the November, 1949 convention of the CIO, the die was cast. The ACA criticized the convention's expulsion of the UE and then Selly commented on the forthcoming CIO hearings against Communism as follows:[9]

> The question must reasonably be asked, 'Why does the powerful CIO descend to such vicious un-democratic procedures? What are they trying to hide?' The 'trials' increasingly reveal that the leadership of the CIO, like all power-hungry people who resort to un-democratic oppression, do it for the purpose of concealing their own crimes against the working people of America. These people have abandoned the principal objective and policies of the CIO, which ACA helped to establish.

The CIO revoked the ACA charter at the recommendation of the Executive Board committee which held the hearings.

Following the expulsion of the ACA, the national CIO encouraged pro-CIO elements in ACA to join Steinberg's American Radio Association, an offshoot of the already weakened ACA, which had been chartered on May 21, 1948.

HARRY BRIDGES AND WEST COAST SHIPPING

The west coast shipping industry was one of the most important locales of Communist influence in union organization investigated by the CIO.

In any discussion of the CIO and west coast shipping the name of Harry Bridges looms large. Born in Australia, he came to the United States in 1920 as a seaman and settled down as a dockworker. A haze surrounds the details of his life between his arrival in the United States and the 1934 waterfront strike, but it is known that he was involved in the publication of *The Waterfront Worker,* a militant bulletin advancing the Communist party position, which first appeared secretly in 1932 as a mimeographed sheet on the San Francisco waterfront. In describing the 1934 strike Minton and Stuart, a writing team allied to the Communists, said:[10]

> . . . The Red scare fell on deaf ears. 'I neither affirm nor deny that I am a Communist,' Bridges replied to newspaper charges, and pointed out that political beliefs had nothing to do with the issues of the strike.
>
> Yet Bridges did not hesitate to accept aid from the Communist Party. Two years later, John L. Lewis also learned to welcome all support from workers regardless of their political affiliations. To Harry Bridges, it was obvious that the Communist Party would not only cooperate wholeheartedly and effectively with the maritime workers, but could also give invaluable advice on the conduct and development of the strike. In addition, the rank and file of the waterfront unions found that the Communist workers were the most militant, the most self-sacrificing, and the most consistent element in their ranks. The membership of the various unions adopted the *Western Worker,* official party organ, as the official newspaper of the strikers.

With the advent of the NRA, a longshoremen's local was formed on the west coast which received a charter from the International Longshoremen's Association. The new union demanded control of hiring halls, better wages and conditions, and went on strike in 1934 when the demands were refused. The sailors quickly joined the longshoremen and a Joint Marine Strike Committee was formed under Bridges' leadership. When the police intervened and two pickets were killed, a protest general strike of 147,000 workers was launched in San Francisco on July 17th. The strike crumbled, but the union finally won its hiring halls.[11] In June, 1936, Harry Bridges took over the Pacific District of the ILA, and was elected president of the West Coast district of the International Longshoremen's Association. He was, of course, a strong advocate of industrial unionism. In June, 1937, he led the members of many maritime unions, federated in the Maritime Federation of the Pacific, into the CIO.

Bridges' Communist affiliations have been a source of public and judicial controversy for many years. On March 2, 1938, a warrant for his arrest was issued by the U.S. Department of Labor, which had jurisdiction over immigration matters at that time. Hearings were conducted by Harvard Law School Dean James M. Landis from July 10 to September 14, 1939. In a decision released December 29th, Landis concluded:[12]

> That Bridges' aims are energetically radical may be admitted but the proof fails to establish that the methods he seeks to employ to realize them are other than those that the framework of democratic and constitutional Government permits.

Landis took note of Bridges' "opposition toward 'red-baiting'; his acceptance of aid and assistance in his industrial struggles from the Communist party—indeed, his solicitation of that aid; his expressed disinclination to disavow that help; his "association with persons admittedly Communists . . ."; but he stated this evidence "falls short of the statutory definition of affiliation." He concluded: "The evidence therefore establishes neither that Harry R. Bridges is a member of nor affiliated with the Communist Party of the United States of America."

It wasn't until May 28, 1942, following the second hearing before Judge Charles B. Sears from March 31 to June 12, 1941, that the United States Government, through Attorney General Francis Biddle, ruled: "that after entering the United States the alien had been affiliated with the Communist Party."

Judge Sears had pointed out that Bridges'

> . . . cooperative and sympathetic attitude toward various Front Organizations of the Communist Party and toward certain Communist-sponsored programs and policies . . . viewed as a whole, form a pattern which is more consistent with the conclusion that the alien followed his course of conduct as an affiliate of the Communist Party, rather than as a matter of coincidence.

Meanwhile, Bridges was being both attacked and defended recklessly. Bridges Defense Committees were set up all over the country. CIO officials and unions, non-Communist as well as fellow-traveler, lent their names and energies to oppose what they considered to be anti-labor attacks. James B. Carey, who was later to spearhead the drive to rid the CIO of Communists, in commenting on Estolv E. Ward's pro-Bridges hero-worshipping account of the Landis trial said:[13]

> I had planned to read a few chapters of this book and then glance through the rest; but I read every word of it. It reveals vividly the colossal forces locked in struggle behind the facade of the 'trial' of Harry Bridges. Today, as in the days of Christ, the world finds those self-sacrificing leaders of men it so badly needs largely among the ranks of people who work for a living.

A number of the pro-Communist unions in the CIO used the Bridges trial to portray Communism in a favorable light. This is best illustrated by a story in the August-September, 1939 issue of *Government Guide,* official newspaper of the SCMWA. Reporting on the trial, the story was headed "Bridges Trial Educates America," and it said:[14]

> What (Communists) do teach, according to these witnesses, is this: As the people of a nation, victimized more and more by unemployment and a lower standard of living, (attendant on the inevitable decay of capitalism), utilized their democratic form of government to improve their conditions by passing more and more legislation of a social and socialistic character, the minority who owns the means of production will engineer a violent anti-democratic revolution. In such an event the people will defend themselves, and their government and, as a defense measure, take over the means of production. The Communist Party, the witnesses said, teaches that the people should be prepared to meet such a situation so that they would be victorious in the struggle.

One of the first CIO unions to break away from the defense of Harry Bridges was the American Newspaper Guild, whose executive board in 1945 declined a request to participate in a "Harry Bridges Victory Committee." President Milton Murray explained:[15]

In the first instance, some years ago it appeared that the attack on Harry Bridges was an attack upon him because of his labor activities. In the light of that attack, I was one of his defenders. I thought it incumbent upon all labor to resist such an attack for such a purpose. Subsequent developments have made it clear that Harry Bridges is not a leader of labor. He is a mis-leader, and he is a wrecker of honest trade unionism. He has demonstrated this on the West Coast, where he has flouted the established and announced policies of the CIO.

At a time when national service legislation was proposed and was being desperately opposed by the CIO, Harry Bridges took it upon himself to support that legislation. At a time when labor is struggling desperately to maintain its no-strike pledge under extreme provocation, and solely because of labor's intention to win this war in spite of the Averys and the Girdlers, Harry Bridges sold out the working people of this country with a quisling announcement that he favored continuation of the no-strike pledge after the war.

At a time when the United Retail, Wholesale and Department Store Employees were struggling to oppose the most fascistic and reactionary elements in our country, Harry Bridges and certain elements in the organization which he leads, allied themselves with those fascistic and reactionary elements and did their utmost to destroy the efforts of honest trade unionists.

I see no compulsion upon us or upon any other believers in trade unionism to support, in any fashion whatsoever, this quisling in our ranks. I therefore oppose taking any action in favor of Harry Bridges.

All during this time Bridges was building up a strong union on the west coast, gaining power in the CIO, and forming alliances with other pro-Communist leaders. He participated "in numerous secret meetings" at which Communist Party functionaries "instructed the union officers as to the Party line and as to the positions that they were to take in the CIO and in their unions."[16]

M. Hedley Stone, National Maritime Union officer who was an active member of the caucus, later testified that the first meeting of the caucus in the CIO took place in late 1937 "to discuss the setting up of a longshore organizing committee on the East Coast to take over Ryan's (AFL) outfit."[17] Bridges was present at the meeting, as was Roy Hudson and Al Lannin, "a waterfront section organizer, and at that time a member of the National Committee of the CP," who was to be in charge of the drive.

Stone called the meeting "a closed meeting of the Communist Party," said the decision to appoint Lannin was made by Hudson, whom he identified as "a party functionary ... in charge of the waterfront activities for the entire United States." He also said that ninety percent of the people who went to work as organizers in the union drive "were members of the Communist Party, attended unit meetings, were given directives." Later in 1942 and 1943, when it became clear that the longshore drive on the east coast had failed, Bridges entered into negotiations with Arthur Osman, head of Local 65 of the CIO Retail, Wholesale, and Department Store Workers Union, whereby Local 65 would leave its own international and join the ILWU. This, Stone said, was worked out at Communist strategy meetings and was "in order to give the ILWU a solid base on the East Coast."[18]

Stone also reported that in 1939 during the CIO convention in San Francisco, he and Bridges attended a meeting of the CIO Communist Party fraction at the Whitcomb Hotel and that similar meetings were held at every CIO convention and at most of the CIO Executive Board meetings.[19] Stone also made it clear, however, that although he believed that those present, including Bridges, were members of the Communist Party, he "could not swear that they were dues-paying members."[20] He was himself a dues-paying member and he assumed the others were as well. Furthermore, he specifically declared that he believed Bridges to be a member.[21]

The fraction, Stone said, prepared very carefully for its activities within the CIO. Its members agreed on resolutions beforehand and distributed speaking assignments for the convention floor or the board meetings. In this connection it is of interest to quote an exchange between Stone and William Steinberg, president of the CIO American Radio Association who questioned Stone at the ILWU trial: [22]

Q. Did any of the people, any of the trade union leaders at these particular meetings ever raise the question with the party people that they couldn't carry out the party wishes until they had secured permission from their rank and file?

A. No. Our job was to get it carried out. The rank and file would always accept a program that we handed down. The proof of the pudding is in the record of our respective unions up to the

time where those of us that were Party leaders and trade union
leaders, when we didn't take the Party line, why it just didn't
go down, and there wasn't any revolution in the rank and file.

Q. Then you might say that trade union leaders, representatives of
international unions who attended these Party meetings, had
the duty to carry out these Party decisions and do everything in
their power to see that the rank and file went along with it. Is
that correct?

A. That's right.

Q. And if it ever happened that in some session of one of the
International unions the rank and file happened to vote against
that proposition would you say that that would be an unusual
happening?

A. Very unusual. . . .

Q. Can you say as a former member of the Communist Party that
it was the duty of each communist to resort to all sorts of strata-
gems, maneuvers, illegal methods, evasion and subterfuge in
order to penetrate the trade unions, to remain in them and to
carry on Communist work in them at all costs?

A. Well, I had a personal experience on that. I believed in the
sincerity of the thing and when I went into this thing I wanted
to be known as a communist. I went to Roy Hudson, who was
the head guy in that particular phase. I also talked to Jack
Stachel on it, and I said: 'I think I should come out and declare
myself openly as a Communist.' He laughed and he said: 'You
certainly won't be helping the cause if you do that. We will tell
when we are ready to have you come out in the open as a communist.' And so it was with those that I had known . . .

An analysis of the ILWU's public policy statement showed
further close correlation with the official position of the Communist
party "line." Prior to the Stalin-Hitler Pact, the union supported
Roosevelt's foreign policy and called for amendments to the Neutrality Act designed to permit the shipment of arms to Europe: it
called for the boycott of Germany; condemned isolationism; and
as late as June, 1939 requested closer collaboration between the
U.S. and the USSR "for the protection of their mutual interests
against any provocation within the Rome-Berlin Tokyo Axis."[23]

This position was suddenly reversed after the Nazi-Soviet Pact,
and Roosevelt was attacked for giving assistance to the Allies,
"while millions of Americans suffer unemployment and poverty."
Bridges declared in April, 1940 that the U.S. "can have no

concern" in the war "except the protection of the investments of the large bankers and industrial interests of the country."[24] The union adopted the slogan, "The Yanks Are Not Coming," and helped sponsor the American Peace Mobilization.

When Germany attacked Russia in June, 1941 and the initials "APM" came to mean American People's Mobilization, Bridges and his union followed suit and adopted the war. The union became a "win-the-war agency." Not only did they now reverse themselves and support convoys, but the ILWU in fact urged that our country join the war even before Pearl Harbor. Bridges said:[25]

> ... the American trade unions have a real decision to face and make today. We are on the verge of having to start making motions or passing resolutions as to whether we shall not only support the President in an actual declaration of war to stop Hitler, but as to whether we will insist that such a declaration be made.

Only a few short months before the invasion, the ILWU had supported John L. Lewis at the 1940 CIO convention and had encouraged him in his opposition to Roosevelt. Lewis, however, soon became "the single most effective agent of the Fascist powers within the ranks of labor," and a "black disgrace to the laboring men and women of America."[26]

Meanwhile, the union declared that war unity meant the subservience of the union's "economic agency" function. "No longer do we think of employers as a group. Our judgement of employers is predicated on their participation in the war." Wages, hours, and working conditions "had to be measured in terms of maintaining efficiency and morale of our members and providing a free flow of war production." We have seen how the ILWU, during this period, helped break a strike against Montgomery Ward sponsored by the Retail, Wholesale, and Department Store Union[27].

The proposed National Service Act was supported in January, 1944 in spite of the national CIO's opposition to the program, because "The right of the people to be secure against the enemy certainly transcends any fancied individual rights." The ILWU also urged that the wartime no-strike pledge be extended into peace time.[28]

By 1946, however, and the collapse of wartime collaboration

between the Soviet Union and the United States, the ILWU began declaring, as it did in an issue of *The Dispatcher,* its newspaper, "Strike time is here." Harry Bridges opposed a loan to Britain on the ground that "the so-called British Labor Government has made it crystal clear that it has no intention of freeing the slave peoples now held captive by the Empire." Britain, he said, would use the money against Russia, which "exploits no colonies of its own and seeks to exploit none," and is naturally in favor of freedom and independence for all peoples."[29]

The ILWU declared in 1947 that the Truman Plan for Greek and Turkish aid was akin to "international gangsterism of Hitler." An editorial in *The Dispatcher* said the aid program would keep "those two Fascist-type governments in power" and "permit them to keep the people in subjugation and prevent the rise of any kind of democracy."[30] Later, the union said that "Truman's real purpose is to strengthen the hold of American monopoly on Middle East oil and to relieve the British Empire of a burden it can no longer bear."[31]

The ILWU policy was also one of support for the Communists in China. Speaking at the 1947 ILWU convention, Bridges said:[32] "If the Communists of China are wrong, so were the people in this country who overthrew the British in the American Revolution."[33]

When the Marshall Plan was announced it was condemned as a "monstrous plot against freedom and living standards," and an attempt to impose "Wall Street puppet dictatorship," as compared to the program of the Soviet Union which supported "coalition governments of nations which are pledged to programs whereby the common people of foreign countries obtain greater ownership and control of raw materials and protection for the greater good of the majority of the peoples of those countries." Our State Department, the union said, "does not speak for or in the interest of the American worker and people."[34]

Henry Wallace became an ILWU hero during this period. When the CIO Executive Board, in January, 1948, announced its support of the Marshall Plan and its opposition to a third Party, Bridges replied that the "ILWU would stand by its determination to give all-out support to the Third Party movement and would continue to oppose the Marshall Plan."

It was these issues, as we have seen, which served to dramatize the growing split within the CIO and which irrevocably separated the ILWU from the national leadership of the CIO. The split on these issues extended itself throughout the trade union structure, and transcended traditional CIO loyalties to such an extent that Harry Bridges supported the efforts of a group of insurgent pro-Communist locals to withdraw from the CIO American Radio Association and join the AFL.

The American Radio Association had been chartered by the CIO on May 21, 1948, to offset the pro-Communist American Communications Association. The leaders of the ARA were anti-Communist, with the result that a group of pro-Communist west coast insurgents explored the possibility of leaving the CIO for the AFL International Brotherhood of Electrical Workers. They consulted with Harry Bridges. The Minutes of a May 22, 1948 meeting held by the insurgents reads: "The discussion was held to determine whether or not the Radio officers could be assured the continued support of the ILWU in case the Radio officers decided to affiliate with the IBEW." The minutes show that Bridges gave them assurances of support: "The shipowners may not recognize the Radio operators in their present status but the unions would."[35]

Bridges never reported his conversations to the leaders of the CIO or the ARA. When in June, the following month, ARA head, Steinberg, went to Bridges for help against the insurgents, he was refused. Steinberg reported the conversation as follows: "Bridges told me point blank, he said, 'Look, we do not support unions on the basis of their affiliation, whether they are CIO or AFL, or independent. The only reason we support unions is on the basis of their program.' "

Steinberg asked for further explanation: "Harry said, 'Well, we have the issue of the Third Party; we support the Third Party. We have the issue of the Marshall Plan. We oppose the Marshall Plan.' "

In view of Bridges' attitude, Allan Haywood, national CIO vice-president and director of organization, wired him in July to adhere to CIO loyalties.

On August 11, the ARA pro-IBEW insurgents wired Steinberg: "... any communication which you may wish to address to this organization relative to any matter will be accepted only when and if contents of same are preferred in writing to us to the International Office of the ILWU acting as your intermediary." This led Steinberg, on August 19, to write CIO regional director, Tim Flynn: "It is a well known fact that the key people leading the AFL move are closely allied politically with Bridges in the third party movement...." Steinberg later was the one who in 1949, at the CIO national Executive Board meeting, moved that the pro-Communist international unions be tried for violating the CIO constitution.

Throughout this period, the ILWU continued to support the Soviet Union and its policies.[36] The union opposed the Baruch proposals for atomic control. It declared the North Atlantic Pact would permit the United States to dominate Europe. It applauded the Communist coup in Czechoslovakia as an ousting of "reactionaries." It said Russia's Berlin blockade was nothing more than an attempt to preseve the Potsdam Agreement. It supported the Russian-dominated World Federation of Trade Unions and called the CIO withdrawal from the organization a "sellout of American workers." It viewed the Chinese Communist revolution as "creating a new force of unprecedented proportions and turning it to the satisfaction of human needs."

ILWU speeches, resolutions, and publications also reflected a tendency to Stalinist terminology in addition to a sympathy for the Soviet Union. *The Dispatcher's*[37] strongest term of opprobrium, for example, was "Trotskyite" and "Norman Thomas Socialist." The Soviet satellites in Europe and China were called "peoples' democracy." When the Soviet Union declared it was granting autonomous rights to its constituent republics, Bridges wrote:[38]

> The vicious lie that both philisophies (i.e. Communism and fascism) have the same basic anti-democratic totalitarian foundation was never more clearly exposed than by the willingness and the determination of the Soviet Union to allow each of its component republics full freedom to choose its way of life and granting full equality for all the people in such republics regardless of race, creed, or color.

During the war, the March 24, 1944 issue of *The Dispatcher* said: "The realistic way in which England and the United States have acted with respect to the harboring of Axis' spies in Ireland recalls the howls that went up in America from the poor-dear-little-Finland crowd when Russia found it necessary to act against the plotters of Mannerheim."[39]

The U.S. loan to Britain after the war and the military aid to Greece and Turkey were opposed as "pages from Hitler's *Mein Kampf.*" An editorial in *The Dispatcher* read:[40]

> The Tories of Britain and the reactionaries of America raise huge cry against the Soviet Union. They broadcast unspeakable slander and pretend that every democratic tendency shown by people bordering the Soviet Union is due to Russian 'expansionism.'

Also

> Their cry against Russia is precisely because Russia insists that the peoples of all countries have the right to organize unions and choose their own forms of government.

With this background, it was understandable that the ILWU would be brought to trial under the terms of the 1949 CIO convention resolution against Communists.

Before entering into a discussion of the trials it is necessary to review one other facet of Bridges' activities within the CIO —his expansionism.

On a number of occasions, Harry Bridges attempted to extend his influence throughout the maritime industry, particularly on the east coast. This interest was evident as early as 1937 when Bridges had wanted to set up a longshore organizing committee to rival the AFL International Longshoremen's Association. In this effort he had had the support of the CIO pro-Communist caucus. Again, during the war, Bridges entered into negotiations with Local 65 of the CIO Retail, Wholesale, and Department Store Workers Union in an attempt to develop a solid base for the ILWU on the east coast. These efforts were not successful.

Late in December, 1945, Bridges tried again, using a different approach. As ILWU president, he wrote a letter inviting all the maritime unions to a conference to be held in February, 1946 in Washington, D.C. The AFL unions rejected the invitation. Present at the meeting were delegates from the National Maritime Union, the Marine Cooks' and Stewards' Association, the Marine Engineers' Beneficial Association, the American Communications Association, the Inland Boatmen's Union, and the International Longshoremen and Warehousemen's Union.[41]

The aim of the meeting was to set up a single national organization to be made up of the participating unions. Plans were formulated for a delegate conference of the constituent unions at San Francisco on May 9, 1946. A Committee for Maritime Unity was established, with Harry Bridges and Joseph Curran as co-chairmen.

The maritime field had traditionally been one of concentration of Communist operations, not only in the United States but abroad as well. The significance of the industry to a nation's economy and particularly to a nation's international activities is, of course, only too apparent. Every CIO maritime, longshore, or shipping union, therefore, with the exception of the Shipbuilding Workers, found itself under the influence of the Communist party. This included the American Communications Association, the International Longshoremen's and Warehousemen's Union, Inland Boatmen's Union of the Pacific, International Union of Fishermen and Allied Workers, Marine Cooks and Stewards Association, National Maritime Union, and the Marine Engineers Beneficial Association.

The stated purpose of the CMU was to establish cooperation between the participating unions, and bring about common support in cases of employer difficulty. Its latent objective, however, seemed to be organic unity in a subfederation within the CIO.[42] There were furthermore, indications that the CMU was another attempt in Bridges' empire-building, designed to counter the growing anti-Communism within the CIO. The earlier attempts had failed and this new, more subtle project was undertaken.

The CMU prospered during the first days of its existence in 1946, primarily because a series of strikes was undertaken in which the CMU acted as an effective clearing house for all the CIO unions in the industry. Those same 1946 strikes, however, served, as we have seen in our discussion of Joseph Curran and his NMU, to widen a rift between Bridges and Curran and their respective unions. Curran wanted to avoid the strike and believed that Bridges prevented a settlement. This split eventually weakened and finally caused the dissolution of the CMU. Some time later Curran accused

Bridges of having damaged the interests of the strikers by meeting with Communist leader, William Z. Foster, during the shipping tie-up. "He met with them (Foster and Communist leaders) unbeknown to us, but the press smeared our strike with all kinds of phony stories."[43]

To salvage the CMU at these signs of its floundering Bridges tried to develop a new approach. The week following the CIO Atlantic City convention in 1946, Bridges visited New York and suggested to Mike Quill the creation of a new "separate federation of land sea transport." This was clearly an expansion of the existing CMU concept. In reporting this conversation later to the national CIO officials, Quill said: "His proposition was that he had worked out an agreement with A. F. Whitney of the Brotherhood of Railroad Trainmen and that we should unite Transport, National Maritime Union, Longshoremen's and Warehousemen's Union, the CIO Communications Workers, and the Brotherhood of Railroad Trainmen into one separate federation of land and sea transport." To Quill's question as to whether he had discussed the proposal with Murray, Bridges reportedly answered: "Hell, no; that is beside the point."[44] Quill was under the impression that Bridges was approaching him in accordance with a Communist party decision, but he had no evidence of that and believed it might also have been simply "a means of boxing Curran in."[45]

Whitney had spoken to the CIO convention the week before, and there had been an invitation sent by the CIO to the Brotherhood of Railroad Trainmen asking them to affiliate with the CIO. In his speech, Whitney had referred to the similarity of policies and the progressive spirit of the members of the CIO and the BRT. He had also been liberal with praise for Murray, but announced to the convention that "the Brotherhood reluctantly refrained from accepting at this time the invitations extended on behalf of the CIO to affiliate formally with you. . . . We decided against formal affiliation, but will cooperate with you 100 percent."[46]

It is, of course, difficult to know whether Bridges actually came to an understanding with Whitney, as Quill was led to believe. The railroad union leader, a man well along in years, may have considered a proposal by Bridges to be a way to "cooperate with you 100 percent." It is clear from his speech to the CIO convention that he would not have been wary of Bridges' Communist affiliations. His speech had warned the CIO:[47]

> "The lesson is clear! The measure of a man's leadership is not his political beliefs. . . . Labor leaders who preach no doctrine more radical than the Sermon on the Mount are charged with being Communists in an effort to undermine their position and deprive labor of their leadership. . . . I speak to you out of a lifetime of experience. Do not let this issue divide you. . . . Do not allow yourselves to become the tools of Fascist or reactionary forces."

To return now to the charges brought against Bridges and the ILWU, we will find Steinberg's accusations to be quite pointed:[48]

> . . . I charge that the policies and activities of the . . . (ILWU) are not designed to unite the working men and women of America into labor unions for their mutual aid and protection but to unite them for the purpose of advancing the interests of the Communist Party . . . Finally, and most important, I charge that the goal of the (ILWU) . . . has not been to perpetuate the cherished traditions of our democracy but has been to destroy and to seek the imposition upon the workers of America of a Communist form of government.

After listening to the evidence, the CIO trial committee concluded that,

> Each of the four major shifts in policy made by the Communist Party during the period since 1938 was faithfully followed by the ILWU. At no time during that twelve year period has there been one single instance of ILWU's deviating in any appreciable degree from the line of the Communist Party.[49]

The committee also decided:

> that the policies of the International Longshoremen's and Warehousemen's Union are consistently directed toward the achievement of the program and the purposes of the Communist Party rather than the objectives and policies set forth in the CIO Constitution.[50]

And one additional point was made clear:

> The question of whether Bridges is or was a member of the Communist Party is not, in the judgment of the Committee, rele-

vant to the purpose of the present inquiry. The Committee is not concerned with anything more than whether the ILWU followed Communist Party policy.... The Committee finds, that Bridges did participate in Communist Party fraction meetings and did receive at these meetings instructions from Party representatives as to the line that was to be carried out, not only in the ILWU itself but also within CIO. The documentary evidence, almost all of it official ILWU material, further clearly proves that the efforts of the Party to control the policies of ILWU were highly success-ful.[51]

Following the CIO committee recommendation, the ILWU was expelled by the CIO Executive Board. The same fate also befell the International Fishermen and Allied Workers of America, which had merged with the ILWU.

Bridges met the committee recommendation to oust his union from the CIO with an attack on the CIO. The ILWU Executive Board instructed its leaders

to initiate the calling of a national conference of those unions already expelled from CIO or about to be expelled, in order to make appropriate plans and to take all possible constructive steps toward such unions working collectively for their own mutual pro-tection and advantage.[52]

Following the expulsion of the ILWU from the CIO, news-papers reported signs of "rank and file revolt" against Bridges. *The New York Times* for July 25, 1950 wrote of a growing opposition "faction" which "might possibly now include a majority of the mem-bership."

Bridges refused to endorse the UN intervention in Korea. The Communist-dominated Maritime Federation of the World, which he headed as honorary president, had ordered a world-wide boycott against ships that would aid the UN intervention. To meet this, every major ILWU local, "representing the vast majority of the West Coast's dock workers" voted to guarantee that crews would be supplied to load ships bound for Korea. All but one of the major locals pledged all-out support of the UN intervention.

A few weeks later, a policy caucus of the ILWU voted to end connections with the World Federation of Trade Unions and its affiliate, the Maritime Federation of the World. The vote was 63 to

9,[53] "indicating that left-wing elements, which had organized the caucus and . . . had beaten off other right-wing moves, did not seriously oppose the withdrawal resolution." This tactic was interpreted as an attempt by the Bridges group to avoid debate on the resolution, since they were not certain of their strength.

The national union of Marine Cooks and Stewards, headed by Hugh Bryson, was likewise expelled from the CIO at the same time as the ILWU following a similar trial. The CIO investigating committee in recommending expulsion declared: "At no time during the twelve year period since 1938 has there been one single instance of MCS's deviating in any substantial degree from the line of the Communist Party."[54]

Following the union's expulsion, Joseph Curran, president of the CIO National Maritime Union, announced that his union would start an all-out organizing drive to take over the expelled union's 7,000 membership.[55] Curran's program was not successful. The failure was due to a number of causes, not the least of which was inadequate organization and an inability to cope successfully with a growing pattern of violence that characterized the efforts of the MCS to hold on to its membership. But one other factor must be noted. The MCS was able to develop a loyalty to the union on the part of its Negro members. The Negroes in the stewards department on vessels from the West Coast ports were since 1947 the source of some of the strongest union support. Negroes became increasingly common on the ships' rosters of stewards. Many Negroes entered the union and received jobs at a time when jobs were denied them by other shipping unions on the West Coast. The MCS made much of the fact that it was the only organization on the West Coast that came to their aid as a union. The union leadership insisted that any anti-MCS talk was in fact anti-Negro talk. The union leadership saw to it that Negroes entered into the ranks of the leaders. For this reason the N.M.U. was unable to use the issue of Communism successfully in its efforts to undermine the M.C.S.

Harry Bridges, following the CIO expulsion, took the smaller Communist dominated sea unions on the West Coast, such as the MCS, under the wing of his international union. He successfully withstood efforts by the CIO and AFL to take away the bulk of his membership and today remains a leading figure on the

West Coast and in Hawaii. Efforts by the United States Government to deport him have been thwarted in the courts. As a result of his own personal leadership power and the strategic position of his union in servicing West Coast shipping and the lifeline between San Francisco and Hawaii, he remains a continued threat to anti-Communists in and out of the labor movement."[55a]

INTERNATIONAL FUR AND LEATHER WORKERS

On the eve of the scheduled hearing before the CIO Executive Board Committee appointed to investigate the charges against the International Fur and Leather Workers Union, David J. McDonald, chairman, received a telegram from Ben Gold, union president, informing him that the union, at its 18th biennial convention, had condemned the charges as "false and dishonest," the proceedings as a "kangaroo hearing," the CIO officials for "raiding, splitting, union wrecking and strike-breaking," the CIO foreign policy for wanting "to unite with Fascists in third world war," and therefore, "decided overwhelmingly to disaffiliate with CIO with only three opposing votes."[56]

The CIO committee nevertheless proceeded with its hearing and found that:

> ... the policies and activities of the IFLWU have been in the past, and are today, directed toward the achievement of the purposes of the Communist Party rather than the objectives set forth in the Constitution of the CIO ...

Ben Gold, president of the union, was one of the few openly avowed members of the Communist party in the American labor movement and was, for a time, a member of the national and New York State committees of the Communist party. In 1931 and 1936 he ran for the New York State Assembly on the Communist party ticket and in 1933 he was the Communist party's candidate for president of the New York Board of Aldermen.[57]

Irving Potash, manager of the union's Furrier Joint Council of New York and second in command of the international, had likewise been for many years a high official of the Communist party; he was one of the eleven party leaders convicted under the Smith Act for conspiring to advocate the overthrow of the United States government by force and violence.

The Fur Workers Union started its activity in 1910 and formally organized in 1912 after a general strike. It joined the AFL the following year, and by 1920 had organized about eighty percent of the industry,[58] most of which was in New York. During the twenties, however, factionalism began to weaken the union, with the Communists becoming very active in New York. Finally, in May, 1925, over the opposition of the anti-Communist officers of the international, the Trade Union Educational League slate won in the New York Joint Board. Ben Gold became the new manager.

As early as December 4, 1926, a special AFL committee headed by Matthew Woll and Edward F. McGrady warned:

> It has been demonstrated beyond peradventure of a doubt that Communistic and destructive leadership has gained ascendancy in the New York Furriers' Union Joint Council.

The report went on to explain:

> ... to secure Communistic control of the International Fur Workers Union is not an end in itself, but merely a means to a greater end, which is the complete destruction of the American trade-union movement and the substitution of a revolutionary Communistic reign of terrorism and corruption and dictatorship in its stead.[59]

Friction between the AFL and the Gold faction continued until 1935. During that time, the AFL set up a rival group called the Furriers Joint Council, headed by Edward F. McGrady.[60] In late 1928, the Gold group formed the Fur Workers Industrial Union and affiliated with the Needle Trades Workers Industrial Union which became, in 1929, a section of the Trade Union Unity League. After 1930, the AFL Furriers Joint Council in New York lost out and had virtually ceased functioning by 1932.

In the spring of 1935, following the change in the Communist party trade union approach, the Fur Workers Industrial Union was dissolved. The left-wing returned to the AFL International Fur Workers Union and in 1935 Ben Gold again became New York manager. Gold became president of the international in 1937.[61]

An anti-Communist opposition within the union continued, called the United Progressive Furriers, but it remained weak.

The union joined the CIO in 1937 and actively became part of the pro-Communist caucus.[62] In 1939, after a merger, it became the International Fur and Leather Workers Union. During the "popular front" period, the IFLWU strongly urged support for "the principle enunciated by President Roosevelt. We must quarantine the war-makers." It supported a boycott of Japanese goods and joined the American League for Peace and Democracy.

Soon after the Nazi-Soviet Pact of August 11, 1939, however, the union reversed its position. In November, 1939, Ben Gold denounced a proposed modification of the Neutrality Act, even though earlier that very year the union's convention with his support had called for just such an amendment to distinguish between aggressor nations and their victims.

The June 22, 1941 attack by Germany on Russia became the IFLWU's Pearl Harbor, and led it to reverse its foreign policy again. John L. Lewis, the former IFLWU hero, fell completely from grace and was denounced in June, 1942 as a "traitor" by Ben Gold. Gold sent "fraternal greetings" to Stalin on the 1943 anniversary of the October Revolution:

> We join with many millions the world over, hailing October Revolution and building of Soviet Union as one of the greatest achievements of mankind. . . . Fur and Leather workers of United States and Canada salute great Socialist country, Soviet Union, erected on indestructible foundation of Marxism-Leninism-Stalinism.

In December, 1943, the union newspaper had a picture of Irving Potash presenting a fur-lined coat from the fur workers to George Dimitroff, prominent Bulgarian Communist.

A call for a "second front" characterized the union's foreign policy position until Teheran in December, 1943. With this new period, the IFLWU leadership became satisfied with American-Russian cooperation and seemed content to trust the war's leadership to Roosevelt. The Officers' Report to the 1944 convention declared that Teheran represented "the priceless and decisive triumph of the peoples of the world"; it continued:

... the International Executive Board in December, 1943, stated that the declarations of Moscow, Cairo and Teheran will without doubt take their place with such historic documents as the Declaration of Independence, the Bill of Rights, the abolition of chattel slavery by the Emancipation Proclamation, and the Constitution of the U.S.S.R.

With the ending of the war and the developing tensions between the U.S. and the U.S.S.R., the IFLWU became critical first of Britain and then of the United States. The union also became more frank in its espousal of Marxist and Stalinist doctrine. The Soviet Union was, of course, considered a "democratic land." In October, 1945, the union officers, Ben Gold and secretary-treasurer, Pietro Lucchi, again sent greetings to Stalin on the Bolshevik Revolution:

> Our members fully appreciate the great contributions of Soviet Union toward victory in the Pacific. . . . We know that in the world's first socialist country, there will be no unemployment, no exploitation or oppression of people or of nations; no discrimination against national minority groups because of race, color, or religion. . . . Long live the Union of Socialist Soviet Republics and its great leader, Generalissimo Joseph Stalin.

Ernest Bevin and the British Labor party were called "phoney" socialists with imperialist fangs. The November, 1945 issue of the IFLWU newspaper said:

> They are 'Socialists' like the Social-Democrats in Germany back in 1932 who refused the plea of the Communists to unite the ranks of the working class in order to prevent the seizure of power by Hitler. . . . They are 'Socialists' like the Social-Democrats in New York City who split away from the American Labor Party, made a coalition in the recent election with Governor Dewey and made a profession out of red-baiting and disunity.

The same issue of the newspaper congratulated Communist Ben Davis upon his re-election to the New York City Council.

At the 1948 convention of the union, the Third Party plan was strongly supported, as was Henry Wallace throughout the presidential campaign. During the Berlin Airlift, the union supported Russia. The Atlantic Pact was attacked as well.

All during this time, the IFLWU newspaper praised the Soviet Union and carried stories of its accomplishments. The August, 1949 issue, for example, carried a letter from one William Gropper, reporting on his visit to Russia:

> There is plenty of food and clothing; there are luxury items. The shops are full of goods and people buying. I have experienced the thrill of seeing dancing and listening to singing, not only at concerts and ballet, but with people on the street. . . . There are no police watching me. . . . There is no anti-semitism. . . . The peasants today ride in automobiles. . . . They are wealthy and educated. . . . They own original paintings by the top Soviet artists, among many other luxuries.

The conflict between the union and the CIO national organization became quite open and pronounced. In denouncing the Atlantic Pact, Ben Gold did not blame Wall Street alone. He also blamed the CIO and those union leaders who failed to raise their voices against the "murderous" Truman Doctrine and the "so-called" Marshall Plan. He warned that when "judgement day" arrived, these leaders would have much explaining to do.

The IFLWU accused the CIO of being a handmaiden of the State Department and explained the withdrawal of the CIO from the Soviet dominated World Federation of Trade Unions in those terms. The Union tied the Taft-Hartley issue with foreign policy as well and in resolutions would join "the Taft-Hartley slave labor law, the Truman Doctrine, and the Marshall Plan."

Finally, after the 1949 CIO convention in Cleveland, the IFLWU began to attack the CIO for not securing wage increases, not sincerely attempting to repeal Taft-Hartley, and not championing civil rights legislation. After the Supreme Court upheld the constitutionality of the non-Communist affidavit provision of the Taft-Hartley Act, the union accused the CIO of being responsible for the decision and of having "embraced that fascist act," even though it was Philip Murray's Steelworkers Union which had carried the case to the Supreme Court.

Interestingly enough, the union, following its ouster from the CIO, found it necessary to submit to the provisions of the Taft-Hartley law to protect itself against raiding from other unions. It requested its officers to sign the non-Communist affidavit in August,

1950, with the result, according to *The New York Times* of August 29, 1950, that Ben Gold openly announced his resignation from the Communist Party but at the same time insisted on his loyalty to the party's principles.

The CIO investigating committee recommended the expulsion of the IFLWU and that soon took place. This expulsion had no effect on the strength of the union in the main segment of the industry in New York. The union remained strong, continued to maintain harmonious relations with most of the employer associations, and, due to its strength, successfully repulsed all attempts either from within its own union or from employers to weaken its hold on the New York industry.

The expulsion did have an effect, however, on the fortunes of the union outside of the New York area. More important than the expulsions, moreover, was the indictment by the United States Government of Irving Potash, for violating the Smith Act against subversion. Potash was one of the eleven top Communists convicted in 1951 of membership in an organization that advocated violent overthrow of the government. The move against Potash strengthened the elements within the union who were opposed to Communism and who hoped to break the union away from Communist control. Finally, in 1954, Ben Gold was indicted by the Justice Department on a charge of perjury in connection with the Taft-Hartley non-Communist affidavit.

Following Gold's conviction, the NLRB on May 30, 1954 gave notice to the union that its facilities would not be available to the union until it elected new officers who could and did comply with the Taft-Hartley Act. The Board was overruled by the court, but the controversy upset the stability of the union.

Internal dissent reached its peak in the Boston area. When the CIO national convention met in Los Angeles in December, 1954, there was present for the first time a small delegation representing approximately nine thousand members from the Leather Division of the union. Their spokesman, Richard O'Keefe, announced to the convention that his own local of four thousand Leatherworkers was prepared to leave their parent union and rejoin the CIO. He asked the CIO to set up an organizing committee which would carry forward the work of "liberating" members of the union from the Communist leadership.[63]

The CIO responded by appointing Hugh Thompson of Boston as director of the newly created CIO Leather and Tannery Workers Organizing Committee. Within a matter of weeks, Local 21 voted to break with the Fur and Leatherworkers and affiliate with the CIO organizing committee.[64]

Meanwhile, the leadership of the International Fur and Leather workers Union, although still strong in the fur trade, made an effort to strengthen itself and gain stature by attempting to affiliate with the American Federation of Labor. Negotiations were undertaken in 1954 with the leaders of the Amalgamated Meat Cutters and Butcher Workmen. These negotiations proceeded quickly and rather successfully to the point where both unions were prepared to sign an agreement for unity under which the fur union would be completely absorbed into the meat union. The merger steps were temporarily halted, however, when the AFL Executive Council, representing the national leadership of all the AFL unions, rejected the plan as "completely contrary to the long-time position of the AFL in opposition to the control and domination of American workers by Communist agents." To the plea by the meat cutters that the new leaders of the fur workers had all signed non-Communist affidavits, the AFL Executive Committee said that this "in no way meets the problem of Communist domination from the viewpoint of the AFL."

Patrick E. Gorman, secretary-treasurer of the meat union, replied that under the terms of the merger agreement the plan would be to "de-Communize" the fur union. He pointed out the fur group was to be dissolved as an international union, its Executive Board disbanded, and its treasury of more than $1 million turned over to the meat union, although the local unions affiliated with the fur workers would retain control of $8 million in funds and property now in their possession. Mr. Gorman also pointed out that his own international union had a clause in the constitution barring "subversives" from membership and that all locals and joint councils would function under the direct supervison of the meat union's international executive board. The fur union would be obliged to discontinue its own newspaper and other publications under the terms of the agreement, and if there was any evidence of continued Communist activity by the union, the AFL group would have the right to expel it without trial or stated cause at any time within a five-year probationary period. Also understood was that Gold would be barred from holding any office, paid or unpaid, in the new organization.[65]

It was clear from these terms that the International Fur and Leatherworkers Union was prepared to go to great lengths in order to get into the American Federation of Labor. They agreed that the meat union could put a trustee in control of any of the fur locals if they found evidence that the local was carrying on Communist activities or promoting Communist causes. If the charges are sustained after a trial, the meat union could expel the offending local and confiscate its treasury.[66]

The national AFL leadership indicated, however, that it would be necessary for 19 leaders of the fur group to be excluded from the new merged union before it would approve the plan. At this point, the new president of the fur union, Abe Feinglass, demurred. The leaders of the meat cutters union went on to state that a "fine relationship" had been established between the officers of the two unions and expressed hope that an amalgamation would provide a united front for meeting the problems of workers in the meat, leather and fur industries.

The two unions merged in February, 1955. The fur workers union sought respectability in its affiliation with the AFL, and the meat cutters union sought the new funds and the 70,000 new members. The national leadership of the AFL continued to criticize[67] the merger, and for a time threatened the union with expulsion. Eventually, however, the leadership of the meat cutters union actively engaged in eliminating Communist leadership and influence in the fur worker segment and won the praise of the AFL leadership for its energetic efforts.

---

[1] Mr. Haddock later became Washington Legislative Representative of the National Maritime Union.
[2] House Report 1311, 78th Congress, 2nd Session, *op. cit.,* pp. 158-161.
[3] Stolberg, *Story of the CIO, op. cit.,* p. 151.
[4] House Report 1311, 78th Congress, 2nd Session, *op. cit.,* p. 171.

5 CIO, *Report of Executive Board Committee Appointed by President Murray to Investigate Charges Against the American Communications Association* (mimeographed), pp. 9-10.
6 House Report 1311, 78th Congress, 2nd Session, *op. cit.*, p. 172.
7 *Ibid..*, p. 173.
8 CIO, *Report of Committee to Investigate ACA, op. cit.*, p. 11.
9 *Ibid.*, p. 14.
10 Minton and Stuart, *op. cit.*, p. 185.
11 "The Maritime Unions," *Fortune*, Vol. 16, September, 1937, pp. 123-128.
12 Estolv E. Ward, *Harry Bridges On Trial* (Modern Age: New York, 1940) p. 231.
13 *Ibid.*, statement on back cover of book.
14 CIO, *Report of Committee on Public Workers, op. cit.*, p. 14.
15 Levenstein, *op. cit.*, pp. 175, 176.
16 CIO, *Report of Executive Board Committee Appointed by President Murray to Investigate Charges Against the International Longshoremen and Warehousemen's Union* (mimeographed) p. 17.
17 CIO, *Hearings to Investigate ILWU, op. cit.*, pp. 593-595.
18 *Ibid.*, pp. 597, 598.
19 *Ibid.*, p. 598.
20 *Ibid.*, p. 645.
21 *Ibid.*, pp. 628-630.
22 *Ibid.*, pp. 605, 606, 609, 610.
23 CIO, *Report of Committee to Investigate ILWU, op. cit.*, p. 10.
24 *Ibid.*, p. 10, 11.
25 CIO, *Hearings to Investigate ILWU, op. cit.*, pp. 375, 376.
26 *Ibid.*, and CIO, *Report of Committee to Investigate ILWU, op. cit.*, p. 12.
27 *Supra*, p. 33.
28 *Ibid.*, p. 16.
29 *Ibid.*, pp. 12, 13; and CIO, *Hearings to Investigate ILWU, op. cit.*, pp. 287, 288.
30 *Ibid.*, pp. 389, 390, 400; and CIO, *Report of Committee to Investigate ILWU, op. cit.*, p. 13.
31 When Harry Bridges was confronted with this statement in 1950 during the CIO committee hearings on the charges that his union was pro-Communist, he exclaimed: "We sure call them, don't we?" (CIO *Hearings to Investigate ILWU, op. cit.*, pp. 389, 390, 400).
32 *Ibid.*, p. 391.
33 Upon hearing this statement read at the CIO trial on the charges made against his union, Bridges shouted, "Hooray." *Ibid.*
34 *Ibid.*, pp. 394, 396, 397.
35 *Ibid.*, pp. 686, 700.
36 CIO, *Report of Committee to Investigate ILWU, op. cit.*, pp. 14, 15.
37 At the CIO trial on the charges brought against the ILWU, Bridges said: "... we won't attempt to deny anything that appeared in the ILWU official papers. We will take full responsibility for anything that appeared in our official paper *The Dispatcher*."
38 CIO, *Report of Committee to Investigate ILWU, op. cit.*, p. 16.
39 CIO, *Hearings to Investigate ILWU, op. cit.*, pp. 383, 384.
40 *Ibid.*, pp. 389, 390.

[41] Taft, "Unlicensed Seafaring Unions," *op. cit.*, pp. 208, 209.

[42] Barbash *op. cit.*, p. 229.

[43] *New York World Telegram*, July 14, 1947.

[44] CIO, *Hearings to Investigate ILWU*, *op. cit.*, p. 65.

[45] *Ibid.*, p. 94.

[46] CIO Eighth Constitutional Convention, *op. cit.*, pp. 160, 161.

[47] *Ibid.*, pp. 164, 165.

[48] CIO, *Hearings to Investigate ILWU*, *op. cit.*, pp. 38-40.

[49] CIO, *Report of Committee to Investigate ILWU*, *op. cit.*, p. 10.

[50] *Ibid.*, p. 23.

[51] *Ibid.*, p. 19.

[52] CIO, *Report of Committee to Investigate ILWU.*, *op. cit.*, p. 22.

[53] *The New York Times*, August 19, 1950.

[54] CIO, *Report of Executive Board Committee Appointed by President Murray to Investigate Charges Against the National Union of Marine Cooks and Stewards* (mimeographed), p. 6.

[55] *The New York Times*, January 13, 1951.

[55a] The ILWU today, under Regional Director Jack W. Hall, out on bail after being convicted on a charge of conspiracy to overthrow the United States Government by force and violence, represents some 23,000 workers in Hawaii's key industries. Its influence and power is attested to by a recent testimonial dinner for Hall, with Bridges as principal speaker, which was attended by Hawaii's Attorney General, Edward Sylva. (*New York Herald Tribune*, December 10, 1956) Bridges himself, meanwhile, has shown signs of either political metamorphosis or new political tactics. It was rumored in labor circles that he favored Eisenhower in the 1956 elections and in a signed column for the December issue of his union publication, *The Dispatcher*, he made what some believe to be his first public criticism of Soviet policy. In his column he states: "In a world as tense as ours is today, the Russian action in Hungary and the British-French action in Egypt are equally harmful and destructive to world peace." (*The New York Times*, December 11, 1956)

[56] CIO, *Report of Executive Board Committee Appointed by President Murray to Investigate Charges Against the International Fur and Leather Workers Union* (mimeographed), p. 2.

[57] House Report 1311, 78th Congress, 2nd Session, *op. cit.*, pp. 115, 116.

[58] Joel Seidman, *The Needle Trades* (Farrar Rinehart: New York, 1942) pp. 135, 136.

[59] House Report 1311, 78th Congress, 2nd Session, *op. cit.*, pp. 115-117.

[60] Seidman, *op. cit.*, p. 123.

[61] *Ibid.*, pp. 207, 208.

[62] CIO, *Report of Committee to Investigate IFLWU*, *op, cit.*, pp. 10-17.

[63] *Daily Proceedings of the 16th Constitutional Convention of the CIO*, Thursday, December 9, 1954, page 41.

[64] *CIO News*, January 10, 1955, p. 11.

[65] *The New York Times*, December 16, 1954.

[66] *The New York Times*, January 3, 1955.

[67] *The New York Times*, March 27, 1955.

PART IV

Chapter 14

THE C.I.O. AND
WORLD LABOR

14 | THE CIO AND WORLD LABOR

The Communists, therefore, are on the one hand, practically, the most advanced and resolute section of the working class parties of every country, that section which pushes forward all others; on the other hand, theoretically, they have over the great mass of the proletariat the advantage of clearly understanding the line of march, the conditions, and the ultimate general results of the proletarian movement.

The immediate aim of the Communists is the same as that of all the other proletarian parties; formation of the proletariat into a class, overthrow of the bourgeois supremacy, conquest of political power by the proletariat.

Karl Marx
Communist Manifesto

The growth of the United States as a world power has been paralleled in the international labor field. Karl Marx strove for the development of an international labor movement whose dynamism and desting-conscious strength would overcome the high protective walls of the nation-state. To date, however, it is a dream that has failed of realization even for ideologically-tied socialists, let alone for trade unions.

Karl Marx's first International Workingmen's Association broke up in 1872 after eight years of political controversy, the socialists, syndicalists, and "reformists" going their separate ways. Political issues have ever since been haunting the efforts of trade unionists to achieve world unity. Political controversies and national loyalties continue to dominate world labor and contribute toward an explanation of the peculiar role which the CIO has played in that scene during recent years.

227

The First International of 1864 was the first significant crossing of national boundaries to realize the idea of labor unity. It arose out of the internationalist and socialist ideas produced in the revolutionary period of the 1830's and 1840's. The first Provisional Central Committee of the IWA consisted of 21 Englishmen, 10 Germans, 9 Frenchmen, 6 Italians, 2 Poles and 2 Swiss. American trade union leaders participated only passively via German political refugees residing in the United States.

From the very beginning, however, two major trends began to vie with each other for supremacy in the organization: the trade unionist orientation of the British and the political orientation of the Germans. The former orientation was well formulated by George Odger, British union leader, who said:[1]

> We find that whenever we attempt to better our social conditions by reducing the hours of toil, or by raising the price of labor, our employers threaten us with bringing over Frenchmen, Germans, Belgians to do our work at a reduced rate of wages, and we are sorry to say that this has been done, though not from any desire on the part of our Continental brothers to injure us, but through a want of regular and systematic communication between the industrial classes of all countries. Our aim is . . . not to allow our employers to play us all one against the other.

Karl Marx, who became spokesman of the organization and represented the political emphasis, supported the need for unity to achieve the immediate aims of reform, but also urged that the first duty of the working class was to acquire political power.

These strong national and ideological differences led to the end of the First International soon after it reached its greatest strength in 1869, when it included representatives of the labor movements of most of the countries of the world. Marx won the battles with the British within the organization, but after the smoke cleared away he found he had no army. The nationalism of the 1870's gave the organization its death blow.

The second attempt to establish international labor unity came in 1889 at a Paris meeting of labor and socialist parties which launched a second Socialist International.[2] No effective labor union internationalism was achieved however until 1901 when the International Labor Secretariat of Trade Union Centers was set up in Copenhagen. Here again the ideological differences of the revolutionary, conservative, and reformist groups weakened the organization. No stability was achieved until 1909 when the French Confederation of Labor and the American Federation of Labor joined. In 1913, at the suggestion of the AFL that the term "secretariat" was meaningless to American workers, the name was changed to International Federation of Trade Unions.[3]

The organization reached its greatest strength in 1914, with nearly 9 million members. It was dominated by the German labor movement, with the British remaining primarily uncooperative, but the central body exercised no real authority since decisions could only be binding if unanimously adopted. Its chief function was to distribute and collect information and statistics, collect strike assistance, and curtail the use of mobile labor for strikebreaking.

The outbreak of war in 1914 marked the breakdown of both the Second Socialist International and the IFTU. Labor lined up in defense of "flag and country" and union solidarity could not resist the "call to the colors." Communication ceased between the labor movements of the opposing sides.

Repeated efforts were made to bring about renewed contact between the opposing sides, with no success until October 1, 1917, when a conference was held in Berne which labor representatives of the Allied, Neutral, and Central powers attended. Samuel Gompers opposed the inclusion of "enemy" countries, so the AFL did not participate.

This break between the AFL and the European labor movement was the beginning of a long period of estrangement between the two. Out of the Berne Conference came a demand that trade union representatives should participate in the making of the peace treaty, particularly the economic and social sections. They wanted the reestablished IFTU to be labor's spokesman in official proceedings dealing with international labor legislation. A labor Charter demanding an eight-hour day, free compulsory education, weekly rest periods of 26 hours, social insurance, and social legislation for seamen, women, and children was drawn up to be presented as labor's demands when the peace treaty would be established.[4]

As a result of Woodrow Wilson's efforts, however, Samuel

Gompers was given the task of writing Part XIII of the Versailles Peace Treaty and it fell below the standards formulated at Berne. The Berne group, which held a Congress in Amsterdam in July and August of 1919, pointed to the discrepancies between the Berne Charter and Gompers' Part XIII and bluntly opposed the latter.

Gompers became quite comtemptuous of the European labor movement. In his autobiography, he described a conference with French Socialists and recalled that he "listened to their fantastic and irrational proposals as long as I could endure them."[5]

European labor leaders reciprocated with similar feelings. Sidney Webb, for example, requested a member of the American Embassy to keep certain American labor delegates out of England and France because "they had a disturbing influence on labor and socialist circles in France."[6]

The international labor movement following World War I, therefore, was in the main a European movement. The Amsterdam International of 1919 gave way to a reborn IFTU in which the German influence for the first time was quite small. The IFTU came to represent 23 million workers in 22 countries and commanded some attention, but the AFL did not rejoin until 1937.[7]

During this time the AFL in its international activities was emphasizing the strengthening of the Pan-American Federation of Labor, created in 1918, which evolved a "labor Monroe Doctrine," and resented efforts of the IFTU to recruit members among Latin American unions.

The IFTU program was primarily committed to democratic socialism through nationalization of industries, collective bargaining, progressive reforms, and support of the League of Nations as a road to liberty and peace. It developed consultative relations with the International Trade Secretariats, groups of unions in the various trades which worked on an international basis to improve the conditions, wages, and hours of the respective industries. The IFTU also supported the International Labor Organization, formed following the peace treaty after World War I, as a means of raising standards.[8]

An ideological split in 1921 separated the Communists from the IFTU. They organized the Red International of Labor Unions (RILU), with headquarters in Moscow dedicated to the establishment of "revolutionary unions." The RILU policy was to bore into IFTU unions at the same time as it called the IFTU "betrayers of the working class" and "social-Fascists." Its program also included mass strikes "in such a way that it be turned against the entire capitalist system." Workers were asked to choose whether to "struggle under the banner of communism or betray the interests of the labor classes under the banner of social democracy."[9]

At its peak in the 1920's, RILU claimed 14,000,000 members: 10,248,000 in the USSR; 2,800,000 in China; 525,000 in France. It also claimed "minority groups in IFTU unions," of which 1,000,000 were in Germany and 235,000 in the United States. Actually, the RILU affiliates in the United States—the Trade Union Unity League and the Trade Union Educational League—never had a membership of more than 100,000.

The IFTU lost its initial sympathy for the Bolshevik revolution and looked upon the RILU unions as "agents of Moscow."

This split, reflecting the growing Socialist-Communist schism, severely battered the IFTU in most European countries as Communist-dominated unions attempted to divide, bolshevize or liquidate the non-Communist trade unions. Although the RILU never achieved any real standing, the IFTU steadily declined in power and influence. This was further accelerated as the rise of fascism to power in Italy in 1923 destroyed the labor movement of that country, the victory of Hitlerism over the German people in 1933 ended the life of that influential labor movement, and the Austrian and Czechoslovak movements were liquidated in rapid succession. The Franco victory in Spain likewise tore another important labor movement out of the European trade union collective. Furthermore, the depression of the 1930's added to the weakness and lethargy.[10]

By the time the AFL rejoined the IFTU in 1937, the latter had little substance left and indeed fitted Gompers' characterization: a rope of sand. The international labor movement failed in its major objectives of averting economic disaster and stopping war and fascism. It had called without success for international economic planning, rational control of raw materials, economic stability, effective boycotts of German and Japanese goods, and League of Nations action to stop Franco and aggression. It had abandoned its early pacifist demands for disarmament and had called for "determined opposition to the brutal and unbridled aggressors," declaring that "the international trade union movement . . . is fully prepared to instruct its affiliates to shoulder the risks and responsibilites thereby entailed." As a final step to avert war, in 1939 it advocated a joint peace front of Britain, France, Poland and the USSR, but the Nazi-Soviet Pact of 1939 put an end to the scheme.

It is not completely clear why the AFL decided to rejoin the IFTU in 1937. Part of the reason was undoubtedly a growing consciousness of internationalism as war and fascism threatened. Part of the reason may also have been a rivalry with the CIO which had just been organized. There was some suspicion within the IFTU that the AFL decision was designed to prevent the CIO from gaining prestige through joining the international labor movement, since the IFTU had a long-standing "one center only" tradition which barred the admission of more than one trade union center from any one country. This tradition had been built up in a period of serious internecine strife within the trade union movement in Europe and was a powerful preventive of internal splits. In spite of those doubts, however, the predominant IFTU sentiment was to accept the AFL eagerly and hope that labor unity in the United States would be re-established with some IFTU encouragement.[11]

The CIO was thus effectively kept out of the international picture until World War II. John L. Lewis, in fact, did not seek such affiliation or contact and seemed to prefer developing hemispheric relations with the labor movements of Latin America.[12] This was consistent with Lewis' isolationist tendencies.

With the war, however, the CIO, as the strongest trade union group in the United States war industries, assumed greater international importance. The British trade unions, the bulwark of the IFTU, showed signs of wanting to establish relations with the CIO in spite of their friendship for the AFL, which frowned on the CIO as a "dual union." During the war Sir Walter Citrine was president of the IFTU and also general secretary of the British Trades Union Congress. In the latter capacity he established a friendship with the CIO which the AFL resented.[13]

With the outbreak of World War II, the IFTU became a trade-union-movement-in-exile in England. As the war progressed and as Allied victory seemed likely, there arose an active interest in restoring international trade union association.

The CIO as early as 1941, meanwhile, had begun calling for an "all-embracing international labor body,"[14] and for "the convening of an international trade union conference of representatives of the labor movements of all the United Nations."[15]

A United Nations effort meant the inclusion of the Soviet labor movement, and under IFTU rules the admission of Russian unions was forbidden. Sir Walter Citrine thereupon formed, acting as representative of the British TUC rather than as head of IFTU, an Anglo-Soviet Trade Union Committee. The British TUC issued a call to all labor organizations of "free nations" to meet at a world labor conference in London, February 6, 1945. Invitations were issued to the CIO as well as to the AFL and to the Russians. This call had been recommended in 1944 by the joint Emergency International Trade Union Council, representing the IFTU and the International Trade Secretariats. Interestingly enough, the Emergency Council also recommended that there should be "no political or religious tests" as a "condition of affiliation, nor must there be any racial discrimination."[16]

The AFL refused to attend the world labor conference and strenuously objected to an IFTU decision, made a few days prior to the world conference, allowing the admission of Russian unions and of more than one national labor organization from any one country. William Green explained the AFL position as follows:[17]

> The invitations were addressed to some organizations which are not free trade unions and to others which are government dominated and to many which fail to recognize the need of domestic trade union unity.
>
> The American Federation of Labor maintains that, until the Soviet labor organization can establish its bonafide character, that is, of a movement of workers for workers, we cannot co-operate with such an organization to establish policies mutually binding upon us.

The World Trade Union Conference took place from February 6–17, 1945 in London. The Preparatory Committee for the Congress had included representatives of the British Trades Union Congress, the All-Central council of Trade Unions of the USSR, and the

CIO.[18] CIO representatives at the February conference were Sidney Hillman, R. J. Thomas, Albert Fitzgerald, John Green, Sherman Dalrymple, James Carey, Allan Haywood, Joseph Curran, Reid Robinson, Martin Kyne, Michael Ross, and John Abt. All IFTU affiliates were represented in the conference except the AFL. Despite the fact that the war was still on, 64 organizations, representing 40 nations and claiming a membership of 60 million, were present.

A determined effort was made to steer the conference away from ideological differences. R. J. Thomas, then head of the United Automobile Workers and a CIO delegate, stated the objective well:

> This conference cannot be dissolved on the slightest pretext of disagreement between us because we must not have disagreement. If democracy is to win the world, I say we must come closer and closer together.[19]

The atmosphere at the conference was quite heavily political, however, and on the one important difference between the Soviet and British unions with regard to the future of the IFTU, the Russians won, with the support of the CIO. Great Britain wanted to save the IFTU by having Russia and the CIO enter it. Phillip Murray, speaking for the CIO, expressed his organization's "firm opposition to any effort to reconstruct" the IFTU, explaining it had "largely ceased to function."[20]

On a second issue that threatened to divide the meetings, the CIO succeeded in devising a compromise. With the 37,000,000 members claimed by the unions of Russian and Eastern Europe, and the 11,000,000 claimed by the Communist-dominated unions of France and Italy, the Communist forces were easily in a position to dominate the meetings and any future organization that might be set up. A report was submitted to the delegates providing for the admission of unions from Poland and ex-enemy countries, Finland, Bulgaria, Rumania, Hungary, and Italy, and for the making of decisions by a majority vote. At this, Sir Walter Citrine jumped to his feet opposing the entry of the new Eastern European countries since "the only information we have has been received through Moscow by telegram, a claim to represent blank number of trade unionists." He likewise opposed formal voting:[21]

The Soviet delegation to this conference is half the total voting strength. I do not think the Soviet delegation would claim that they are as important as all the other delegations put together. . .

Albert Fitzgerald, UE head, had been the CIO delegate on the Committee which had brought in the unanimous report to which Citrine objected. Carey, also a CIO delegate and the man Fitzgerald had defeated in the UE, suggested within the CIO delegation that the whole report be referred back to committee. A compromise was worked out between Citrine and R. J. Thomas under which the committee report would be adopted except for the part dealing with the ex-enemy countries and Poland, which would be referred back. A compromise on voting was also agreed upon, through Mr. Hillman's efforts, by a formula which virtually meant decisions would be adopted by general consent.

One other difference between the British and Russian labor representatives revolved around the selection of a Secretary General of the permananent organization. This question came up at the Paris meeting of September 25, 1945 to effectuate the organization of the World Federation of Trade Unions. It was agreed that Citrine would be chairman, but the Russians were not willing to accept his choice of the Belgian IFTU General-Secretary Walter Schenevels to hold the same post in the new setup. They insisted rather on the French resistance leader, Louis Saillant, and they carried the day as Citrine withdrew his opposition.[22]

The WFTU program adopted at London and reaffirmed at Paris demanded labor representation in all international organizations, sovereign rights and democratic self-government for all peoples, an end to international cartels and the colonial system, and other programs in line with the IFTU tradition. Major resolutions asked for the severing of relations with Franco; legislative reform all over the world to eliminate racial discrimination; the severing of relations with Argentina's fascist regime; a national homeland for the Jewish people in Palestine at the same time "respecting the legitimate interests of other national groups and giving equality of rights and opportunities to all its inhabitants"; a stronger UNRRA; complete German disarmament and punishment of Nazi war criminals with the proviso that in the administration of this program and German occupation "the countries that have been directly injured by German invasion and occupation and have effectively opposed the occupation should have representation," and strong support for the UN "in accordance with the general principles formulated at Dumbarton Oaks ... the Atlantic Charter, and ... the Moscow and Teheran Conferences."[23] The latter resolution included the following statement of principle:

> This World Conference, indeed, considers it to be the duty of the Goverments of the United Nations to deny recognition to States whose political and economic systems are opposed to the principles embodied in the Declarations made at the Atlantic meeting and at the Conferences of Moscow and Teheran. The struggle for the uprooting of militarism and Fascism, which has involved the working people in unaccountable sacrifices, is an integral part of their struggle for a stable and lasting peace, and of their fight to remove the last vestiges of militarism and Fascism ...

In a very significant sense, the WFTU was formed with the same hope in mind that accompanied the birth of the United Nations itself in the same year. In fact, the CIO made that comparison in explaining its position to the country and to its members:[24]

> The world wants peace, liberty and security.
> Towards that end, the United States government and the governments of almost every other freedom loving country joined the United Nations.
> Towards the same end, the CIO helped create the World Federation of Trade Unions.
> The UN is the machinery through which a war torn world seeks lasting peace and common understanding.
> The WFTU is the organization through which union men and women from every section of the globe seek to help attain that common understanding on world problems.
> The UN is based on recognition of the national sovereignty of its various constituent nations. That sovereignty is protected in the UN constitution. UN doesn't try to tell the United States how to run its elections or what it should do about combatting inflation.
> The WFTU likewise recognizes the independence of its affiliated labor organizations, in the same way that the CIO doesn't attempt to interfere with the functioning of its member international unions.

The report went on to say "If WFTU were to try to tell those Detroit auto workers, or Liverpool longshoremen or Omsk taxi drivers how to run their union business, the result would be simple and quick; the unions affected would leave the WFTU."

At the 1946 convention of the CIO, Philip Murray, in referring to the unanimous resolutions of the Russian and American WFTU delegates "on a wide variety of problems" said it was "in sharp contrast with the bickerings and disagreements of diplomats and governments."[25]

Sir Walter Citrine, however, seemed to appreciate the pitfalls that lay ahead and made an effort to meet them at the very outset. But the CIO, divided within itself, made a show of unity and appeared determined to ignore the basic differences of political philosophy between the Soviet and democratic societies, for the sake of forming and preserving the organization. In fact, in the process of achieving this "unity," the CIO committed itself to a number of positions it later had cause to regret. First, in reporting to the CIO, the delegates accepted the Soviet system as a "democratic" one.[26] In an official publication in 1946, the CIO explained the need for the WFTU by stating that "Fascism still lives"—pointing to "former Nazis," "Japanese big businessmen," "Franco Spain," and "many sections of the globe—including the USA—where reactionary forces see oppression of the working class as their key to quick riches and power." The name of the Soviet Union in this analysis was conspicuous by its absence.[27]

To solidify its alliance with the Soviet trade union, a delegation of 11 CIO leaders, led by James B. Carey, secretary-treasurer, made an eight-day survey of trade unionism in Russian in late 1945. The result, in spite of an inner-delegation difference of opinion, was in effect an apology for the Soviet Unions and "their excellent activities in promoting the interests of the workers." The report concluded: "Our observations have increased our pride at being associated with such a great trade union movement through the World Federation of Trade Unions."[28]

The Soviet delegates, during the formation of the WFTU, made a good impression on most other delegates. Cautious, they refrained from exercising the power they had from the numerical superiority of their delegations. Their chief object was to elect Saillant for the full-time post of WFTU General Secretary and in this they succeeded.

An uneasy balance was decided upon for the WFTU governing bodies. The General Council, meeting annually, was roughly divided into twelve who would follow the Communists and nine others. The important Executive Bureau of the WFTU, meeting four times a year, had members from Britain, the United States, the Netherlands, and France on the one side, with members from Russia, Latin America, and Italy, plus Saillant, on the other side. China's delegate held the balance.[29]

The WFTU had an ambitious program and worked to fulfill it. It was able to secure a consultative status with the UN Economic and Social Council, the ILO, and UNESCO, in spite of obstacles placed in the way by the United States delegation to the UN. The U.S. delegation, at the insistence of the AFL, had stopped a move to give the WFTU a vote on the Economic and Social Council.[30] It pressed resolutions within the UN condemning Franco Spain. It obtained partial recognition from the occupation authorities in Germany to aid in the reconstruction of the German trade union movement.[31] It sent missions all over the world, concerning itself with economic questions and civil liberties in a number of countries, including Greece, Iran, and Indonesia, where incipient Communist revolutions were beginning to make noises of varying degrees of intensity.[32] For Greece, the WFTU urged the restoration of "trade union liberties . . . on the basis of proportional representation of all trade union tendencies and opinions, excluding none."[33]

The WFTU was an extremely helpful arm to the Soviet Union during this period. The CIO and the British trade unions provided the organization with a prestige of apparent impartiality, and tended to place the Soviet trade union structure on a par with that of the American and British in the minds of many workers in the world. Attacks upon the West were given the appearance of general labor views rather than Communist propaganda. With the heightening of international pressures, the affiliation of the CIO and the WFTU served to confuse and blur the differences between free and totalitarian-oriented labor, to the detriment of the democratic labor movements and the countries in which they operated. It was, therefore, inevitable that as the CIO moved to rid itself of Communists in its own organization, it would have to stop assisting Communism abroad. The preliminaries for this move were laid down at the 1948 national convention of the CIO.

When the WFTU split finally did come, Carey, speaking for the CIO, and Arthur Deakin, for the British, admitted the WFTU report on Germany had omitted the "abuses" committed by the Soviet in the Eastern zone, and that other WFTU reports were similarly slanted. They said that "for the sake of maintaining international trade union unity," they "paid the price of abstention from protest against violation of this same liberty in the bolshevized countries."[34]

The formal split in the WFTU took place on January 19, 1949 when the representatives of the CIO, the British, and the Dutch unions walked out of the Executive Bureau meeting after it had refused to approve a British motion to suspend the organization temporarily until the international situation would permit resumption. The British motion was based on the fact that the organization had stopped functioning as a united movement in 1947, when the "cold war" started between East and West. The bitterest controversy had been over the Marshall Plan. Communist-led unions in France and Italy had called a series of national strikes in the winter of 1947 which the non-Communists had described as attempts to prevent operation of the Marshall Plan. This had led the unions favoring the Plan, including the American Federation of Labor, to establish a separate Trade Union Advisory Committee to combat Communist influence in Europe.[35]

At one point, Arthur Deakin, general secretary of the British Transport and General Workers Union, who had succeeded Citrine as WFTU president, accused the Paris headquarters of the WFTU of acting under Soviet control in not calling an Executive Bureau meeting to discuss the European Recovery Plan. Louis Saillant had refrained from calling a meeting at the advice of V. V. Kuznetsov, head of the Soviet Central Council of Trade Unions. Deakin said: "If, therefore, the position is now that the WFTU is to be merely a political body dealing only with those questions acceptable to the USSR, we know where we stand."[36]

Within the CIO, Communist-led unions and councils made

efforts to associate themselves with the WFTU in Europe to defeat
the Marshall Plan. A communication on the Taft-Hartley law, for
example, from Paul Schnurr, secretary of the San Francisco Council,
to WFTU-affiliated Communist-dominated labor federations in Italy
and France was used by the Communists in Europe against the ERP.
It read: "This law which seeks to destroy our free trade unions
is the domestic program of American imperialism which now attacks
free trade unions in the European countries as well. . . ." This
led to a strong rebuke by the CIO national office, with the adoption
of a rule that all communications to WFTU people must be chan-
neled through the national office.

The Marshall Plan was not the only divisive issue. The non-
Communists accused the WFTU leadership of seeking centralized
Communist control over Germany's labor movement, and Saillant
retaliated by charging the West with "sabotaging" German trade
union unity. The Communists charged the CIO and the British
with having "interfered with the rendering of assistance to the labor
movement of the colonial countries." In turn, the Communists were
charged with using the WFTU to further Soviet policies in Greece,
Japan, Korea, Indonesia, and other areas by "exciting backward
peoples to rise in revolt against the Western democracies to
embarrass the latter and facilitate the propagation of Communism."
The Soviet Union entered the fray when *Trud*, the official organ
of the Soviet unions, called upon the WFTU to rid itself of its
"reformist leaders."[37]

During the first days of this struggle within the WFTU, the
CIO defended its earlier position in forming the organization. James
Carey, in a number of speeches, said that the CIO membership
in the WFTU allowed the CIO to present the merits of the
Marshall Plan to European workers. "We were able to talk to the
French workers and other labor leaders in the language of labor.
With the CIO taking a position in support of the Marshall Plan it
is difficult for them to call it a scheme of Wall Street," he said.[38]

When Matthew Woll, vice-president of the American Federation of Labor, urged the CIO, in an open letter, to leave the
WFTU, Carey replied with characteristic vigor that the WFTU
"is no place for cream-puffs." He said:[39]

At issue is the question of whether or not the labor movements of the world will be taken over by reactionary totalitarianism. The CIO has elected to enter the arena and engage in the struggle; Mr. Woll prefers to loll in his ivory tower.

Carey said the CIO has "outstanding committments" to democratic union forces in Europe belonging to the WFTU. "These folks have their coats off, and we have our coats off too," he continued.

Sure we'll get our faces and hands dirty. We are not prepared to write off as lost to real democracy Czechoslovakia, Eastern Germany, Hungary, Yugoslavia and the people of the other nations, that have fallen within the Communist orbit.

Mr. Woll apparently is prepared to write them off and allow the free labor forces of other European countries to be written off along with them. . . .

Our past and continuing contributions to the welfare of the American people lead us to believe that our presence and participation inside and outside the WFTU alongside the free labor unions of Europe will inspire their confidence.

Shortly after this exchange, however, conversation started between the AFL, the CIO, and the British Trades Union Congress with regard to the formation of a new international labor organization. Following the 1948 CIO convention, preparations were made by the CIO for a break. In January 1949, a delegation consisting of James Carey, L. S. Buckmaster, Emil Mazey, and David McDonald went to Europe and consulted with British and European trade union leaders, including Vincent Tewson of the British Trades Union Congress, and Leon Jouhaux of the French *Force Ouvriere*. In March, the British leaders came to the United States to meet with both the CIO and the AFL.[40]

On April 28, 1949 a CIO-AFL conference brought forth a "friendly discussion" and a significant measure of agreement as to the nature of the new organization, with a further understanding that they would continue to consult together "in an effort to reach a common policy."

Finally, in May, 1949, the CIO Executive Board formally announced its disaffiliation from the WFTU, tracing the background of its relationship with the WFTU, and describing particularly developments of the last year during which Saillant was charged with committing the WFTU to political rather than trade-union action. The CIO revealed disagreements beginning in June 1946, when Saillant had decided that WFTU union affiliates should carry on political strikes to force their countries to blockade Franco Spain. The CIO had vigorously objected on the ground that only its constituent unions themselves could authorize strikes by their members and that no official WFTU vote urging an embargo had been taken.[41]

Further evidence used by the CIO against the WFTU was its propaganda against the Marshall Plan in spite of an early WFTU resolution calling for economic reconstruction in Europe. The CIO objected to a WFTU executive decision preventing Carey, in November 1947, from presenting CIO's arguments in support of the Marshall Plan to a WFTU meeting. Efforts to resolve these differences, the report continued, had failed. The report was here referring to Carey's attempt in May 1948 to arrive at a showdown with WFTU leaders. A meeting had been held in Rome at whch the WFTU majority was conciliatory. Saillant had agreed to act as an impartial officer. Two months later, however, another incident found WFTU in the active Communist camp.

In July 1948 a young Italian monarchist had shot Palmiro Togliatti, leader of the Italian Communist Party. Giuseppe Di Vittorio, Communist leader of the Italian General Confederation of Labor, had been head of the WFTU at this time. As part of a series of political strikes designed to cripple Premier De Gasperi's government, Vittorio had called a general strike of his Italian unions. The next day, a telegram from Saillant on behalf of the WFTU read as follows:[42]

> Assure Togliatti of our sentiments of fraternal solidarity. Convey to him our best wishes on behalf of the executive of the WFTU. Antifascist militants must be protected by general solidarity. The criminal campaigns which furnish the weapon to assassins must be met by a wide front of all working people.

The CIO and British unions had interpreted this wire as an open endorsement of a political strike against a free, anti-Communist government.

The decision of the CIO to split from the WFTU reflected

the realization that in the struggle between East and West the European labor movement would hold a key position and that in fact the struggle was in the main one for the allegiance of European workers.

With the split, the WFTU's remaining strength was estimated to be between 54,000,000 and 61,000,000, the bulk of which was in Eastern Europe, the Soviet Union and Communist China. As against that was an estimated 41,000,000 to 50,000,000 workers mainly in the United States and Western Europe.[43] The hope of the democratic trade union forces was to gain added strength from the unions in Asia, Latin America, and the undecided ones in Europe by isolating and labelling the WFTU a "Communist Front."

On June 25, 1949, the British TUC convened a Preparatory International Trade Union Conference in Geneva. The AFL and CIO were represented; Carey and Michael Ross were the CIO delegates, with John Brophy and Elmer Cope as alternates. The Geneva Conference appointed a 16-member Preparatory Committee to draft a constitution and program and convene a World Conference formally to establish a new international body.

A world conference was called for November 28 in London. It resulted in the creation of the International Confederation of Free Trade Unions. There were more than 260 delegates present from 70 national centers in 53 countries, with an aggregate membership estimated at 50 million.[44]

The establishment of the ICFTU opened up a new phase of international labor organization. It represented a departure from the pattern of its predecessors in that its main well spring was no longer European trade unionism. The presence of both the AFL and the CIO in the organization provided it with an American orientation, both because of the financial resources of the American labor movement and because of the conscious understanding that the ICFTU was allied with the interests of the democracies, under the leadership of the United States, against the Soviet movement. Furthermore, the ICFTU recognized the strength of the labor movements outside of Europe and North America when it chose eight of the nineteen members of the Executive Committee from Asia, the Middle East, Latin America, Africa, Australia, New Zealand, and the West Indies.

The new non-European orientation made it easier to accept the conclusion, as one participant in the deliberations observed,

> that the vital line of demarcation dividing mankind today, within every nation as well as among the nations, is drawn not between those who would have the government own some industries and those who would have such industries remain under private enterprise, but between those who have contempt for the dignity of human life and those to whom human values, rights and liberties are paramount.

It seemed true that the "word Socialism" had "lost much of its luster in the eyes of labor as a result of 'National Socialism' in Germany and the 'Socialist paradise' in the Soviet empire." With the understanding that Marxism had indeed been buried at Moscow, Marx was buried at London.[45]

The first manifesto of the ICFTU, however, did attempt to utilize Marxist symbols and was called "For Bread, Peace and Freedom." In discussing freedom it equated the "tyranny of Communist, Fascist, Falangist, and any other form of totalitarianism," and the "domination and exploitation of concentrated economic power in the hands of cartels and monopolies!" It asserted: "We reject the false theory that workers must sacrifice political and spiritual freedom to obtain economic security and social justice." The words "political democracy" appeared frequently in the document.

A special resolution was adopted declaring:[46]

> ... the so-called trade unions of the countries of Central and Eastern Europe under the domination of Communist totalitarian regimes imposed against the will of those peoples are not free, independent and democratic organizations which defend the interests of the workers but governmental instruments designed for the organized exploitation of workers for the benefit of a state capitalism serving the U.S.S.R., the principal beneficiary.

The resolution went on to protest against "the concentration camps, forced labour camps and military organization of workers' units and against the supression of civil rights."

The battle between world communism and the forces for political liberty has gone through many phases since 1950. There has been bloodshed and the struggle for men's minds. In all of this, there has been pitted against each other the communist-led WFTU and the ICFTU.

Today, Soviet Communist Party Chief Khrushchev is calling for increased harmony between the two worlds and, as part of the new communist drive, has proposed a united front with non-communist unions in other countries. Free labor's answer came from ICFTU General Secretary J. H. Oldenbroek, who said: "There is no 'point of contact' with the Soviet-controlled organization such as the W.F.T.U."

Recalling past efforts at working within the WFTU, Mr. Olden-broek reiterated the basic indictment against communists in the labor movement whose real aim was "the infiltration of free unions" and the "subordination of the international trade union movement to the political aims of the Soviet Union."[47]

With this WFTU policy and with the conclusions that no common ground can be found with the communists abroad, the CIO remained united and in agreement. The 1955 merger of the CIO with the AFL only served to strengthen and fortify this resolve.

[1] J. B. S. Hardman and Joseph Paull, "World Federation of Trade Unions," *Labor and Nation*, December, 1945, Part Two, p. 2.

[2] See *passim The Second International 1889-1914*, by James Joll (New York 1956).

[3] Hardman and Paull, *op. cit.*, p. 3.

[4] *Ibid.*, p. 4.

[5] Adolf Sturmthal, "World Strategy for Unions," *The Nation*, Vol. 157, August 28, 1943, p. 233.

[6] *Ibid.*

[7] Adolf Sturmthal, "Russia and World Labor," *Current History*, Vol. 8, May, 1945, pp. 385-390.

[8] David Lasser, "Labor and World Affairs," *Foreign Policy Reports*, Vol. XXV, no. 13, November 15, 1949, p. 151.

[9] *Ibid.*, p. 151, quoting from a report of A. Losovsky, secretary of the RILU, to Fifth World Congress, Moscow, in *Pravda*, September 2, 1930.

[10] Hardman and Paull, *op. cit.*, pp. 4, 5.

[11] Sturmthal, "Russia and World Labor," *op. cit.*

[12] Sturmthal, "World Strategy for Unions," *op. cit.*

[13] Sturmthal, "Russia and World Labor," *op. cit.*

[14] Hardman and Paull, *op. cit.*, pp. 5, 6.

[15] CIO, *Daily Proceedings of the Fifth Constitutional Convention* (Boston, Massachusetts, November 9-13, 1942), p. 190.

[16] Lasser, *op. cit.*, p. 152.

[17] Hardman and Paull, *op. cit.*, p. 6.

[18] British Trades Union Congress, *Report of The World Trade Union Conference* (London, February 6-17, 1945), p. 1.
[19] Hardman and Paull, *op. cit.*, p. 6.
[20] CIO, press release, January 10, 1945.
[21] Hardman and Paull, *op. cit.*, p. 15.
[22] *Ibid.*, p. 8.
[23] BTUC, *Report of World Conference, op. cit.*, pp. 237, 238.
[24] CIO, *You and the WFTU*, publication no. 139, 1946.
[25] Murray Kempton, "Global Labor War," *Plain Talk*, May, 1949, p. 17.
[26] CIO, *Report on World Unity*, publication no. 127, 1945.
[27] *You and the WFTU, op. cit.*
[28] Kempton, *op. cit.*, p. 16.
[29] Lasser, *op. cit.*, p. 153.
[30] CIO, press release, March 15, 1946.
[31] WFTU, *Report of the Commission of the World Federation of Trade Unions to Investigate Conditions of Germany*, 1946. The CIO representatives in this WFTU effort were Sidney Hillman and John Abt.
[32] Lasser, *op. cit.*, p. 154.
[33] CIO, press release, September 24, 1946.
[34] Kempton, *op. cit.*, p. 17.
[35] Lasser, *op. cit.*, p. 154.
[36] *The New York Times*, February 9, 10, 11, 1948.
[37] Lasser, *op. cit.*, p. 155, quoting *Trud*, November 16, 1947.
[38] *The New York Times*, January 3, 1948.
[39] *CIO News*, August 2, 1948.
[40] *CIO News*, October 31, 1949.
[41] *CIO News*, May 23, 1949.
[42] Kempton, *op. cit.*, p. 18.
[43] Lasser, *op. cit.*, p. 155.
[44] International Confederation of Free Trade Unions, *For Bread, Peace and Freedom*, (London, 1949) p. 5.
[45] David Dubinsky, "World Labor's New Weapon," *Foreign Affairs*, April, 1950, pp. 6, 8.
[46] ICFTU, *op. cit.*, p. 26.
[47] *The New York Times*, March 24, 1956.

PART V

Chapter 15

CONCLUSION

15 | CONCLUSION

In reality there is no such thing as Communist trade unionism; there are merely Communists who work for the Party inside the trade unions. And, once it is taken over by the Communists, a trade union ceases to be a trade union, for all that it may retain the charter and outward appearance of a trade union.

A. Rossi
A Communist Party in Action

The trade-union may be termed 'the all-embracing organization of the working class'...They are a school of Communism.

Joseph Stalin

It is clear, in summarizing the story of the CIO and the Communist Party, that the American labor movement did not seek a death struggle with Communist trade unionism. In the logic of international developments, however, the break was inevitable; and once it came, the high stakes were plain for all to see. Not only was the integrity and survival of the trade union heritage at stake but more important was the national self-interest of the United States. For the CIO to have remained aloof from the battle between Communism and democracy would have stopped it from playing any significant role on the American scene.

The decisiveness of the CIO victory over the Communist Party is in a measure illustrated by the fact that Communist-led unions in 1949 claimed a membership of more than two million and are today estimated to represent no more than two hundred thousand workers. The real measure and significance of the outcome, however must be spelled out in broader terms. Equally important are the lessons learned from the experience.

There is no compartment of life in the 20th Century America

which is not a concern of the American labor movement, even though the economic function of a trade union is the one which most firmly grips the loyalty of union members. Unions in our democracy are also frequently social units providing wage earners and their families with an opportunity to fulfill their fraternal and social needs. They are educational institutions as well, both in the narrow sense of the term when they train apprentices and train and elevate leaders from their ranks, and in the broader sense of the term as they provide an opportunity for participation in decision-making. These economic, social, educational, and political functions have been decribed by one political scientist as "one of the plurality of governments which constitute a free state."[1]

Whether we accept this theory of pluralism or not, the trade union is an important seat of power in a democracy. The fact, therefore, that communist unionism has suffered a defeat in the American labor movement during recent years is of great importance. The Marxists allege that a revolutionary trade union movement is necessary for their success. A Communist movement which does not have its roots firmly in the labor movement is like a house without a foundation. Therefore, the Communist party suffered a significant reverse when the eleven unions under its control were either ousted or forced to resign from the CIO.

The CIO was very proud of its decision to expel the Communist-led unions. In an editorial in an issue of the *CIO News* which appeared one year after the expulsion,[2] the editor said "To put it bluntly—and factually—the CIO in a year has broken the back of the Communist party in the United States." This is, of course, an exaggerated statement. Some Communist-led unions still operate independently today and exercise influence in a few of the industries where they operate. The CIO has significantly diminished the power of Communist unionism in the electrical industry, but it has not been able to affect the control which Communist unions have in the west coast shipping industry and in the copper mines. The problem is a diminishing but still a serious one and is intensfied as America's defense needs become urgent, and as the interests of the United States and the Soviet Union continue to conflict in the world.

One of the questions raised by a study such as this is how does a union leadership continue to maintain its hold on the membership while carrying the union through contortions which lead ultimately to a thoroughly unpatriotic political position The power of nationalism and patriotism is great, and their hold on American citizens has been a potent fact in our history. Yet many thousands of American citizens have supported Communists as their union leaders, and even today continue to vote for those leaders in secret elections under Government supervision in the face of a barrage of hostile editorial comment, speeches, and Congressional investigations which expose their leaders as Communists.

Finding the answer to this question is a challenge which requires the expertise of political and social psychologists and not of the political scientist and labor economist alone. Various explanations, however, do suggest themselves from this study.

To begin with, we must note the climate which permitted the Communists to gain their initial influence and control. The period beginning with 1933 was characterized by increasing acceptance of the Soviet Union in public opinion and intellectual circles. It was also a period of extraordinary fluidity in the labor movement, since new organizational vistas were opening and there was a dearth of competent union leadership to explore them. It is also clear in retrospect that where established unions had firm leadership, as in the garment and clothing trades, the Communists made little headway, but where that leadership was not strong, as in the electrical and automobile industries, or was corrupt and ineffective, the Communists were able to fill the vacuum and establish control.

Second, Communist success in gaining and keeping influence and control is partially explained by their mastery of the techinques of group organization and manipulation. Decision-making within a Communist-dominated union is always, as we saw demonstrated within the Mine, Mill and Smelter Workers, the seamen's unions, and the Transport Workers Union, controlled by the party fraction. On occasion, the party fraction will utilize "front" leadership; thus Albert Fitzgerald, a Catholic, became president of the Electrical Workers. Even where "front" leadership exists, however, key members of the Communist party are placed in strategic positions within the union; the office of secretary-treasurer is one such post, the editorship of the union newspaper is another.

The manipulation of democratic procedures so as to yield results beneficial to the Communist minority is an established technique of Communist control. One of the important and significant characteristics of American trade unions, just as it is a characteristic of the American political scene, is membership apathy. The typical union member frequently has little desire to attend a meeting after his day's work is done. He would far rather go to a movie, watch television, or seek other forms of personal pleasure. He is quite content to leave all business matters of his union in the hands of his officers and a few active members. This is true so long as these offices and leaders are able to win economic gains. Union leaders interested in developing membership participation have had to resort to such devices as door prizes and fines to stimulate participation. Union leaders interested in maintaining minority control merely take advantage of this apathy.[3] Communists usually come to union meetings well organized and well caucused. Many of them will be fully instructed, with resolutions all prepared in their pockets. The evidence is likewise clear that the caucus is usually trained and disciplined and prepared to stall all night at a meeting in order to exhaust the non-Communist members present.

Another well calculated technique used by the Communists is that of undermining and discrediting the opposition. This is usually accomplished by slogans, violent denunciations, and disciplinary action against opponents, who are labelled "racists," "Taft-Hartleyites," "labor saboteurs," and "scabs," among other things.

An additional refinement of this technique is the occasional use of violence and intimidation. The National Union of Marine Cooks and Stewards affords a good case in point. A thorough study of that union's control mechanism was undertaken in 1952 by the Senate Subcommittee on Labor and Labor-Management Relations with the cooperation of the National Labor Relations Board. Senator Hubert H. Humphrey in his introduction to the study pointed out that the leaders of the union were able to remain in control "by terrorizing the real and imagined dissidents within the union, by depriving critics of their jobs, by slander, villification; by intimidating Government witnesses to its illegal activities, by perverting the union's judicial machinery into an instrument of reprisal, by intimidating the employers into becoming parties to their totalitarian methods. In brief, this Communist-dominated union has remained in power by corrupting the basic democracy of a union to create a little totalitarian system all of its own."[4]

The intimidation was both physical and economic. In one case, the wife of a member of the opposition group was beaten in her home. Anti-Communists risked being beaten or threatened by officers of the union or by hangers-on around the union hall when then came in the vicinity. Attempts by anti-Communists to obtain jobs also met with great difficulty because of the union hiring hall provision which had been entered into between the union and the management. The hiring hall, normally a useful mechanism for stabilizing the hiring policies in the maritime industry, was perverted into an instrument of attrition against opposition elements within the union.[5] Employers, to avoid trouble, permitted themselves to become agents through which the union leadership imposed its rule of terrorism and discrimination against all who dared to oppose its Communist policies.

A third possible explanation for Communist control within the American labor movement is the fact that union members have frequently demonstrated their ability to compartmentalize their loyalties. The members of the United Mine Workers had proven their trade union loyalty to John L. Lewis on many occasions, but then voted for Roosevelt and not for Willkie in 1940. The labor movement in Ohio is a strong one, with a loyal membership which has gained many concessions from employers, but union members did not follow the leadership of their trade union officers in 1950, when these leaders urged support of Mr. Ferguson against Mr. Taft for United States Senator. In the same way it is clear that members of Communist-led unions continue to support their trade union in collective bargaining arrangements while they often silently ignore the political recommendations of the unions' leadership.

There is a fourth possible explanation. Most of the Communist-led unions which we have investigated had achieved maturity, stability, and harmonious relations with management. A union such as the Fur and Leather Workers, for example, has been able to realize high wages, reasonable hours, and good working conditions within the industry. One labor historian evaluated these factors in the following manner:[6]

254

CONCLUSION

Like the rank and file workers in other industries, members of the Fur Union are concerned with immediate improvements and pay little heed to the ultimate goals and objectives of the union leadership. The fact that Communists dominate the union has not frightened members, especially since many of the members have radical inclinations. Nor are they deeply interested in the part that the union plays in the larger labor movement, as long as wages go up, hours go down, and working conditions improve.

In the fur industry, the union's position has been so strong as to establish a feeling among many of the smaller fur manufacturers that the union could force them out of business if it should be so inclined. The great economic strength of the union—which has meant great economic gains for the members—has kept many members loyal to it in spite of the political views of its leaders. This is equally true in many other Communist-led unions.

Fifth, we have also seen that the cry "Communist" has been used so often by anti-labor employers and editorial writers to besmirch the legitimate aspirations of trade unionism that many workers have become immune to the charge. This observation is no small factor in arriving at an understanding of why it is that Harry Bridges is able to continue his control over the west coast longshoremen and that the Communist leadership of the International Union of Mine, Mill and Smelter Workers has retained power.

Finally, we must understand that the revolutionary political philosophy of Communist trade unionism is most frequently not discernible in the collective bargaining policy of the unions. Collective bargaining has not been used by the Communists to achieve communism in America nor to achieve the economic revolution they advocate. It would be difficult to distinguish between the CIO International Union of Electrical Workers, and the independent Communist-led United Electrical Workers, on the basis of the minimum contract standards of these two unions. The economic demands of Communist-led unions have on the whole been orthodox trade union demands.[7] In fact, no innovation in collective bargaining techniques or demands can be attributed to the Communists or to their unions. Product royalties for welfare funds, for example, were pioneered by the miners and by the musicians; unemployment assistance by the International Ladies' Garment Workers Union and the Amalgamated Clothing Workers Union; pensions by the miners, steelworkers, and auto workers; the guaranteed annual wage by the UAW and UE and Steelworkers; health benefits by the Amalgamated Streetcar Employees and the ILGWU.

The differences arise where the interests of the Soviet Union are involved. Prior to World War II, during the Communist "isolationist" period, there were Communist-led strikes in plants doing defense work, such as North American, Vultee Aircraft, and Allis Chalmers. During the war, Harry Bridges led his union into an active policy of collaboration with employers and no-strike pledges on the waterfront. During the war, too, the UE and other Communist-led unions actively supported wage incentive plans as their contribution to a "win the war program," a line which ran counter to the traditional opposition of American unions to "speed-up" in industry.

There is very little evidence to prove that the goal of the Communists in the trade union movement is to achieve economic revolution or the overthrow of capitalism. There is, however, overwhelming evidence to prove that the goal of Communists in the trade union movement is support of Soviet strategy in foreign affairs, regardless of what that strategy happens to be at any particular moment. Communist unionism, therefore, does not so much represent a trade union philosophy in any meaningful sense of the term as a system of power.

The traditions of the American labor movement are quite hostile to the philosophy of Communism. The philosophy of the American labor movement, insofar as it is possible to speak of its philosophy, is one of humanism. This explains why it is that the American labor movement has not considered itself as representative of narrow class or sectional interests, but rather of the broad mass of the population.

The American labor movement has been a staunch advocate of progressive measures designed to humanize man, to educate him, to enlarge his moral vision and his material possessions. Trade unions have struggled to humanize labor not only by improving working conditions, but also by attaching to industrial labor a significant status value. It is this function which has attracted so many intellectuals, who would not ordinarily be trade union members, into the labor movement.

Samuel Gompers expressed this philosophy of humanism well when, in addressing the 1909 convention of the American Federation of Labor, he said:[8]

> There is not a wrong against which we fail to protest or seek remedy; there is not a right to which any of our fellows are entitled which it is not our duty, mission, work, and struggle to maintain. So long as there shall remain a wrong unrighted, or a right denied, there will be ample work for the labor movement to do.

Again addressing the 1918 convention of the AFofL, Gompers said:[9]

> The trade union movement, true to its history, its traditions and its aspirations, has done, is doing, and will undoubtedly continue to do more in the interests of mankind to humanize the human family than all other agencies combined.

The modern counterpart of that expression of labor humanism can be found in a statement by the late Philip Murray, CIO President:[10]

> Labor in America seeks the quickest possible perfection of ... the human welfare state. The human welfare state preserves the best of our American traditions. It promotes and expands the basic concepts of human liberty. It encourages the enterprise system which has helped make this nation great.
>
> The human welfare state seeks earnestly to protect its citizens from fear, from want, from human degradation. It is not a paternalistic government; it does not rob its citizens of initiative, or bind them in slavery to an all-powerful dictatorship.
>
> The human welfare state does—and must—work for its citizens. It is not—and it must not become—an overpowering machine which sacrifices the liberty of the people in return for security or reforms.
>
> We in American labor value beyond all else the rights and dignity of the individual. We in American labor will fight totalitarianism from the right or from the left. We regard the human welfare state as America's middle way. It should be neither right nor left, but liberal, progressive, openminded and daring.

Sidney Hook summarized the belief system of the labor movement as follows:[11]

... that human values are primary to all others; that social institutions must be judged ultimately not by the intentions or rationalizations of those in the seats of power, but by their effects on the work-a-day lives of individuals; that all social principles and doctrines must be justified by their fruits in enriching the quality of personal experiences here and now; and that human beings have the resources in themselves and in nature to fulfill all their reasonable needs.

This tradition of humanism within the American Labor movement helps explain why the Communists, in spite of their skill, zeal and dedication, were not able to make even greater headway than they did. A study of labor history shows that there have never been any AFL international unions under Communist control. There are today no unions under Communist control in the newly merged AFL-CIO. And even at the height of their influence within the CIO, Communist-controlled unions accounted for no more than 25 percent of the total CIO membership.

The Communist party could not successfully adjust to the prevailing philosophy of humanism within the American labor movement. Its inflexible loyalty to the immediate interests of the Soviet Union eliminated any resilience within its group and made it impossible for the Communist party, and for Communist-led unions, to withstand the ebb and flow of American attitudes toward the Soviet Union. The Communist party member could demonstrate his loyalty only by absolute conformity. As a result of the conspiratorial environment in which the Communist party operates the practicing Communist "regards himself as a professional revolutionist along the Soviet model."[12] He could not, dared not, and did not criticize the Soviet Union. Communist trade union leaders, unlike ordinary politicians—even those with firm political commitments who find it tactically wise on occasion to remain silent or dissent from the pattern with which they are usually identified, did not indulge in this tactic.

It is this characteristic of inflexibility and rigidity in behalf of the Soviet Union on the part of the American Communist movement which has made it possible to identify Communist trade union leaders and thus strengthen those who would negate their influence. Here, indeed, is the Achilles' heel of Communist trade unionism in America.

[1] Marshall E. Dimmock, "Labor's Part in War and Reconstruction," *The American Political Science Review*, Vol. 35, April 1941, p. 219.

[2] *CIO News*, Nov. 20, 1950, p. 4.

[3] Joel Seidman, *Union Rights and Union Duties* (Harcourt Brace: New York, 1943) p. 48.

[4] *The Marine Cooks and Stewards Union*, A Staff Report to the Subcommittee on Labor and Labor-Management Relations of the Committee on Labor and Public Welfare, United States Senate, 82nd Congress, 2nd Session, 1953. The author of the report is Julius Draznin.

[5] *Ibid.*, p. 137.

[6] Robert D. Leiter, "Fur Workers Union," *Industrial and Labor Relations Review*, Vol. 3, no. 2, January 1950, p. 186.

[7] Jack Barbash, "Communist Unionism—Aims and Means," (an unpublished manuscript, 1952).

[8] Lois MacDonald, *Labor Problems and the American Scene* (Harper: New York, 1938) p. 386.

[9] *Ibid.*

[10] Labor Press Associates, press release, January 15, 1949.

[11] Sidney Hook, "Humanism and the Labor Movement," in *European Ideologies* (Philosophical Library: New York, 1948) pp. 1059-1063; See also, Frank Tannenbaum, *A Philosophy of Labor*, (Knopf: New York, 1951).

[12] Barbash, *op. cit.*

APPENDIX

APPENDIX:
LEGISLATION ON
COMMUNISTS IN UNIONS

We have examined in quite some detail the history of Communist infiltration into an important part of the American trade union movement, and the efforts made within that organization to combat the totalitarian threat. The stakes in the struggle were high and affected not only the CIO, but the nation as a whole. The battlefield was the trade union meeting hall, but the rest of the American community were more than disinterested observers. It was, therefore, perfectly understandable that the American people speaking through its government concerned itself with the problem of Communist trade unionism and was not content for the decision to be made only in the union halls.

The first serious legislative proposal in the Congress relating to Communism in labor unions came during the 80th Congress. It passed in the form of Sec. 9(h) of the Labor-Management Relations Act of 1947, the Taft-Hartley Act. The provision required the execution of an affidavit by each officer of any labor organization which desired to operate under the Act, to the effect "that he is not a member of the Communist Party or affiliated with such Party, and that he does not believe in, and is not a member of or supports any organization that believes in or teaches, the overthrow of the United States Government by force or by an illegal or unconstitutional methods.[1]

President Truman vetoed the Act, and in his veto message singled out this section for specific attention to the effect that its only result "would be confusion and disorder, which is exactly the results the Communists desire..." He went on to say "I consider that this provision would increase, rather than decrease the disruptive effects of Communists in our labor movement..."[2]

The American labor movement reacted negatively to the affidavit requirement. For a number of months, organized labor considered opposing the affidavit as a matter of principle and threatened non-compliance. It wasn't long, however, before most of the trade unions recognized the necessity to comply as a means of carrying out their collective bargaining objective and all but a few of them, notably the United Steelworkers and the United Mine Workers, decided to have their officers file the affidavits. Communist trade unions, therefore, had the choice of either finding ways and means of complying with the affidavit requirements or not signing and taking the risk of being in a difficult competitive relationship with other unions.

The Communist trade union leaders developed three major techniques for meeting the affidavit threat. First was the resignation from the Communist party of some of the leaders. Max Perlow, secretary-treasurer of the United Furniture Workers started this trend. In a statement to the press on June 5, 1949, Perlow stated that his union had decided to file the affidavits and thus prevent raiding from other unions. He said he was faced with a choice of continuing either as a union officer or as a member of the Communist party. He still believed in Communist doctrine and his right to advocate it, and he asserted that he had never kept his long-standing membership a secret from the union members. He then used this occasion to further advance the Party's interest by saying:

> It is because of the teachings of this party that I came to the conclusion that there can be no higher privilege, no greater principle, than to serve the working people in their struggle for a higher standard of living, for higher wages, for job security, for greater and greater guarantees for the workers to live decently and bring up their children as free people without fear to face the future ... Marxism is the best expression of the hopes and aspirations of mankind to free itself of the mounting evils which threaten the world today.[3]

It is clear the Perlow's action violated the spirit and intent of Sec. 9(h), but the general counsel of the National Labor Relations Board, Mr. Denham, felt that "the maximum limit" to which he could go was to refer the affidavit to the Department of Justice.[4] "The act does not direct or authorize either the general counsel or the Board to police these affidavits or to pass judgment upon their truth or falsity. While Mr. Perlow's published statements, if they accurately quote him, would tend to throw considerable doubt on the good faith in his affidavit, nevertheless, we are required by the law to take the affidavits as they are submitted . . ."[5]

The NLRB supported Mr. Denham's position by a 4-1 majority when, in a decision dated July 19, 1949, they placed the Furniture Workers on a ballot for the first time since passage of the Taft-Hartley Act. The Board claimed that it was not the intent of Congress to have the authenticity of the affidavits questioned by the Board.

Perlow's successful effort was emulated about a month later by Maurice Travis, secretary-treasurer of the Mine, Mill and Smelter Workers, who "reluctantly" resigned from the Communist Party, signed the affidavit and pledged he would "continue to fight" for Communist goals "with all the energy and sincerity at my command."[6] Travis said a "great sense of indignation" accompanied his decision since "an American has as much right to be a Communist as he has to be a Republican, a Democrat, a Jew, a Catholic, an Elk or a Mason."

Donald Henderson of the Food and Tobacco Workers of America followed the same line. In August, 1950, Ben Gold, head of the Fur and Leather Workers Union also officially resigned from the Communist Party to sign the Taft-Hartley affidavit thus allowing his union to qualify and protect itself from raiding.[7]

The Department of Justice was quite reluctant for a number of years to begin prosecutions for perjury in connection with Sec. 9(h). The statute provides that an officer of the union must file an affidavit stating that he "is not" a member of the Party. The use of the present tense led the Justice Department to believe that prior or future membership in the Communist party was not controlling if at the instant of taking the oath the signer of the affidavit was not a party member. The difficulty of proving actual membership at the time of the signing was for a time considered an insurmountable obstacle by the Department. Subsequently, however, the Department obtained indictments against several union leaders who were convicted and sentenced by the courts. These included Anthony Valentino of the Packinghouse Workers Union in 1952; Melvin Hupman, United Electrical Workers, in 1954; Maurice Travis of the Mine, Mill and Smelter Workers Union, and Ben Gold, Fur and Leather Workers Union, in 1954. The NLRB for a time considered the indictments to be sufficient for it to declare that Sec. 9(h) was not complied with, but the courts on two occasions overruled the Board on the ground that the indictment itself did not prove guilt.[7a]

A second strategy to avoid the intent of the Act was to amend the union constitution and juggle union offices. The first NLRB test of this ruse was furnished by the United Shoeworkers which changed its constitution so that there were only two national officers of the union. Other leaders remained at their old posts, but without officer titles. At first, the Board allowed the ruse to operate.[8] It soon, however, changed its ruling after it became clear that other unions were following suit. The board adopted its new ruling in the case of Donald Henderson and his Food and Tobacco Workers Union. Henderson had been named "national administrative director" after resigning as president. The Board disallowed this change and claimed it would be necessary for Henderson to comply if the union was to be considered in compliance.

The third method of evading Sec. 9(h) was simply to ignore charges of Communist domination and sign the affidavit on the assumption that fraud and perjury would have to be proved by the Department of Justice.

It is difficult to evaluate the effect of the 9(h) provision on the decline of Communist influence in the trade-union movement and in the CIO in particular. There can be no question but that a final break with the Stalinists was inevitable. Differences as to the Marshall Plan and the Wallace Progressive Party were the developments that stimulated action. It does appear, however, that the affidavit requirement helped in a number of local situations to identify the Communists and to facilitate their ouster. This was particularly true during the first days following the passage of the Taft-Hartley Act.

The affidavit shifted the anti-Communist struggle from the political to the economic level. Communists within unions had been attacked by congressional committees, employers, the press, and within the unions themselves. The issues, however, had been political—i.e., "Red fascism," Marshall Plan, third party—but these issues did not seem to cause many union members too great a concern. With the Taft-Hartley affidavit, however, the union's welfare itself was at stake. If the officers did not sign, it could mean economic hardship, union raiding, loss of contracts, perhaps strikes.

After the passage of the Taft-Hartley Act, a number of bills were introduced in the Congress to change its anti-Communist provisions. These came from two directions. On the one hand, suggestions came to eliminate Sec 9(h) completely, or to make it applicable to employers as well so as to remove the implicit assumption that the national security need only concern itself with Communists in the labor movement and not among the employer group. On the other hand, proposals were made to strengthen the Department of Justice's hand with regard to enforcing violations of Sec. 9(h) by clarifying the language.

Efforts were made also to change one other provision in the Taft-Hartley Act, which had an effect on the Communist problem. The law's section dealing with union shop agreements, prevented a union under the terms of a collective bargaining agreement from getting any person discharged from his position for any reason other than non-payment of dues. This meant that membership in the Communist party was not adequate reason for a union to obtain discharge of a person under union shop agreements. A number of legislative proposals were introduced which would permit labor organizations to bar Communists from membership and which would permit employers to discharge such persons.

A rather intensive and thorough study of the whole problem was made during the 82nd Congress by the Senate Subcommittee on Labor and Labor-Management Relations under the chairmanship of Senator Hubert H. Humphrey of Minnesota.[9] The Subcommittee analyzed existing practice and discussed a number of suggestions that had been made for further government action. In discussing the adequacy of existing legislation, it described the Atomic Energy Commission's solution of the problem of dealing with the UE. The General Electric Corporation, pursuant to a Wagner Act certification, had recognized the United Electrical Workers as the representative of its organized employees. When GE undertook to operate a government-owned atomic installation at its Schenectady plant, it proceeded to recognize the UE for that operation as well. This concerned the AEC because even though all employees engaged on classified atomic energy work were subject to security clearance, the recognition of UE as the bargaining representative raised additional security questions over and above those of individual security clearances. The Commission, therefore, decided to direct the General Electric Corporation not to recognize the UE at the new atomic energy installation. It did so on the ground that there were circumstances at Schenectady conducive to Communist-inspired action adverse to the atomic energy program and the nation's security and that it was necessary to remove from lines of influence over employees on atomic energy work any representative of "undependable loyalty." The UE protested this directive and went to the courts where the AEC ruling was upheld. A new election was held with both the UE and the CIO IUE on the ballot. The NLRB prior to the election stated that any certification following the election would have to be conditional upon compliance by the certified unions with the security requirements of the AEC. UE lost all of the elections in that plant pursuant to that directive.

The Department of Defense, when questioned by the subcommittee, claimed that it did not have the legal authority to follow in the footsteps of the AEC. Its own program was primarily one of denying access to individuals found to be security risks, a program which "does not in itself substantially reduce the threat of possible sabotage which might be carried out at the instigation of Communist-dominated unions."

Interesting testimony was presented to the Humphrey subcommittee recommending ways of dealing with Communist-dominated unions. One of the suggestions was to treat those unions in the same way as the law now treats company-dominated unions, namely, by allowing the NLRB to order such unions disestablished and to have employers withdraw recognition from them on the grounds that they are not legitimate and *bona fide* trade unions. The NLRB itself did not relish assuming that responsibility and suggested that if the policy was a desirable one another agency should be given the responsibility of making the determination on the ground that the NLRB itself did not have the expertise or the techniques to make such determinations intelligently.

Mr. Benjamin Sigal, an attorney for the IUE, suggested that administrative action rather than legislation was the answer and he proposed that agencies like the Munitions Board be given the authority within the Department of Defense to police security regulations by establishing a tripartite board to determine if unions were Communist-controlled.

In its recommendations, the Humphrey subcommittee urged that the National Labor Relations Board be given authority "to protect its own processes from abuse," if it did not have that authority. The refusal to testify under oath as to the truth of a non-Communist affidavit or as to membership in the Communist Party, or a conviction for false swearing in a non-Communist affidavit, said the sub-committee, should be adequate for the Board to put the union on notice either to purge itself of the officers whose affidavits are found lacking in good faith or be considered in non-compliance with the statute. The subcommittee felt that Sec. 9(h) had served some function in helping to identify the Communist-dominated unions and should not be taken from the law until all Communist domination has disappeared in the vital industries. The Justice Department was also urged to give more careful study to the possibility of prosecuting alleged Communist violations of Sec. 9(h). The Munitions Board, the AEC and the FBI were urged to develop specialized competence in dealing with security implications of Communist-dominated unions, and the President was urged to have an in-service training program for these various agencies through the Bureau of the Budget.

The subcommittee also took to task those employers who saw rivalry between a Communist union and a non-Communist and anti-Communist union as simply ordinary trade union competitiveness and who sought to take advantage of that competitiveness. The General Electric Corporation was specifically singled out for criticism for its "plague on both your houses" attitude and for informing its workers that there was little choice between "left-wingers" and "right-wingers." "It is this attitude on the part of some employers which has made the opposition to the real Communists in the unions very difficult and explains in large part why the Communists have been able to retain as much as they have," said the subcommittee. Not to make a distinction between Communist unionism and liberal or radical groups in the American labor movement, said the subcommittee "is to play the Communist theme song."

No anti-Communist legislation affecting the trade unions was enacted by the 82nd Congress. In the 83rd Congress, however, Public Law 637 was enacted which included an amendment to the Subversive Activitites Control Act of 1950 to provide for the determination of the identity of certain Communist-infiltrated unions. The bill provided in effect that any union that had aided Communist-front groups within the last three years or whose leaders had been consistently identified with Communist groups in the last two years could be brought before the Subversive Activities Control Board by the Department of Justice and if found to be "Communist infiltrated" would lose its collective bargaining rights. Contracts entered into by that union could be invalidated and 20 percent of the workers could ask for an NLRB election to determine a new bargaining agent.[10]

The Department of Justice has now moved quite decisively against the Mine, Mill and Smelter Workers Union. In July 1955, it asked the Subversive Activities Control Board to determine that the Union was a Communist-infiltrated organization as defined by the Communist Control Act. These proceedings are now pending. Again in November 1956, it obtained indictments against 14 officials of the same Union, including Maurice E. Travis, former president, who had been sentenced to 8 years imprisonment for filing false non-Communist oaths in 1951 and 1952, for conspiracy to file false Taft-Hartley affidavits with the National Labor Relations Board.[11]

It is clear that Communist-dominated unions pose a sufficient threat to our security by sabotage and espionage to warrant government action. No private group has inherent immunity from public regulations on the point of security. The decisive question is whether the proposed action is wise and a democratic exercise of public authority.

The solution of the problem of Communist trade unionism must be a joint one between voluntary self-regulation and government action. As a result of this joint action, Communist-dominated unions are on the run. Only Harry Bridges has been able to maintain a degree of power.

It is clear that as of this date the Communist problem is of little moment numerically in the American labor movement. NLRB election results demonstrate that American workers are abandoning the unions with Communist-line histories. A study made of four of the expelled unions shows that in five years, they lost more elections than they won compared to a national average of seven out of ten union victories over the "no union" proposal. Commenting on these statistics, Joseph A. Loftus, distinguished labor reporter for *The New York Times,* concluded "Thus, the election process is gradually eroding the unions with Communist-domination marks on them."[12]

[1] For much of the material used in this analysis, I am indebted to David I. Shair, "How Effective It The Non-Communist Affidavit?" *Labor Law Journal,* Vol. I, No. 12 September 1950, pp. 935-944; and Walter L. Daykin, "The Operation of The Taft-Hartley Act's Non-Communist Provisions," *Iowa Law Review,* Vol. XXXVI, No. 4, Summer 1951, pp. 607-628.

[2] *The New York Times,* June 21, 1947, p. 4.

[3] *The New York Times,* June 6, 1949, p. 1.

[4] NLRB Release—R-202, June 14, 1949.

[5] Mr. Denham's opinion was consistent with a decision of the NLRB on March 4, 1948, *In the Matter of Craddock-Terry Shoe Corporation and United Shoeworkers of America, CIO,* Case No. 5-C-2087, 76 NLRB 842.

[6] *The New York Times,* August 16, 1949, p. 7.

[7] *The New York Times,* August 29, 1950.

[7a] On December 10, 1956, the United States Supreme Court ruled that a non-Communist oath taken falsely by a union officer does not expose the union to penalty even if the union members are aware of the crime. The court held in cases involving the Fur Workers and Mine, Mill, that the Congress did not intend to give the NLRB the power to disqualify unions. (*The New York Times,* December 11, 1956). Also *Supra,* pp. 185-188.

[8] Craddock-Terry Shoe Corporation 76 NLRB 842.

[9] See *Public Policy and Communist Domination of Certain Unions,* Report of the Subcommittee on Labor and Labor-Management Relations to the Committee on Labor and Public Welfare, United States Senate, 82nd Congress, 2nd session, 1953.

[10] Important studies of the problem include:
Taft, Philip: "Communism in Trade Unions"
  77 *Monthly Labor Rev.* 139 (1954)
"Labor Law—Non-Communist Affidavits by union officers—union knowledge of falsity" (Farmers v. International Fur Workers, 35 LRRM 2448, N. Y. U. *Law Rev.* 30-1132, May 1955
"Control of Communist Unions: A New Approach."
  NW. U. Law Rev. 50: 396, July, Aug. 1955
"Labor Law—Non-Communist Affidavits—authority of NLRB to declare labor unions not in compliance with Sec. 9 (h) of Labor Management Relations Act" (Farmers v. International Fur Workers, 221 F. 2nd 862), *Geo. Wash. Law Rev.* 24:150, October 1955.

[11] *The New York Times,* November 17, 1956; also see *Supra* p. 185, 187.

[12] *The New York Times,* March 28, 1955.

BIBLIOGRAPHY

BOOKS, MANUSCRIPTS

ABERNETHY, BRYON, R.: *Liberty Concepts in Labor Relations,* American Council on Public Affairs, Washington, D.C., 1943.

BARBASH, JACK: *Labor Unions in Action,* Harper & Bros., New York, 1948. "Communist Unionism—Aims and Means," unpublished manuscript, Washington, D.C., 1952.

BARNES, JOSEPH: *Wilkie,* New York, 1952.

BRITISH TRADES UNION CONGRESS: *Report of the World Trade Union Conference,* London, February 6-17, 1945.

BROWDER, EARL: *Communism in the Uinted States,* International Publishers, New York, 1935.

CARROLL, MOLLIE RAY: *Labor and Politics,* a Ph.D. dissertation, University of Chicago. 1820.

COLEMAN, MCALISTER: *Men and Coal,* Farrar and Rhinehart, 1943, 350 pp.

COMMUNIST PARTY OF USA: *The Way Out,* 1934.

CROSSER, PAUL K.: *Ideologies and American Labor,* Oxford University Press, New York, 1941, 221 pp.

FOSTER, WILLIAM Z.: *From Bryan to Stalin,* International Publishers, New York, 1937.
   Misleaders of Labor, 1929.
   Toward Soviet America, New York, 1932.

GITLOW, BENJAMIN: *I Confess,* E. P. Dutton, New York, 1939.

GLICKSMAN, JERZY: *Tell the West,* The Gresham Press, New York, 1948, 358 pp.

HARRIS, HERBERT: *Labor's Civil War,* A. A. Knopf, New York, 1940.

HOOK, SIDNEY: "Humanism and the Labor Movement," *European Ideoligies,* edited by Felix Gros, Philosophical Library, New York, 1948, pp. 1059-1063.

International Confederation of Free Trade Unions: *For Bread, Peace and Freedom,* London, 1949.

JENKINS, M: *The Communist Nucleus,* New York, 1928.

JOLL, JAMES: *The Second International,* New York, 1956.

JOSEPHSON, MATTHEW: *Sidney Hillman,* New York, 1952.

Labor Research Associates: *Labor Fact Book,* New York, Vol. 1—1931; Vol. 2—1934; Vol. 3—1936; Vol. 4—1938; Vol. 5—1941; Vol. 6—1943.

272   BIBLIOGRAPHY

LANG, FREDERICK J: *Maritime,* Pioneer Publishers, New York, 1943.
LANGER AND GLEASON: *The Challenge to Isolation,* New York, 1952.
LENIN, V. I.: *"Left-Wing Communism, An Infantile Disorder"* in *Selected Works,* Vol. X, Lawrence & Wishart Ltd., London, 1938.
LEVENSTEIN, AARON: *Labor Today and Tomorrow,* Knopf, 1945.
LEVINSON, EDWARD: *Labor on the March,* Harper & Bros., New York, 1938.
MACDONALD, LOIS: *Labor Problems and The American Scene,* Harper & Bros., 1938.
MARX, KARL: *Communist Manifesto,* Charles H. Kerr & Co., Chicago, 1940.
MILLIS, HARRY A. and ROYAL E. MONTGOMERY: *Organized Labor,* McGraw-Hill, New York, 1945.
MINTON, BRUCE and STUART, JOHN: *Men Who Lead Labor,* Modern Age, New York, 1937.
MORRIS, GEORGE: *The Trotzkyite 5th Column in the Labor Movement,* New Century Publishers, New York, 1945.
MURRAY, PHILLIP, and JOHN BROPHY, JAMES CAREY, I. F. STONE: *The CIO and National Defense,* American Council on Public Affairs, Washington, 1941.
NAFTALIN, ARTHUR: *A History of the Farmer-Labor Party of Minnesota,* a Ph.D. dissertation, Political Science Department, University of Minnesota, 1948.
O'NEAL, JAMES and WERNER, G.A.: *American Communism,* New York, 1947.
PERLMAN, SELIG: "History of American Labor" (mimeographed), a series of six lectures presented at the University of Wisconsin School for Workers, Madison, 1947, 11 pp.
and PHILLIP TAFT: *History of Labor in the United States, 1896-1932* Vol. IV, The MacMillan Co., New York, 1935.
A History of Trade Unionism in the United States, New York 1937.
PUTNEY, BRYANT: *Labor in Politics,* Editorial Research Reports, New York, 1940, 23 pp.
RESEARCH INSTITUTE OF AMERICA: *The Communist in Labor Relations Today,* (special report prepared for members), March 28, 1946.
RIKER, WILLIAM H.: *The CIO in Politics 1936-1946,* a Ph.D. thesis submitted to the Department of Government, Harvard University, Cambridge, Massachusetts, April, 1948.
ROSSI, A.: *A Communist Party in Action,* New Haven, 1949.
SAPOSS, DAVID J.: *Left-Wing Unionism,* International Publishers, New York, 1926.
SCHNEIDER, DAVID M.: *The Workers' (Communist) Party and American Trade Unions,* Johns Hopkins University Study in Historical and Political Science, Baltimore, 1928.

SCHWARTZ, DONALD A: *The 1941 Strike at Allis Chalmers,* (unpublished M.A. thesis), University of Wisconsin, 1943.

SEIDMAN, JOEL: *Union Rights and Union Duties,* Harcourt Brace, 1943. *The Needle Trades,* Farrar Rinehart, New York, 1942.

SMITH, WILLIAM J.: *Spotlight on Labor Unions,* New York, 1946.

STEINBERG, JULIEN: *Verdict of Three Decades,* Duell, Sloan and Pierce, New York, 1950.

STALIN, JOSEPH: *Foundations of Leninism,* International Publishers, New York, 1932.

STEINBOCK, JULIUS: *The Emergence of the Liberal Party in New York State: A Study in Minor Parties,* (unpublished M.A. thesis), Ohio State University, 1947.

STOLBERG, BENJAMIN: *The Story of the CIO,* Viking, New York, 1938. *Tailor's Progress,* Doubleday Doran, New York, 1944.

TAFT, PHILIP: *Civil Rights in the National Maritime Union,* a report prepared for the American Civil Liberties Union, August, 1950. (released January 18, 1952).
Economics and Problems of Labor, Stackpole, Harrisburg, 1942.

TANNENBAUM, FRANK: *A Philosophy of Labor,* Knopf, New York, 1951, 199 pp.

TONER, REV. JEROME L.: *The Closed Shop,* American Council on Public Affairs, Washington, 1942.

UNITED STATES GOVERNMENT: *Congressional Record*
Department of Labor, Bureau of Labor Statistics. *Brief History of the American Labor Movement,* October, 1947, 19 pp.
House of Representatives, Special Committee on Un-American Activities, 78th Congress, 2nd Session, H. Res. 282, *Investigation of Un-American Propaganda Activities in the United States,* House Report No. 1311, 1944.
House of Representatives, Committee on Education and Labor, 80th Congress, 2nd Session. *The Distributive Trades of New York City,* House Report no. 16, (interim report), December 17, 1948.
House of Representatives, Committee on Un-American Activities, 80th Congress, 2nd Session. *Annual Report for Year 1949,* March 15, 1950.
House of Representatives, Committee on Un-American Activities, 81st Congress, 2nd Session. *Hearings Regarding Communist Activities in the Cincinnati, Ohio, Area,* Part I, July 12, 13, 14, and 15, 1950.
National Labor Relations Board. *Fifteenth Annual Report,* 1950, 257 pp.

WARD, ESTOLV E.: *Harry Bridges on Trial,* Modern Age, New York, 1940.

WECHSLER, JAMES A.: *Labor Baron,* W. Morrow & Co., New York, 1944.

WHITE, KENNETH: *Labor and Democracy in the United States*, University Press of Liverpool, London, 1939.

NEWSPAPERS, PERIODICALS, INTERVIEWS

ASSOCIATION OF CATHOLIC TRADE UNIONISTS: *Wage Earner*, March 29, 1946.

AVERY, ANDREW: "The Communist Fifth Column," *Chicago Journal of Commerce*, June 24-July 11, 1946.
    "Communist Power in U.S. Industry," *Chicago Journal of Commerce*, January 13-31, 1947.

BARBASH, JACK: "Unions, Government, and Politics," *Industrial and Labor Relations Review*, Vol. 1, No. 1, October, 1947, pp. 66-79.

BELL, DANIEL: "The Coming Tragedy of American Labor," *Politics*, Vol. 1, pp. 37-42, March, 1944.

BENDINER, ROBERT: "Politics and People," *The Nation*, December 18, 1948.

BERNSTEIN, IRVING: "John L. Lewis and the Voting Behavior of the CIO," *The Public Opinion Quarterly*, Vol. 5, pp. 233-248, June, 1941.

BRAUNTHAL, ALFRED: "American Labor in Politics," *Social Research*, Vol. 12, No. 1, pp. 1-21, February, 1945.

BROUN, HEYWOOD: "Shoot the Works," *The New Republic*, Vol. 93, p. 280, Jan. 12, 1938.

Catholic Worker, January, 1937—August, 1937.

CHASAN, WILL: "Philip Murray," *The American Mercury*, Vol. 64, pp. 147-155, February, 1947.

COMMUNIST PARTY OF THE U.S.A., *Fight*, September, 1937.
    Youth Bulletin No. 1.

Counterattack, August 8, 1947.

Current Biography, "Max Yergan," September, 1948, pp. 57-59.

Daily Worker

DAYKIN, WALTER L.: "The Operation of the Taft-Hartley Act's Non-Communist Provisions," *Iowa Law Review*, Vol. 36, No. 4, pp. 607-628, Summer, 1951.

DIMOCK, MARSHALL E.: "Labor's Part in War and Reconstruction," *The American Political Science Review*, Vol. 35, pp. 217-231, April, 1941.

DUBINSKY, DAVID: "A Warning Against Communists in Unions," *The New York Times Magazine*, May 11, 1947, pp. 7, 61-65.
    "World Labor's New Weapon," in *Foreign Affairs*, April, 1950, pp.3-14.

FOUNTAIN, CLAYTON W.: "Labor in the Community," *The Antioch Review*, Vol. 5, No. 2, pp. 285-297, Summer, 1945.

Fortune, "John Llewellyn Lewis," Vol. 14, No. 4, pp. 95 f., October, 1936.

Fortune, "The Maritime Unions," Vol. 16, pp. 123-128, September,1937.

Fortune, "Alternating Currents in United Electrical, the Communist Party's Last Base," Vol. 39, pp. 175-177, March, 1949.

FRANK, NELSON: Personal Interview, July, 1947.

FRANK, WALDO: "Labor's Coming of Age," *Labor and Nation,* Vol. 3, pp.7-9, July-August, 1947.

George Washington Law Review, October, 1955.

GOULD, HELEN M.: "The Negro and the CIO." *Common Ground,* Vol. 5, No. 2, pp. 73-75, Winter, 1945.

HARDMAN, J. B. S. and JOSEPH PAULL: "World Federation of Trade Unions," *Labor and Nation,* Part Two, December, 1945.

HERLING, JOHN: "Two Conventions," *Labor and Nation,* Vol. 3, pp. 14-16, November-December, 1947.

KEMPTON, MURRAY: "Global Labor War," *Plain Talk,* May, 1949, pp. 13-18.

KROLL, JACK: "Why Labor is in Politics," *The New York Times Magazine,* October 27, 1947.

Labor Leader, July 25, 1947.

Labor Press Associates

LASSER, DAVID: "Labor and World Affairs," *Foreign Policy Reports,* Vol. XXV, No. 13, November 15, 1949.

LEITER, ROBERT D.: "Fur Workers Union," *Industrial and Labor Relations Review,* Vol. 3, No. 2, pp. 163-186, January, 1950.

LEWIS, JOHN L.: "What Labor is Thinking," *Public Opinion Quarterly,* Oct. 1937.

MILLS, WRIGHT C.: "The Trade Union Leader: A Collective Portrait," *Public Opinion Quarterly,* Summer, 1945.

Milwaukee Journal

Minneapolis Star

Minneapolis Tribune

Minnesota Labor

MURRAY, PHILLIP: "Labor's Political Aims," *American Magazine,* Vol. 137, p. 28, February, 1944.

MURRAY, PHILLIP: "Labor Should be in Politics," *The New York Times Magazine.* April 21, 1946, p. 13.

New Leader

Newsweek, Vol. 11, No. 22, pp. 7-8, May 30, 1938.

New York Post

New York Herald Tribune

New York World Telegram

New York University Law Review, May 1955.

Northwestern University Law Review, July, August, 1955.

PM

PORTER, PAUL: "Factions and Unity in the CIO.," *The American Scholar,* Vol. 8, No. 2, pp. 131-143, Spring 1939.

Progressive, September 1, 1947

RASKIN, A. H.: "Drive on Communists Gains Momentum in the C.I.O." *The New York Times,* December 12, 1948.

ROMER, SAMUEL: "Distruption in CIO," *The New Leader,* September 6, 1947.

ROSENFARB, JOSEPH: "Labor's Role in the Election," *Public Opinion Quarterly,* Fall, 1944.

ROVERE, RICHARD H.: "Labor's Political Machine," *Harper's Magazine,* Vol. 190. pp. 592-601, June, 1945.

St. Paul Pioneer Press

SHAIR, DAVID I.: "How Effective is the Non-Communist Affidavit?" *Labor Law Journal,* Vol. 1, No. 12, pp. 935-944, September, 1950.

Socialist Call, October 10, 1947.

STOLBERG, BENJAMIN: "Inside Labor," *The American Mercury,* Vol. 55, pp. 174-183, August, 1941.

STURMTHAL, ADOLPH: "World Strategy for Unions," *The Nation,* Vol. 157, pp. 233-235, August 28, 1943.

STURMTHAL, ADOLF: "Russia and World Labor," *Current History,* Vol. 8, pp. 385-390, May, 1945.

STURMTHAL, ADOLF: "Crisis in the International Labor Movement," *American Perpective,* May, 1949.

STURMTHAL, ADOLF: "The United States and European Labor," *American Perspective,* Winter, 1950.

TAFT, PHILIP: "Labor's changing Political Line," *The Journal of Political Economy,* Vol. 45, No. 5, pp. 634-650, October, 1937.

"Attempts to 'Radicalize' the Labor Movement," *Industrial and Labor Relations Review,* July, 1948, pp. 580-592.

"The Fate of the WFTU," *The New Leader,* October 2, 1948.

"The Association of Catholic Trade Unionists," *Industrial and Labor Relations Review,* January, 1949.

"Unlicensed Seafaring Unions," *Industrial and Labor Relations Review,* Vol. 3, No. 2, pp. 187-212, January, 1950.

"Communism in Trade Unions," 77 *Monthly Labor Review,* 139, (1954).

The New York Times

The Shield, July, 1947.

TYLER, GUS: "The Gompers Heritage," *New Republic,* May 8, 1950, pp. 12-15.

Wage Earner

Washington Post

WEINBERG, JULES: " Priests, Workers, and Communists," *Harper's Magazine,* November, 1948, pp. 49-56.

WOLTMAN, FREDERICK: Personal Interview, July, 1947.

WOODCOCK, GEORGE: "Trade Unions Under Nationalization," *Labor and Industry in Britain,* Vol. V, No. 6, June, 1947.

C.I.O. NEWSPAPERS, PERIODICALS, REPORTS, STATEMENTS

CAREY, JAMES B., "Address at Twelfth Annual Convention of the Industrial Union of Marine and Shipbuilding Workers Of America," September 24, 1946.

"Labor and the Community," (unpublished manuscript), 1947.

CIO's 1940 Legislative Program, CIO Publication No. 38, 14 pp. 1940.

CIO's 1941 Legislative Program, CIO Publication No. 52, 1940.

COMMITTEE ON LATIN AMERICAN AFFAIRS, *The Argentine Regime: Facts and Recommendations to the United Nations Organization*," 1946.

COWAN, NATHAN E.:"Testimony Before House Select Committee on Post-War Military Policy," June 13, 1945.

"Testimony Before the House Military Affairs Committee on H.R. 515," December 4, 1945.

Daily Proceedings of the First Constitutional Convention, 1938.

Daily Proceedings of the Second Constitutional Convention, San Francisco, October 10-13, 1939.

Daily Proceedings of the Third Constitutional Convention, Atlantic City, N.J., November 18-22, 1940.

Daily Proceedings of the Fourth Constitutional Convention, Detroit, Michigan, November 17-22, 1941.

Daily Proceedings of the Fifth Constitutional Convention, Boston, Massachusetts, November 9-13, 1942.

Daily Proceedings of the Sixth Constitutional Convention, Philadelphia, Pennsylvania, November 1-5, 1943.

Daily Proceedings of the Seventh Constitutional Convention, Chicago, Illinois, November 20-24, 1944.

Daily Proceedings of the Eighth Constitutional Convention, Atlantic City, New Jersey, November 18-22, 1946,

Daily Proceedings of the Ninth Constitutional Convention, Boston, Massachusetts, October 13-17, 1947.

EBY, KERMIT, "Testimony Before Sub-Committee of Senate Committee on Education and Labor," August 31, 1944.

"Testimony Before House Immigration and Naturalization Committee Supporting the Luce-Cellar Bills" March 7, 1945.

"Testimony Before the House Committee on Armed Services," July 10, 1947.

Economic Outlook

GOODMAN, LEO, "Testimony Before House Immigration and Naturalization Committee on H.R. 3663," March 20, 1946.

Guaranteed Wages the Year Round, CIO Publication No. 124, 1945.

Guild Reporter

Hearings Before the Committee to Investigate Charges Against International Longshoremen and Warehousemen's Union, (transcript), Washington, D.C., May 17, 18, 19, 1950.

Hearings Before the Committee to Investigate Charges Against International Union of Mine, Mill and Smelter Workers, (transcript), 2 Vol., Washington, D.C., January 18, 19 and February 6, 1950.

INTERVIEWS. John Brophy, James Carey, Eugene Cotton, Nathan Cowan, Kermit Eby, John Edelman, Leo Goodman, John T. Jones, Tom Owens, George L-P Weaver, July, 1947.

Keeping Score to Win the War, CIO Publication No. 87, 1943.

Labor Political Action, CIO Publication No. 89, 1943.

LABOR'S NON-PARTISAN LEAGUE, *Organizing Letter* and *National Bulletin National Bulletin*, 1937-1942.

   Press Information, 1937-1938.

   Labor's Non-Partisan League—Its Origin and Growth, Washington, 1939.

   War, 1940.

"Letter from CIO National Office to all Industrial Unions and Organizing Committees, State and Local Industrial Union Councils, CIO Regional Director and Local Industrial Unions," (issued irregularly).

LEWIS, JOHN L., *Labor and the Nation*, CIO Publication No. 11, September, 1937.

   The CIO Crusade, CIO Publication No. 15, 1937.

   Jobs, Peace, Unity, CIO Publication No. 40, 1940.

Local Review, UE Local 1102, St. Louis, May, 1947, June, 1947.

Memoranda and Press Releases, (issued regularly).

"*Minutes of CIO Legislative Department Meetings and its Executive Committee.*"

MURRAY, PHILIP, "The Objectives of the CIO," address before Assembly of Wharton School of Finance and Commerce, University of Pennsylvania, *Wharton Assembly Addresses*, May 6, 1937.

   Plan for Strengthening National Defense Program, December 19, 1940.

   "Statement to the Senate Committee on Foreign Affairs Regarding S. 275," February 5, 1941.

   We'll Work to Win, CIO Publication No. 64, 1942.

   Labor's Political Aims, CIO Publication No. 102, 1944.

   "Statement in Support of H.R. 2910, the Stratton Bill to the Sub-Committee on Immigration of the House Judiciary Committee," 1947.

   "Memorandum Submitted to the President of the United States on Basic Principles to Govern Aid to Europe," *Labor and Nation*, Vol. 3, pp. 4-7, November-December, 1947.

NATIONAL MARITIME UNION OF AMERICA, CIO, *Proceedings of the Fifth National Convention*, New York City, July 2-13, 1945.

   Pilot, 1947.

"Note on Strategy in the Fight to Abolish the Poll Tax," (confidential manuscript), 1940.

Political Primer for All Americans, CIO Publication No. 93, 1943.

Report on World Unity, CIO Publication No. 127, 1945.

Report of CIO Delegates to USSR, CIO Publication No. 128, October 12-19, 1945.

Report of the Commission of the World Federation of Trade Unions to Investigate Conditions in Germany, 1946.

Report to President Philip Murray by Committee Appointed to Investigate Break Within the International Union of Mine, Mill, and Smelter Workers, CIO, May 16-17, 1947.

Report of Committee Dealing With UAW-FE Dispute, April 4, 1949.

Report of the Committee to Investigate Charges Against the International Union of Mine, Mill and Smelter Workers, (mimeographed), February, 1950.

Report of Executive Board Committee Appointed by President Murray to Investigate Charges Against the International Longshoremen's and Warehousemen's Union, (mimeographed), 1950.

Report of Executive Board Committee Appointed by President Murray to Investigate Charges Against the National Union of Marine Cooks and Stewards, 1950.

Report of Executive Board Committee Appointed by President Murray to Investigate Charges Against the United Office and Professional Workers of America, 1950.

Report of Executive Board Committee Appointed by President Murray to Conduct Hearings on United Public Workers of America, 1950.

Report of the Committee to Investigate Charges Against the Food, Tobacco, Agricultural and Allied Workers of America, 1950.

Report of the Committee to Investigate Charges Against the United Furniture Workers of America, 1950.

Report of Executive Committee Appointed by President Murray to Investigate Charges Against the International Fur and Leather Workers Union, 1950.

Report of Executive Board Committee Appointed by President Murray to Investigate Charges Against the American Communications Association, 1950.

Report of the Administrative Committee to the Second Annual Convention of the International Union of Electrical, Radio and Machine Workers, December 4-9, 1950.

"Resolution on Condemnation of Un-American Activities of the Dies Committee," 1942.

Retail, Wholesale and Department Store Employee.

"Statement of Congress of Industrial Organizations in Opposition to House Joint Resolution 1 Submitted to the Sub-Committee of the House Judiciary Committee," March 21, 1945.

"Statement on Behalf of the CIO on the Punishment of War Criminals Before the House Foreign Affairs Committee," March 22, 1945.

The CIO and the Negro Worker, CIO Publication No. 63, 1941.

The CIO and the War, CIO Publication No. 34, 1939, 23 pp.

The Program of the CIO, October, 1937.

The Road to Victory, CIO Publication No. 76, January, 1943.

Union News Service, CIO Press Release Service, 1936-1937.

UNITED ELECTRICAL, RADIO, AND MACHINE WORKERS OF AMERICA, *Proceedings of the Eighth Constitutional Convention,* September 7-11, 1942.

Victory Program, January 11, 1943.

"V. J. Statement of Policy," National Executive Officers and Vice-Presidents of the CIO, August 16, 1945.

Working and Fighting Together, CIO Publication No. 85, 1943.

You and the WFTU, CIO Publication No. 139, 1946.

Your Civil Liberties and How to Protect Them, CIO Publication No. 39, 1940.

Your War Job With Congress, CIO Publication No. 81, 1943.

INDEX

INDEX

A

Abraham Lincoln School, 68, 113

Abt, John, 19, 234, 246 f.n. 31

Addes, George, 67, 71, 73, 74 75, 105

Alameda, CIO Industrial Union Council, 157

Alberts, Nathan, 136

Allen, Daniel, 43

Allis Chalmers Corporation, 8, f.n. 13

Allis Chalmers, Strike, 26

Alter, Victor, 31

Altman, Jack, 32, 36, 53, 54

Aluminum Workers of America, 68

Amalgamated Clothing Workers of America, 34, 35, 46, 51, 105, 161, 183, 255

American Committee for Struggle Against War, 174

American Communications Association, 18, 45, 111, 142, 144, 160, 161, 195, 196, 198, 207

American Congress for Peace and Democracy, 122

American Federation of Labor, 3, 7, 8, 9, 10, 11, 12, 14, 15, 37, 44, 59, 90, 122, 145, 207, 208, 216, 221, 222, 229, 231, 234, 238, 239, 240, 241, 243, 245, 256

American Federation of Teachers, 106

American Labor Party, New York, 13, 28, 34, 98, 127, 146, 147, 154

American League Against War and Fascism, 13, 27, 97, 101 f.n. 19, 114, 174, 178, 196

American League for Peace and Democracy, 98, 101 f.n. 19, 113, 122, 150, 171, 172, 178, 217

American Newspaper Guild, see Newspaper Guild, American

American Peace Mobilization, 44, 68, 98, 101 f.n., 19, 113, 123, 124, 127, 150, 171, 172, 179, 205

American Peoples' Mobilization, 205

American Radio and Telegraphists Assoc., 196

American Radio Association, 160, 198, 207

American Student Union, 13

American Youth for Democracy, 43, 117, 128

Americans for Democratic Action, 102, 103, 104, 106, 109

Architects, Engineers, Chemists and Technicians, Federation of, 19, 45, 196

298

INDEX

United States Government

Fair Employment Practices Commission, 41

Federal Bureau of Investigation, 77, 267

Federal Communications Commission, 197

House of Representatives, 26

National Labor Relations Board, 175, 185, 187, 188, 220, 263, 264, 266, 267-269

National War Labor Board, 33, 269 f.n. 7A. See also Legislation, United States

Senate, 20

Supreme Court, 187, 269 f.n. 7A
Atomic Energy Commission 137, 265-267

Upholsterers Union, 100 f. n. (1)

U.S.S.R., See Russia

Utility Workers Union, 36, 46, 47, 153, 161

V

Valentino, Anthony, 264

Vandenberg, Senator Arthur, 74

Versailles Peace Treaty, 230

Vishinsky, Andrei Y., 110, 137, 141

Vultee Aircraft, Strike, 25

W

Wage Earner, 74

Wagner, Martin, 161

Wallace, Henry, 100, 102, 117, 132, 134, 135, 141, 142, 143, 144, 145, 146, 154, 158, 182, 198, 206, 218, 264

Walsh, J. Raymond, 106

War, 180, 181, 205, 255

Waterfront Worker, The, 199

Wayne County Industrial Union Council, 33

Weaver, George, L-P, 109

Webb, Sidney, 230

Weber, Joseph R. (Alias). See Joseph Ruic

Westcott, Raymond, 153, 154

Whisner, Robt., 136, 137

Whitney, A.F., 211

Wiggins, Edward, 113

Wilkes, Phil, 184

Willkie, Wendell, 22, 23, 253

Williamson, John, 50, 69, 142, 144, 168, 176, 190

Wilson, Homer, 176, 177, 182, 188, 189

Wilson, Woodrow, 229

Wisconsin, 55

Wisconsin Industrial Union Council, CIO, 40, 63, 100

Wishart, Robert I, 115, 116, 117, 118, 133

Wolchok, Samuel, 32, 33, 102, 119 f.n. 2

Woll, Matthew, 216, 240, 241

Woltman, Frederick, 122

Woodworkers Association, International, 26

Woodworkers of America, United, 19, 46

Workers Alliance of America, 13, 114